FAST JETS AND OTHER BEASTS

FAST JETS AND OTHER BEASTS

PERSONAL INSIGHTS FROM THE COCKPIT OF THE HUNTER, PHANTOM, JAGUAR, TORNADO AND MANY MORE

IAN HALL

GRUB STREET | LONDON

Published by
Grub Street
4 Rainham Close
London SW11 6SS

Copyright © Grub Street 2017
Copyright text © Ian Hall 2017

A CIP record for this title is available from the British Library

ISBN-13: 9-781-910690-42-0

Design by Daniele Roa

Printed and bound by Finidr, Czech Republic

Publisher's Note:
Unless credited on the specific page, all photographs were taken by, or form part of the author's collection.
The cartoons on pages 26-27, 96 and 98 are by the late Ken Aitken.

TABLE OF
CONTENTS

INTRODUCTION
A CAREER ON THE WING

A working life in aviation. Mostly on fast jets but, towards the end, with the airlines. Such vivid memories, and so much excitement. Jets flown; places visited; people on whom my life depended and with whom I became incredibly close. Friends lost and grieved for. Crazy events and eccentric characters. Job satisfaction and frustration.

I started off flying Hunters on 208 Squadron, then moved to ground-attack Phantoms with 54 Squadron. Another tour on Hunters, this time instructing on 234 Squadron at the TWU, was followed by a short-notice posting to 20 Squadron, flying Jaguars. Then came an interlude flying the Northrop F-5A with 336 Skvadron of the Royal Norwegian Air Force, following which I returned to the Jaguar as a flight commander on 6 Squadron. My final flying tour in the RAF was as the squadron commander of 31 Squadron, equipped with the Tornado GR1. This varied and slightly unusual career pattern came during a period when the RAF, driven by changes in government and defence policy, was continually chopping and changing its equipments and roles. I know many current operators who have spent their entire career on a single type, occasionally moving seamlessly from squadron to squadron. I, however, never flew the same type two tours running, which certainly had much to be said for it in terms of interest and variety. But it also resulted in my spending an inordinate amount of time on conversion courses, as well as on refresher courses for types I was returning to. Leaving aside the fact that this must have been very expensive for the RAF, it had a disadvantage in that I never had the pleasure of arriving on a squadron as a current expert.

All that made for seven flying tours, but I also did my time on the ground. During those three tours I saw all sorts of different aspects of the fast-jet game; from the political viewpoint it all looks different. But during those interludes I nevertheless managed to fly in types I'd always fancied trying, and was constantly amazed at seeing at first hand the various capabilities I'd previously heard of only by repute.

Civil aviation brought a whole new set of experiences. A less frantic, more orderly life than the military? I certainly expected that would be the case, but there turned out to be just as many crazily unexpected episodes on the other side of the fence. As well as at least as many odd scenarios and characters. Indeed, when I mentioned out of courtesy to the director of flight operations at my last airline that I was about to have a book published, his response was: "You should write about this lot – there would be hundreds of stories there."

Although most of the tales which follow are from my own archive, I don't presume to have a monopoly of flying experiences. Therefore I've leavened the text with a few stories from friends and acquaintances. Truly, during our flying times, there was a remarkable amount going on.

And throughout all this mayhem I towed with me my wife and, in due course, my children. A life with the fast jets affects, to perhaps an unsuspected degree, the pilot's nearest and dearest. But before they came on the scene let's return to 1968 and relive the feeling of emerging from the far end of the sausage machine which was the RAF's Flying Training Command. The skies ahead were blue and our horizons were unlimited.

CHAPTER 1
'I'M AN AFME
HUNTER PILOT...'

What a milestone! The point in 1968 at which I and my young colleagues were to be sent onward from advanced flying training to our operational conversion units (OCUs) was an unforgettable moment. We had undergone the rigours of initial officer training, enjoyed trying out our fledgling abilities on the Chipmunk and Jet Provost, and had marvelled that we'd mastered the slippery little Gnat. Now, the choice was essentially between Lightnings and Hunters. Those of us whose names came out of the hat for Hunters were thrilled to bits; not one who was headed for the day-fighter/ground-attack (DFGA) role doubted that we would have a marvellous time tearing around at low level and firing ordnance at ground targets. But it may surprise readers to learn that not all of our friends who were sent to Lightnings were quite as delighted. Of course there were some who had never aspired to fly anything else, and quite clearly the aircraft was an impressively exciting beast. But there was a perception amongst many that the air defence role was, despite the aircraft's proclivity to catching fire and running out of fuel, somewhat boring. Most of us imagined that a Lightning pilot spent his time at high altitude, where there was no sensation of speed, flying on instruments and obeying the instructions of a ground controller. In our ignorance, we never considered the satisfying and demanding aspects of the flying, nor the opportunities for postings to Germany, Cyprus or Singapore. I certainly didn't fancy the Lightning at the time.

Anyway, back when we youngsters arrived at 229 OCU at RAF Chivenor for our next course, all our preconceived prejudices seemed to be confirmed. For those of us headed for Hunters, the unit was an operational conversion unit pure and simple. We were taught all the various facets of the DFGA role: low-level navigation and attack; air-to ground weapons delivery of all types; air-to-air combat and gunnery; and so on. The pre-Buccaneer chaps (our Valley course was the first from which a couple of first-tourists were sent to the RAF's latest jet) got all the low-level stuff but not the air-to-air, and seemed at the time to be generally content with that.

But the pre-Lightning boys appeared to receive the rough end of the stick. There was no low-level fun for them, and their course flying hours were made up with extra instrument practice and night flying. Neither did their night work seem terribly interesting; there was no attempt to introduce practice interceptions, so they simply bored holes in the sky on high-level navigation exercises. Tough luck, thought we DFGA types. We were enjoying ourselves, and that was all that mattered.

The 400-knot wash. A 208 Squadron Hunter releases its 100-gallon tanks at Rashid range, simulating a 50-foot level napalm delivery.

On completing the Hunter OCU I was thrilled to be posted to 208 Squadron at RAF Muharraq, Bahrain. But I still vividly recall my first meeting with my new squadron commander. I was wheeled into his office and saluted smartly. "I suppose I ought to say welcome," said he, "but to be honest I've already got dozens like you and I could well do without another one. Anyway, just for the form, welcome." A greeting never to be forgotten. I don't recall him ever saying another word to me before he was posted away halfway through my tour.

He was right, though, about the vast numbers of first-tourists on his squadron, which had a somewhat unusual structure. The boss was a squadron leader – perhaps one of the last operational COs with that rank, for by that time most front-line units had wing commanders at the helm. The two flight commanders were flight lieutenants and they, together with a couple of QFIs (qualified flying instructors), an IRE (instrument rating examiner) and two PAIs (pilot attack instructors – that qualification soon to be renamed qualified weapons instructors, QWIs), formed the experienced cadre. The remainder of the total of twenty-two or so pilots were first-tour flying officers. This lack of balance led to the rest of the fighter force regarding the Bahrain Hunter squadrons as little more than advanced training units. That wasn't altogether the case – as we shall shortly see – but there was nevertheless a grain of truth in the notion.

The structure was made even odder by the fact that, apart from the flight commanders and the QFIs, the rest of what might be described as the 'top team' were also of flying officer rank. Yes, the two PAIs and the IRE. This derived from the apparent view of those three gentlemen that 'real' pilots would rather not get promoted because of the risk of being sent to staff appointments; they simply wished to keep flying. They wore incredibly old and faded flying suits, adorned with the badges of squadrons on which they'd previously served. I guess this was designed to reinforce to us newcomers that they were terribly experienced operators, but it seemed a somewhat odd habit. Certainly, in later years, accepted practice was that one would only ever wear the badge of one's current squadron; if anybody wished to display his previous flying history, then the wall of his den was the place.

Whether or not the pay rise which would have come on promotion to flight lieutenant was ever a factor I don't know; perhaps it was negligible. But at any rate these characters wore their flying officer rank as something of a badge of honour to show that they hadn't taken their 'B' exam. That routine test would have seen them automatically promoted to flight lieutenant and was, by the way, quite hard to fail.

Some time into my tour we got a new boss, and he decreed that all his flying officers must take the exam at the next annual sitting. Whether he had come under pressure from above or whether it was his own idea I've no idea – anyway, he insisted. Unfortunately, the exam that year was scheduled to be held at Muharraq slap bang in the middle of our annual live weapons (high-explosive, rather than inert) armament practice camp at Masirah. Now this wasn't a major problem for all us young chaps – we were sorry to miss the APC, of course, but there would be others. But to dispatch the squadron on this important weapons event without its two specialist PAIs was a big call. Because I was in Bahrain taking my 'B' exam I have no first-hand knowledge of what actually happened down at Masirah, but the bush telegraph did bring word of a couple of incidents that might have been avoided if the experts had been running the show.

There is another story relating to those three senior flying officers and APCs. They were pretty good buddies as far as I knew, and were all good weaponeers; unsurprisingly, they were very competitive. During this particular APC one of them was scoring too well and, the story has it, his compatriots began to suspect that he must have been firing from closer than the minimum permitted range. They were unable to pin anything on him, because he seemed to be having consistently bad luck with his gunsight cameras; faults repeatedly caused his film to be unassessable. The other two had a good idea that those 'faults' were self-induced and, one day, arranged for his aircraft's G90 camera to be loaded with film. This was a forward-facing camera mounted on the top of the aircraft's nose; I don't recall it being used at all during my time on the Hunter. Anyway, it required no additional cockpit switchery to make it function, so the man under suspicion would have had no idea that it was running during his next firing detail. Sure enough it confirmed the illegal parameters and our friend's scores were instantly zeroed. He went pretty quiet for a while.

This chapter's title stretches the truth, for I was not actually an 'AFME' Hunter pilot. AFME stood for 'Air Forces Middle East', the command organisation which had ruled RAF operations in the area until a couple of years before my arrival. The withdrawal from Aden had prompted reorganisation, following which squadrons operated under HQ British Forces Gulf. But the older hands on the squadron brought with them songs we used to perform in the bar late at night, amongst them the ditty whose first two lines went as follows:

> "I'm an AFME 'Unter pilot and me name is Joseph Soap,
> I left the shores of UK and me 'eart was full of 'ope ..."

We would happily roar away the evenings at Muharraq and Sharjah with a huge repertoire of similar classics, keeping ourselves endlessly amused. Although, I fear, probably not amusing the other residents of those messes.

There was a custom on Hunter squadrons that no two pilots could have the same first name. Therefore if a second Pete, for example, was posted in, he would be given an alternative name. 'Sid' was the favourite substitute, with 'Bert' following close behind. The problem would be compounded when these Sids and Berts were later posted to new squadrons, when it could quite easily turn out that a unit would finish up with, perhaps, two Sids. Should one of them revert to his original name? That could be difficult, for by now he would be well known by and thoroughly used to his new handle. And of course there was always the complication of reverting to 'Pete' when there might be a Pete there already.

One of these characters (I think his real name was Dave) became immortalised in the Middle Eastern Hunter world by virtue of 'Bert's Boat' being named after him. It was common, when trying to rejoin a split formation, to nominate a geographical location over which to RV. For example, "I'm over Doha at 16,000ft in a left-hand orbit". This particular Bert was, one day, trying to find his leader. "I'm over the big boat half-way down the west coast of Qatar," he said. The other guy searched for ages but was unable to find any such boat. Eventually, the story has it, they gave up and returned independently to Muharraq. Naturally, the debrief was quite interesting, especially when they were forced to agree after much map study that the 'big boat' had most probably been the quite substantial island which lay more or less where they both thought they'd been. Ever afterwards, that lump of rock was known to successive generations of Middle Eastern Hunter pilots as 'Bert's Boat' – and a very good RV it always proved to be. Certainly, its new name sounded better than 'Dave's Boat'.

Later in my RAF career we took very seriously the setting for a real or simulated war mission. The political background would be well known to us and would be touched on briefly, followed by the intelligence situation pertaining to the particular mission. But I don't think that, on my first tour, we were at all politically aware. Most of our flying from Bahrain was of the training variety, but on the odd occasions when we received an operational task I don't recall ever hearing any background to it. We knew,

A 208 Squadron Hunter at low level over the Trucial States. The pilot is Terry Heyes.

of course, that the UK had agreements with the Trucial States (broadly speaking, those states which would later form much of the UAE). And we were faintly aware of past unrest within the Jebel Akhdar region of Oman, the fighting during which the SAS had won its Middle-Eastern spurs. As far as we understood, things were generally quiet at the time we were out there, although renegades were known still to be provoking occasional skirmishing.

But for whatever reason we were, from time to time, tasked with 'flag wave' sorties from Bahrain, down across the Akhdar with a landing at RAF Masirah. I remember being awed by the spectacularly wild and rugged terrain of the Jebel, with our little Hunters being dwarfed by mountains rising to almost 10,000 feet. The vistas of agriculture being scraped out on those high, rocky escarpments were simply extraordinary. And I also remember the mess steward on the bleak island of Masirah – a man whom many of us first-tourists recalled from our days at Valley for his magnificent night-flying suppers – serving us in the 40°C heat with doorstep corned beef sandwiches. Yes, they were memorable trips. But were those flag waves designed to reassure loyal Omanis – or to deter rebel groups? What prompted our tasking on those particular occasions? Were we successful? To this day I have no idea.

Similarly, in November 1970 we deployed at short notice to RAF Sharjah with the order to stand by for border patrols. The border in question was, I think, way down south of the Gulf between Abu Dhabi and Saudi Arabia – where today lies the southern extremity of the UAE. I say 'I think', because others with whom I've recently spoken recall the operating area as being up in the Musandam Peninsula. Whichever way, we were issued with loaded pistols to be carried in shoulder holsters, so it must have been serious. But at whom we should have aimed our pistols had we ejected I've no

On standby for border patrol in 1970,
the author dressed for action.

idea. What exactly the problem was and who was causing it I simply can't recall – indeed I'm fairly certain that I never knew.

We were endlessly drilled in tactical formation flying, with the most strictly enforced principle being that, at low level, the element leader was responsible for the terrain clearance of both himself and his wingman. Therefore one never flew below the element leader. Generally speaking this was relatively easy to achieve (as long as you loosened your ejection seat straps, which allowed you to stretch and see more), but in certain situations it became a very demanding exercise. One such scenario was when a four-ship closed up into 'arrow' formation to manoeuvre through mountains and valleys. The leader was now responsible for the terrain clearance of all four, who would be spaced at approximately 200-yard intervals. A second principle which now came into play was that, as an added separation safety-break, nobody ever crossed to the opposite side of the arrow.

It all sounds simple, but now picture the entire ensemble wending its way at 420 knots up the bottom of a narrow, twisty, steep-sided valley. Imagine you're number two on the inside of a turn as the leader cranks on seventy or eighty degrees of bank and pulls around the corner. Unlike in close formation when you stay in the plane of his wings, here you must fly above him. But you're losing sight of him under your aircraft's nose. You can't slide to the outside of the turn to maintain visual because numbers three and four are there. The solution is to apply lots of bottom rudder, which cants the nose of your Hunter down and restores visibility – but you now need to hold off unwanted extra bank by applying out-of-turn aileron. What with the G in the turn, the crossed controls and the inevitable turbulence in the baking-hot, mountainous air it was a pretty uncomfortable way of flying. It was the sort of situation that would have given Biggles, in his Sopwith Pup, an unwanted blast of air on the side of his helmet which would make him correct the sideslip. The method was effective, though, and what we called 'wadi-bashing' was tremendous fun. It must, however, have placed unbelievable strain on the fin post and rudder, and I wonder whether Sir Sydney Camm ever anticipated his beautiful swept-wing interceptor being abused in such a way.

Compared with that, the endless high-level battle formation and cine gunsight-tracking exercises seemed much less exciting, but I guess they also stood me in good stead. Returning to low level, though, some of the weapons delivery profiles were quite hairy. I remember being amazed when, on the initial Hunter course, a series of bombing exercises taught me '50 foot level skip' profiles. Fifty feet above ground level at 400 knots seemed helluva low and exciting, and I could hardly believe that I was being let loose in a Hunter to do this. In the Gulf we practised a variation, a 3° dive profile with a release planned for 75 feet above ground level. As I recall, the minimum authorised height for the recovery from the dive was 35 feet – which was even more helluva low! On one occasion, in the exceedingly hot and humid conditions, the hand of one of the first-tourists slipped off the stick during his 6G recovery and his jet efflux blew the target over. That certainly accounted for one of his nine lives.

To my knowledge we had no iron bombs out there, and that shallow dive profile was designed for the release of napalm – although I never saw or heard of any plan for the preparation of the real thing. Usually, we released small practice bombs, but on occasions there would be a few life-expired 100-gallon external fuel tanks available. These would be filled with eighty gallons of water to simulate the weight of 100 gallons of napalm, and the delivery then became known as the '400-knot wash'. In one instance a surplus forty-ton vehicle was available to provide a realistic, hard target. It took two or three days to drag it out to the range over the soft sand, and it was in position the evening before our planned flights. However, it disappeared overnight, spirited away by the locals.

Those people were well known for scavenging the range for the 30mm brass shell cases which our Hunters ejected when we fired the cannons. Reputedly, the metal was rapidly hammered into 'antique' coffee pots for sale in souks across the Gulf region. Usually the departure of the day's last flight would signal the emergence of a swarm of local Steptoes, hitherto invisible in the vastness of the desert. Occasionally, though, those characters would misjudge their timing and would begin to encroach before close of play. When another pair of Hunters appeared over the horizon to begin firing, their pilots would first have to 'clear the range' with a series of low passes to disperse the intruders. That was always a fun mission!

Our daily routine at Muharraq (or at RAF Sharjah, whence we

A 208 Squadron Hunter wearing its colours on the outboard tanks, specially painted up prior to being dropped on a '400-knot wash'.

It's dawn as Hunters of 208 Squadron stand on the line at RAF Muharraq. In the background are Argosy aircraft of the Gulf's permanent 'Ardet', with resources provided by 114 and 267 Squadrons.

would deploy for our regular weapons practice) ran very predictably. We would rise early, fly a couple of sorties (five days a week, with Saturday being devoted to ground training) and then go to the bar at about 1pm to continue our debriefs. Afternoons would be occupied by a swim or a sleep, followed, perhaps, by an early-evening trip into the nearby town. In Bahrain this would be Manama, a place with plenty of local character but also something of a colonial heritage. From Sharjah we'd visit Dubai, and it's just unbelievable how the fishing and trading port we knew then has mushroomed into today's spectacular city. On return to base there would be an early dinner followed by a return to the bar to resume flying chat.

While in Sharjah we were dependent on taxis for transport, but at home base Muharraq many of us owned small motorbikes. These could be dangerous, especially in the late evenings if we opted to go downtown for a further sharpener. For not only did we tend to travel with three aboard our little machines, but in the high humidity the tarmac road surfaces would take on the characteristic of a skating rink as dew formed on top of the oily sand on the black top. Miraculously, no-one got seriously hurt, but most suffered nasty grazes from time to time – known euphemistically as 'Honda rash'. The camp tailor, Abdul Ghani, was expert at sewing complete new legs into damaged trousers. In all that time did we see much of the local culture? No, I regret to say we did not.

In early 1971 the unusual prospect of a detachment to Pakistan loomed on the horizon; we were to spend ten days in Peshawar with a MiG-19 squadron. This detachment was related to CENTO – the Central Treaty Organisation, a strategic alliance which linked the UK with Pakistan, Iran and Turkey. There was great competition for slots on this trip and, being one of the longer-serving first-tourists, I was in with a good chance.

However, another temptation tugged in the opposite direction. I was due to be married back in England in six weeks. I had not been home for half a year and there had been a postal strike for the last two months or so. Phone calls were difficult to arrange and, while there was much to be said for leaving all the arrangements to the wife-to-be, I was beginning to feel a little guilty. It so happened that three of our Hunters were due to be ferried back to the UK maintenance unit for major servicing at the same time as the Pakistan detachment. So, tempting as it was to leave wedding plans entirely in the hands of the belovèd, conscience insisted that here was an opportunity to get home for a few days to at least show an interest. It would be a shame to give up the chance of a lifetime to fly to Pakistan in an RAF fighter, but it was no contest. In any case, the ferry flight would be fun too.

208 Squadron, before the formation of the RAF, was Naval 8 Squadron. Here, as part of the Christmas 1970 festivities, the senior British naval officer in the Gulf region is enlisted to 'launch' the airmen's billet bar at RAF Muharraq.

At the time of my story, RAF transport aircraft en route the Gulf routinely used what was called the 'CENTO' route for the Cyprus-Gulf sector, flying over Turkey and Iran. We Bahrain-based fighters generally only saw the Iranian mountains from a distance – from the south side of the Gulf or over the Straits of Hormuz – as we were prohibited from overflying the Shah's kingdom. For ferry flights, though, there was a special dispensation, and that's the way we would go this time.

That we could then fly over a country that has been closed to the British military for much of the time since brings home the fact that the world's political map changes very regularly. For example, during my time in Bahrain we were never allowed to fly over adjacent Saudi Arabia. And this despite the UK having sold them Lightnings, which were based at nearby Dhahran and were largely being flown by British pilots.

A stirring performance of 'Zulu Warrior' by pilots of 208 Squadron, with my friend Terry Heyes (with whom I'd gone all through training) taking the lead role. The author is just to Terry's left, pretending not to notice. Our bush jacket uniforms indicate that we'd come from some sort of formal event – although the occasion was clearly becoming rapidly less formal.

Similarly, the pre-Suez and Arab-Israeli war route over Egypt was, during my time, closed to the RAF. Later, and certainly from the time of Gulf War One onwards, RAF aircraft have routinely routed over Saudi and Egypt.

Anyway, when the three of us (two from our sister unit, 8 Squadron, and me from 208) set off on our transit that sunny February morning in 1971, we headed towards unknown territory. Navigation equipment was problematical. We had DME (distance measuring equipment) to measure range from 'eureka' beacons. This was familiar kit to us, but those beacons were few and far between on this route. We also had the ADF radio compass to give us bearings. But, accustomed to clear, middle-eastern weather, we only tended to use that bit of kit on our annual instrument flying check flights. So our level of knowledge of it amounted to little more than how to switch it on, and its coffee-grinder frequency dial was permanently tuned to the frequency of the BBC World Service – for music. Such was the Hunter force's lack of practice with it that I recall an incident at about that time when a Hunter (not from Muharraq) was lost in poor weather near Malta. The pilot was doing an instrument approach using his radio compass, not appreciating that the bearings he was reading were relative to the aircraft's axis rather than to north. I'm not admitting to being quite that ignorant – but we nevertheless prayed fervently for a good weather forecast for our trip!

We set off northward from Bahrain. Tehran, our first stop, lies at an altitude of 4,000 feet in a hollow surrounded by quite high mountains. Winter high pressure means cold, still air stagnating in the bowl – with smoke haze well and truly thickening things up. And so it was for our arrival, with visibility being just a couple of miles. Our inbound track led around a pattern from beacon to beacon; being a fighter pilot, our leader flew this at 400 knots with his wingmen in tactical formation. I was hanging on at the back, and I still remember the leader occasionally asking me for confirmatory bearings from my ADF. Some hopes! But we found the airport and landed safely – although I do remember being startled by a couple of helicopters going in the opposite direction as I flew down the final approach.

As I confirmed much later while working for the airlines, flying an NDB approach is not always the easiest thing in the world, even when one has a good autopilot and the kit is coupled to the flight management system. Perhaps, though, we might have stood a better chance if we'd flown at a sensible approach speed!

We were to continue onwards two hours later and the other two went off to flight plan, leaving me to look after the aircraft turn-rounds. In this, I was assisted by an elderly and wrinkled Iranian airman. As we came to replenish the highly volatile AVPIN starter fluid, he proudly demonstrated his knowledge of the importance of avoiding contamination – by offering to strain it through a dirty and doubtful-looking sock. This AVPIN, which was used on Lightnings as well, caused a minor fire on almost every start, and standard issue for Hunter ground crews was an asbestos glove with which to beat out the flames. At Tehran we had one glove between three pilots, so took turns to stand guard down below while each started his engine. Made-to-meas-ure Hunter ladders weren't available there, so we had to improvise with wobbly substitutes. In any case, once the engines were running it wasn't possible to use any sort of ladder forward of the air intakes. So the last man (me of course) had to get a leg-up via the external fuel tank and onto the wing before wriggling into the cockpit from over the sliding canopy – with the howling intakes horribly close. What with all the scrambling in and out, I managed to get airborne without lacing up the leg-re-strainers (interwoven with the seat straps on that type of bang seat) – and I remember taking most of the climb to 40,000 feet to get the whole ensemble done up properly.

Never mind, we were en route again, this time heading towards the north-west corner of Iran, past the bizarrely-named Van, Tatvan and Batman. It was wild and spectacular landscape, and yes, we could just see over the border into the USSR, a first for all of us. Soon, though, we were over eight-eighths cloud, which persisted all the way down through Turkey, past Diyarbakir, until our landing at RAF Akrotiri. For at least half of the two-and-three-quarter-hour flight we had nothing but dead reckoning and the dreadful ADF to navigate by. It worked out all right though, which was just as well, for we each landed with only 800 pounds of fuel remaining – the same minimum we'd have used for a local training sortie on a fine day. Proof of the power of prayer!

Cyprus is a lovely island and warranted a two-night stop, which allowed us a spot of R & R. There was snow up on the Troodos mountains but it was mild on the coast, so we could ski in the morning and water ski the same afternoon. As Basil Fawlty might have said, 'That sounds very tiring!' Anyway, well fed and watered (if not rested), we then pressed on towards Malta. There was terrible weather all the way, necessi-tating two hours of close formation in cloud. It was nearly dark and pouring with rain by the time we landed at RAF Luqa, and the deluge continued until our departure the next morning. I recall our hosts taking us to see such well-known sights as 'the gut' – where generations of jolly jack tars have relieved their frustrations and been relieved of their money. For us, it was something of a washout.

Weather on the next leg was kinder, and we proceeded to the French test centre at Istres, near Marseilles, for lunch. On this visit, and on pretty well every subsequent trip I made to France with the military, the main characteristic was that our flight-planned route was rejected by French air traffic control. However correct one's plan is according to latest publications and NOTAMs, les Gauloises always find it 'not correct on Thursdays when there's an R in the month' – or something similar. It's a good game, which they always win! Anyway, we made it across the Channel and safely into RAF St Athan, at the same time as the maintenance unit which carried out Hunter major servicing. The final incident I recall concerned HM Customs. The formation leader had only one bottle of spirits with him, which didn't seem unreasonable, but the customs officer demanded payment of duty on it. This so incensed my friend that he poured the Scotch down the drain rather than pay!

It was a great trip – and yes, I did have a good few days with my wife-to-be before taking the VC10 back to the Gulf. I suppose I might have been some assistance in the business of making wedding arrangements, but it could only have been in a minor way. The postal strike was still in full swing when I finally arrived back in the UK just two days before the ceremony, so my wife was fully justified in claiming the lion's share of the credit for the arrangements.

I still, though, have a sneaking wish that I'd seen Peshawar.

Earlier I alluded to the pre-Lightning pilots not getting, at 229 OCU, much that was relevant to their future role. There was a reason for that: the entire Chivenor staff was ex-Hunters, not having a single Lightning hour between them. And this despite the fact that Chivenor had been running pre-Lightning courses for many years. No wonder that my Lightning colleagues (as well as, I learned recently from reading *Buccaneer Boys,* some of my Bucc friends) didn't look back at their time at Chivenor with undiluted pleasure.

That 'Hunter only' staff composition continued for several more years. When I returned from Phantoms in 1974 to the Tactical Weapons Unit (the renamed 229 OCU) to begin a Hunter instructional tour, I believe I was only the second to join the staff who had flown anything other than Hunters. Aside, that is, from those who had been returned to Hunters having had an abortive go at the early Harriers, only to finish upside down too often in cabbage fields – à la 'dead ants'! I certainly, at that point, felt that my slightly wider background meant I had more to offer. In defence of the posting staffs, I've no doubt they must have had their work cut out trying to keep the front line manned; perhaps they simply couldn't spare many Harrier, Buccaneer, Phantom and Lightning pilots for Chivenor.

I'm sure that many of those all-through Hunter people saw themselves as heirs to the excellence that had resided in the old Day Fighter Leaders' School, but I have a feeling that some of them may have over-rated themselves. Possibly, also, the posters simply had nowhere else to put their Hunter-only people.

This last point might still have applied much later in Chivenor's history. Some time after the station had reopened as the second TWU, a man was posted in as its chief instructor who had never flown anything modern. He had, it's true, combat experience – from Aden and the Radfan – but by the time of his arrival there had been no Hunter front line for many years, and the TWUs were exclusively providing tactical lead-in courses for the Buccaneer, Phantom, Jaguar, Tornado and Harrier OCUs. By then the unit's equipment was Hawks, but that made no difference; the Hawk in this role was simply a smaller and more economical Hunter.

One could argue that a DFGA background was adequate for the top job. After all, the unit commander is as much a manager as a pilot, and there's no doubt that, on this basis, the RAF has regularly fitted square pins into round holes. I know, for example, of fighter/bomber aircrew in recent years who have subsequently commanded transport stations. The appointers would say, quite simply, that the best person gets the job regardless of his background.

And this reflects civilian practice where, in the upper echelons of employment, it's not uncommon for people to take jobs for which, on the face of it, they have very little background. The chief executive of a fashion retail chain may have no experience of textiles and fabrics, but the board who appoints him may point to his proven record in management and sales. And I know pilots who, on leaving the RAF, have successfully taken jobs such as managing medical practices.

But still, for me, a doubt remains. Chivenor's students were being prepared to move on to aircraft with the following characteristics: nuclear strike; two-crew operations, with navigators; inertial navigation systems; automated weapon-aiming systems; night all-weather roles; air-to-air intercept radars; air-to-air refuelling systems; and guided missiles, both air-to-air and air-to-surface.

This chap had no experience in any of these areas. He had never flown at night other than to bore holes in the sky, while he had never navigated other than by stopwatch and compass. He certainly fitted in with the ethos of the old Hunter pilots who believed they were god's chosen ones. But might not some first-hand experience of at least some current developments have suited him a little better to that particular job?

CHAPTER 2
JUST LIKE ICARUS

When I took over the reins of my Tornado squadron in 1992 it was my second tour at RAF Brüggen, the first having been on Jaguars in the mid to late 1970s. Many people whom I'd known there earlier were, like me, now back at the German base, and I confess to suffering occasional angst throughout that second tour over the possibility of my 'secret history' becoming public.

Jaguar GR1s of 20 Squadron, on which the author served from 1977-1979. (Crown Copyright)

If it were to have got out I'd have been in for some uncomfortable ribbing. But it never happened. Perhaps those who once knew had forgotten. Possibly they were respecters of privacy – although, knowing the RAF, that seemed unlikely. On the other hand, maybe it hadn't been such an embarrassing incident after all; it could be that my own memory had inflated it into more than it was. Whatever the reason, the story lay dormant for the whole of the second tour. Much to my relief, for running a squadron was a big enough job without additional injects.

But now nearly forty years have passed since the event – over twenty since I left my squadron command and almost as long since I hung up my uniform. The story has, I think, served its penance. With remission for good behaviour it's done its time and has had its parole application approved. I'm satisfied that it is now no longer a danger to society – nor to me. Suitably tagged, therefore, it's safe to be released into the community.

One hot summer's evening in 1978 I was programmed for a stint as duty pilot during Jaguar night flying. I would be the aircrew representative in the air traffic control tower – available to keep an eye on the weather, to recommend diversion airfields and to give advice when required by ATC or by airborne pilots. It wasn't a particularly popular duty, but neither was it, as a rule, very onerous. In normal circumstances it was a good chance to relax, write letters or catch up with secondary duties.

Arriving for my shift I climbed the several flights of stairs to local control, the glass cupola at the top of the tower. Opening the DP's log book I scribbled: '2015 hours – Hall on, ops normal.' I had a coffee with the controller and watched the first wave roar off into the night, reheats blazing. It was a glorious evening – clear, still and very warm. There was no moon though, and outside the arc of the runway lights it was as black as pitch. A ceiling fan barely stirred the torpid air in the local control room. The jets would be gone for nearly an hour and a half, and I settled down to enjoy my book.

Some time on, the coffee having done its work, I headed down a couple of flights to answer a call of nature. Even at this late hour it was absolutely stifling, but halfway down the stairs I sensed a welcome draught of slightly cooler air wafting in through an open door. On impulse I decided to take a little more of this refreshing breeze, and stepped out onto the flat roof of an annex building. Enjoying the balmy atmosphere and the quiet of the night, I meandered towards the far end of the roof, the dark edge of which was clearly outlined against the distant glow of lights from the Dutch town of Roermond. Lovely – after the stuffy tower, it was good to stroll in the open.

And I strolled into thin air. Down ... down ... down. It took only a fraction of a second, but felt like a lifetime. The instant I started to fall, and an age before the crunching impact with the ground, I realised what had happened. OK then, let's try that again. Fast rewind, let's go back a few milliseconds. But one can't, of course. Mistakes are so horribly final. When accidents happen, there's no second chance. One minute you're safely on the pavement, the next you've stepped into the path of a bus.

Whilst still in mid air, it became crystal clear to me that we don't really look at our feet while we're walking, tending more to scan some distance ahead. Because I'd been able to see the far edge I had registered the roof as a continuous structure. But it wasn't. I was falling into the large open courtyard which lay between two flat-roofed buildings. And it was going to hurt.

This must have been how Icarus felt, and it did hurt. A lot. Twenty feet's worth of hurt. To the tune of a broken wrist, together with assorted sprains, cuts, bruises and abrasions. It could have been worse; even as I lay on the ground I could see that I'd fallen into the ATC bicycle park. Despite the shaking up I'd received I was still compos mentis enough to thank my lucky stars that I hadn't landed astride a crossbar or been impaled on a brake lever! Thanks be for small mercies.

There was nobody around so I had little option but to heave myself to my feet and stagger back to the front door of the tower to get help. I couldn't find anybody on the ground floor, so painfully, laboriously, I dragged myself back upstairs. A couple of times I swam in and out of unconsciousness, but I still remember with absolute clarity being struck by the absurdity of the question uttered by the first person I met. As I crawled onto the first-floor landing, covered in dust and blood, cradling one arm with its hand protruding at a ridiculous angle, an airman uttered five unforgettable words: "Are you all right, sir?"

The rest of the story followed a predictable flow: ambulance to Wegburg Hospital; then six weeks off flying – most of which was spent, appropriately enough, acting as duty pilot. My only real complaint was with the medics. A few days after the plaster cast had been applied I felt that it was far too sloppy; I guess the initial swelling had subsided. I drew to the local GP's attention that my arm was loose inside the cast, but he said there was no problem and that I should wait for my routine 'howgozit' appointment the following week. At that meeting the consultant expressed surprise. "Oh dear," he said, "your arm has been rattling around inside the cast and the bone has set crooked. We'll have to re-break it and start again." I was mad; that would mean at least an extra fortnight on top of the standard recovery process.

Officialdom took a fairly neutral view of the incident, although I was tickled to note during my second Brüggen tour all those years later that the spot on the stairway had subsequently been marked by a bit of nonsense bearing the unmistakable signs of the health and safety police. A warning notice had been put up to the effect that 'walking on flat roofs on dark nights can be dangerous'. The phrase that begins 'Bolting the stable door ...' springs to mind!

Of course at the time of the incident my fellow pilots from the four Brüggen Jaguar squadrons had a field day at the expense of my bad luck (as I saw it) – or my stupidity (their view). And for the rest of that first tour the story haunted me. In fact, the mickey-taking started on the evening of the day of the accident, at the hand of the individual who was summoned to take my place in the tower for the remainder of the night-flying period. Normally, at the end of the shift, we would clock off in the duty pilot's logbook. As I discovered when I next visited ATC, he had signed off on my behalf – and with commendable wit:

'2115 hrs – Hall off. Well, not just off. Fallen off the tower, in fact. Bloggs on. Ops back to normal.'

Anyway, a couple of months later I received the news that I was to go on the exchange tour I'd always coveted, a period of three years working with a foreign air force. It was always said that to attract the attention of the posting staff one needed to do something noticeable – it didn't matter whether good or bad. So perhaps that piece of folk wisdom did have some truth in it.

CHAPTER 3
ARMY COOPERATION

The squadron I commanded, number 31, had been designated in its youth an 'army cooperation' unit. In those days there were three officially approved role types: fighter; bomber; and army cooperation. And squadrons so designated had those roles recorded on the frame of their badges. It seemed that my squadron's original badge was destroyed in a fire at their jungle camp in India during 1943, and when their replacement badge was issued in 1956 it came without any role designation. Those of us in the old boys' association who were interested in such things assumed that it was because the squadron had, over the years, changed its role several times. But a gentleman from the RAF Historical Society later enlightened us with the facts. He told us that roles were introduced into squadron titles in 1924, and when the standard badge frame was introduced in 1936 it incorporated these. But in May 1939 air ministry order A.185 announced that roles were no longer to be reflected in the titles of units … the regulation was reiterated in October 1941 (AMO A.899), this time including the specific statement that a unit's role "is not to be included in the standard frame or in reproductions of any kind". This was to reflect that wartime pragmatism had meant that squadrons were being re-roled so that their original label was no longer appropriate – and perhaps also to stop making things unnecessarily easy for enemy intelligence. He continued: "This regulation has never been rescinded. As a result, the original of any squadron badge approved since 1941 has never included the unit's role, and it is still, strictly-speaking, incorrect to reproduce an image of a pre-1941 badge or to include the original role in the unit's designation. So those squadrons that still do it are really out of line."

How interesting, given that the likes of II(AC) Squadron, IX(B) Squadron and 1(F) Squadron continually use their role appendages; perhaps they shouldn't really be according themselves such titles these days. But if it is indeed a technical transgression it seems to me a fairly innocuous one – and one which, arguably, lends a little colour to what can be a dry area. And as it happens my own squadron has, despite having operated over the years in the bomber, transport, reconnaissance and strike/attack roles, returned during recent operations in Iraq and Afghanistan to a role that can be described as nothing other than army cooperation. What goes around certainly comes around.

Anyway, regardless of my own time on 31 Squadron being in strike/attack days, it wouldn't have been possible for me to have spent thirty-two years in the RAF without bumping up against the army in one way or another. And although I made some good friends amongst the brown jobs, their culture always seemed to me to be somewhat – shall we say – 'quirky'. Rather than try to describe to you the occasional army-aviation related oddities I came across during my time I hope you won't mind if I concentrate here on a completely non-flying aspect. It concerns the time I met the Household Cavalry.

The last months of my final tour in the RAF, which was at the ministry of defence in Whitehall, coincided with the period of my daughter's greatest enthusiasm for horses. She was always on at me to hack out with her – but I had never ridden. I was keen to show willing, but equally anxious not to make a complete ass of myself. So after casting around for a suitable way to learn the black art of riding I heard that the Household Cavalry occasionally took on pupils at Knightsbridge Barracks. I don't know whether that's still the case, but the reasons then were twofold. First, they had a fully-equipped riding school, and when their instructors had spare capacity they liked to keep in practice. Secondly, they had hundreds of horses which needed daily exercise. I was surprised to find how many 'extras' helped with this – everyone from members of the nobility, through nannies, army officers keeping current while in staff appointments, to occasional members of other services. Mostly at ungodly hours, prior to going about their own daily business.

So on the premise that I might eventually prove useful to them they were happy to take me on – and I reported very early one morning for kitting out and lesson one. The quartermaster's stores came up with khaki jodhpurs, thigh boots and spurs – and after levering myself into that lot I soon found out why the troops on Horse Guards Parade walk in such an extraordinary manner! The rest of the outfit comprised the top half of my best RAF uniform and a borrowed hard hat.

I waddled, bandy-legged, across the barracks yard to meet my trusty steed for lesson one. 'Patrick' was lovely. A speckled white horse (flea-bitten grey was the technical term, according to my daughter), he was the most handsome and lovely-natured boy. So much so that he was apparently often the mount of a senior officer on ceremonial occasions. I guess his gentle and unflappable nature was as well suited to big dates on Horse Guards Parade as it was to having a complete novice aboard. The height of him was awesome, the view from his back both exciting and terrifying.

My instructor wasted no time, and I was taken on a leading rein to the ring in the indoor school. "Now then sah, this is first gear." Patrick walked nicely around.

...I waddled bandy-legged across the barracks yard...

"Come along sah, heels down, back straight, knees in." I tried frantically to contort myself as demanded. "OK, give him a nudge and we'll try second gear." We broke into a trot; my teeth rattled and my backside thudded against the saddle, my motion precisely one-eighty out with Patrick's. "Happy sah? Third gear now – rev him up!" No, not happy – but surprisingly it all got smoother in the canter. The lesson sped by, and I went off to

AITKEN

...OK Sah - give him a nudge and we'll try second gear...

work. Mentally thrilled with what I'd done; physically stiffening up by the minute.

You'd be mistaken if you take from this that I had an aptitude or was a quick learner. Not at all, but army people don't mess around and the following lessons progressed at an equally breathless pace. Number two was my circuit consolidation in the outdoor ring in Hyde Park, just over the other side of South Carriage Road. Exercise three was a sector recce out along Rotten Row and around the perimeter of the park – traffic and all. Throughout, Patrick looked after me beautifully, never batting an eyelid at the unlikely messages my nervous and inexperienced body movements must have conveyed, whilst at the same time giving me the impression that he was obeying my every command. What an extraordinary sensation it was astride such a huge beast in a fast trot – the power and momentum of the animal really came across. Marvellous. Together we posed for early-morning Japanese tourists, me in my RAF number one uniform. If only they'd known!

I was growing in confidence, but even so the plan for lesson four was alarming. The Household Cavalry hold mass 'trots' through the streets of London in the early hours. Well, they did then, anyway – I assume they still do. All in the name of exercise. Oxford Street, Park Lane – many of the main highways echoed to the hooves of a hundred or more horses on summer mornings before the traffic woke up. I wonder whether they're nowadays subject to the 'congestion charge' if they do it after 7 a.m.! We've all marvelled at the discipline of the animals at Horse Guards. Perhaps, though, they don't stand still just because they're well trained. Maybe they're exhausted after being trotted all around London before their shifts start.

That's by the by; back to the mass trot. You'll imagine how nervous I was about the prospect. I hadn't even done the pre-solo emergencies trip in the Pegasus simulator. What if my steed should take off and head for Tower Bridge? It didn't bear thinking about. And yet my pride wouldn't let me say no. The army was testing this flabby RAF staff officer, and I wasn't about to duck the challenge. But luckily for me, that particular 'trot' was cancelled in favour of an extra trooping the colour rehearsal for the regulars, so I was off the hook. A very close shave.

At the barracks the atmosphere was friendly. Experience in my daughter's horsey environment had taught me that one generally got on best by showing willing and doing one's bit. So in return for riding at Knightsbridge I would have been happy to have done my share of tacking up, grooming and so on. But the army is a very hierarchical organisation, and my horse was always ready for me when I arrived. Afterwards, no matter how I protested, it was always "Trooper, take the group captain's horse away and see to it". "Yes s'a'nt!" I could but try.

It was time for exercise five, my pre-solo check. I was to go out with the riding master, a fierce sergeant major who would certify me as fit to take one of Her Majesty's chargers out into Hyde Park whenever I wished. I was absolutely not ready for this, but again, could I say no? Of course not! So I pitched up at 5 a.m. one summer morning, knees knocking, to be met by two shocks. The riding master was temporarily busy. "Just press on sah, I'll catch you up in the park directly." Oh gawd, I was being sent solo without the reassuring dual circuit detail beforehand. Worse, though, my mount was not to be the trusty Patrick, who was otherwise engaged that morning. I was introduced to 'Burniston', a standard-issue dark brown horse, who stared at me with baleful eye. I attempted to make friends, but was greeted with indifference. I mounted with trepidation – unfortunately, horses can sense that immediately – and headed across Carriage Road into the park. I decided to do a clockwise circuit and indicated this to Burniston. The contrary mare (I make no comment on the gender!) forcefully indicated that she would prefer to go anti-clockwise. Weakly – and of course wrongly – I acquiesced. From then on it was downhill. I won't bore you with the tedious details, but the ride culminated in Burniston casting me off with ease during a spirited demonstration of her aerobatic display. In the time it took me to fall the eighteen hands to mother earth, she shot off to the far side of the park and got amongst the traffic. As I dusted down my uniform and massaged my bruises and ego, I contemplated the humiliating walk back to the barracks, grateful that I'd never see that horse again.

...casting me off with ease during a spirited demonstration of her aerobatic display...

But I was not to get off the hook so easily. As I slunk away, the riding master trotted up. Worse still, he had Burniston on a leading rein. "Here you are, sah! Small mishap? Never mind. She's safe and sound. Up you jump!" I noted that the sergeant major hadn't inquired about my own welfare, and I also swear that the horse was grinning. Declining was clearly not an option, but getting up was all but beyond me. What with the stiff boots,

Top: The author aboard 'Patrick' on Rotten Row. (Jacqueline Hall)

Bottom: The lively 'Burniston' during a rare, calm period.

the tight jodhpurs, a throbbing hip and the lack of a mounting block, it took what seemed about fifteen minutes to get aboard. And I needed the help of Lady Bloggs, Tim Nice-but-Dim and all the other assorted exercisers of HM's horses who had gathered to enjoy the spectacle of this RAF officer making an absolute prat of himself. Together with dogs various and, I shouldn't wonder, a platoon of Japanese tourists snapping the action. Throughout it all, Burniston stood as good as gold. As soon as I was aboard, however, the aeros started again. Despite the close attendance of the riding master I lasted no longer than twenty seconds before biting the dust once more.

What a long way down it is from those huge beasts. And it doesn't half hurt! Amazingly, the sergeant major did get me back in the saddle again and he, the horse and I walked, more or less under control, back to Knightsbridge Barracks. But it was pretty well unspoken that I would not pursue this particular career, and I never went back again. Well, I was leaving the RAF in a few weeks, so not a lot was lost. And I have since ridden a couple of small, docile nags with my daughter, so the aim was at least partially accomplished. I still have a couple of bits of kit as souvenirs – the QM said that they were c-class stores and not required back. And, vainly, I'd asked my wife to come down and photograph me in happier times – mostly on Patrick. So with these mementoes, together with the occasional twinge from the hip which I bear proudly like an old war wound, I have a permanent record of my particular brand of army cooperation. I can still scarcely believe it all happened.

I can't believe, either, that I didn't consider at the time the potential for jeopardising the clean bill of health I needed to get the airline job I was looking for. The whole episode was, in hindsight, pretty unwise – but as so often happens in the military I got away with it.

As a postscript, I noticed when watching the annual trooping the colour broadcast on TV some fifteen years later that the parade commander's mount was one Burniston. I guess the beast whose path I'd crossed all those years ago had, like me, mellowed with age. Alternatively, although I somehow doubt it, maybe she'd learned something from me about army cooperation.

CHAPTER 4
PHANTOM MUD MOVING

As I reached the end of my first tour I waited with bated breath for my next posting. Whilst one or two from 208 Squadron had gone to Buccaneers and to instructor courses at the Central Flying School, I didn't really fancy the former – while the latter rarely attracted volunteers. And in any case most of those before me had headed off to become either Harrier or Phantom pilots. Of those two I much preferred the idea of Harriers. But it wasn't to be and the Phantom came out of the hat for me. At that time 43 Squadron was flying the FG1 Phantom in the air defence role, whilst half a dozen other squadrons were building up with strike/attack FGR2s. Again a choice, and just as the Lightning option hadn't seemed attractive from advanced flying training, so air defence didn't appear, from Bahrain, to be the way ahead. In the end I got my wish and it was to be ground-attack Phantoms. Having said that, and having read the draft of this chapter, I'm quite surprised to see how much air defence material it contains.

It seems strange, now, to think that any of us could have baulked at being sent to any one of these exciting options. From my rocking chair it looks as though we were spoilt for choice – and it was undeniable that the Phantom was an impressive machine. So it would be wrong to describe myself as disappointed, and I headed happily off to 228 OCU at RAF Coningsby. There, I soon found that there were two distinct aspects to the course. The first squadron taught initial conversion and air defence; because all the ground-attack squadrons had an intercept capability, all students completed this part of the syllabus. The second squadron taught those of us who were headed for ground-attack units the mud-moving skills we needed to learn.

The first phase was fascinating. The aircraft was awesome, although I was puzzled by what seemed to me the rather peculiar take-off technique they were teaching: hold the stick back from the start of the roll and then check forward when the nose wheel reared off the ground. That must, firstly, have increased drag and, secondly, reduced nose-wheel stability. I thought for some time that this 'stick back' idea might have come from the aircraft's naval heritage – perhaps it was the configuration for coming off the catapult. But I subsequently learned that the 'cat shot' positioning of the stick was infinitely more complicated. It involved individual aircraft weight and

C of G, wires and crocodile clips attached to the stick in the cockpit, and tailplane angle marks painted on the rear fuselage. I also learned that some USAF Phantom units started their take-off rolls with the stick forward of neutral. So quite where the RAF's unusual procedure for take-off came from I am still none the wiser.

I very much enjoyed the air defence phase, which mainly comprised practice interceptions at medium level. The pilot had a repeater radar screen and was expected to keep a good eye on the intercept. I loved to follow the geometry of the engagement, measuring the target's angle off, range and crossing speed against our intercept angle and turn-in point. There was lots of maths involved. On a parallel reciprocal course to the target, and planning to make a one-eighty turn in behind him, the angle off in degrees multiplied by the range in miles divided by sixty gave the displacement in miles. One could alter one's course to lessen or increase that displacement, making the appropriate adjustment to the angle off to take account of the new heading, until one arrived at the ideal eight miles displacement. Then, at forty degrees off and twelve miles, one would turn in and arrive in the target's stern sector at the perfect range to fire a Sidewinder missile. Altitude difference could be calculated similarly by looking at the radar elevation and target range.

My only previous experience of air defence had come in Bahrain when we'd occasionally been sent up to intercept Vulcans which were transiting through on exercise. The only lessons I had learned there were, firstly, that a Hunter fell out of the sky long before getting into guns range on a Vulcan at 50,000 feet. And secondly, that if the Vulcan chose to turn at that altitude it left the poor old Hunter struggling even more badly.

Now I had a machine with real capability, and intercepts proved to be much more fun than I had ever anticipated; perhaps I'd been wrong all along to think that Lightning pilots' work was boring. There was a difference, though. In the Phantom there was only limited ability for the front seater to control radar and missile functions. However, on the basis that the rear seater might become disabled or, more mundanely, that the intercom might fail, we pilots were given a few opportunities to do the thing from the front seat. The 'one-forty degree look-down with re-attack' is the profile I particularly recall – lots of maths and huge satisfaction when the simulated front and rear hemisphere missiles were both away.

The air-to-air combat phase which followed was exciting. It was an extraordinary experience to use techniques which would have been absolutely alien in the types I had hitherto known. At medium level we were taught the 'robinson loop' as the quickest way of reversing direction: roll inverted, pull to maximum angle of attack, aileron in the opposite direction from which one wished to turn – which through the usually-to-be-avoided aerodynamic phenomenon of 'adverse yaw' would induce a roll in the required direction. Plus, as I recall, a spot of rudder was involved, too. How on earth did anybody (Robinson, I presume) ever manage to invent that bizarre manoeuvre? It was sobering to note that the full 13,000 pounds of fuel carried in a clean (no external fuel tanks) Phantom could be consumed, using full reheat, in seven minutes flat. One ton per minute! But it was all good fun.

Despite all that, however, the atmosphere on that first squadron was flat. The instructors were from various backgrounds: from Vulcans, Canberras, Hunters and Lightnings. They were all good guys and their various histories shouldn't have caused any problem. I was at a loss, therefore, to find the source of the malaise. Much later, I discovered that the 'problem' was the boss. In those days the RAF ran a reporting system that was completely closed; not only did one not have the opportunity to read what had been written, but it wasn't uncommon not even to receive a debrief on the CO's opinion. But years later I had the chance to read my Coningsby course report, and I was taken aback to see that the squadron commander had betrayed a prejudice by committing to paper the following: 'Despite his previous "fighter" experience ...' This was odd, given that he himself had a Hunter background; but he certainly seemed now to have an in-built low opinion of recent Gulf products.

He went on to express in my report his view that 'I have doubts about his ability to walk and chew gum at the same time'. We'd better leave aside the question of whether he was right in that assessment; after all, I guess I'm not the best person to offer an objective view. But the style of reporting is appalling. Perhaps he was demonstrating to those up the chain who would read his words that he was a pretty cool dude who had converted to the Phantom in the States. But I've done enough report writing myself to know that putting seemingly smart comments above one's signature in a closed report shows a distinct lack of class. Moreover, it perhaps reflects more on the instructor than the student. It's all water under the bridge now, but I was pleased to note that he didn't make it much further in the RAF. Perhaps the system proved perceptive in the end.

I wasn't the only one to detect a problem on that squadron at the Phantom OCU. A friend of mine who followed me from Bahrain Hunters fell even more foul of the system, being suspended from the course at that same first stage. He had been a good Hunter pilot and, later, became a very well respected Jaguar pilot and squadron commander. But for whatever reason (I think I can guess) he and the F-4 world didn't click. Ironically, by the way, following his chopping from Coningsby my friend was returned to Chivenor as a Hunter instructor. Teaching, among others, pre-Phantom students. What a complex organisation we lived in.

Having got through that problematic first stage I emerged into the sunlit uplands of the second OCU squadron. Everything about that phase was enjoyable: good instructors; good spirit; good flying. I saw straight away, though, that the brand new, shiny Phantom was not equipped with modern weapons. We were learning to deliver the Hunter's unguided rockets and the Canberra's (Lancaster's?) iron bombs. Never mind, we had a good time on that squadron – and we graduated.

I joined 54 Squadron, also at Coningsby. At the time the unit had four flights, three specialising in ground attack and one in reconnaissance. Number 6 Squadron, our sister unit next door, was similarly constructed. About a year after I joined, the two squadrons' recce flights were spun off to form 41 Squadron, specialising in reconnaissance.

The author with navigator Dave Wilson beside a Phantom FGR2 of 54 Squadron. The Sidewinder armament shows that the squadron was preparing to hand over to 111 Squadron in the air defence role, which dates the picture to spring 1974.

I enjoyed the first three months on my new unit. Suddenly, however, a hammer blow struck. The Phantom had been experiencing engine problems for a while, and these had come to a head. To the effect that flying hours available each month were to be severely cut. There were various ways this could have been dealt with: sorties could have been made shorter and more intense; or crew sorties per month could have been reduced. But our boss decided that the available hours could only keep a reduced number of pilots current. Accordingly, two of us were grounded – and I was one of them. The policy wasn't consistent, for all the navs continued to fly. I'm not sure what conclusion, if any, to draw from the difference in treatment.

It was all very dispiriting. Although my grounding lasted just five weeks, those engine problems had far-reaching effects. Because the OCU was shut down for a good period, no new crews arrived on 54 Squadron for roughly two years. So instead of making the conventional progress up the unit seniority ladder I remained rooted firmly at the bottom.

The engine difficulties stemmed from the nature of the Rolls-Royce Spey. It was a high-bypass ratio engine, a turbofan, and had been performing well in the Buccaneer for some years. But adding reheat to such an engine for the Phantom was a new venture and brought teething problems. The first I saw of these occurred during a night sortie on the OCU. On selection of afterburner at the start of the take-off roll I was startled by a huge bang and a sheet of flame erupting out of the engine air intake – right beside my ear. This was a 'flashback' and was, apparently, a fairly well known phenomenon. At the time it wasn't regarded as particularly harmful to the engine, but it's not hard to imagine the kinds of stresses that such violent, reverse air flow was putting on the blades. It was all exacerbated, I later learned, by the fact that the aircraft's wing flaps and slats were 'blown' – in other words incorporated slots which were fed through ducts with engine bleed air to provide extra lift at low speed. All in all this complex arrangement was proving a little too much for the brand-new reheated Spey.

An interim measure, I seem to remember, was for wing slat bleed air to be disabled. This was accomplished by means of pulling a couple of circuit breakers in the rear cockpit prior to the landing approach. These were difficult to reach, so our highly trained navigators were each provided with a very low-tech gadget mounted on a long stick – with which they could pop the afore-mentioned circuit breakers. Longer term, the engine fix involved drilling the engine blades with a hugely complex labyrinth of air passages, in effect giving each individual blade its own little bit of boundary air control. During this rectification period we were wheeled across to the factory to see the work in action. It was a fascinating day out and the Rolls-Royce management gave us a sumptuous company lunch – but it hardly compensated for being stuck on the ground. In the end, a rethink by the squadron commander on how to manage the problem meant that my grounding didn't last long – but of course it seemed like a lifetime.

The FGR2 was intended only to be temporarily employed in the ground-attack role; the idea was that it would replace the air defence Lightning as soon as something (eventually that proved to be the Jaguar) could take over ground-attack duties. When it entered service it was, in common with the Harrier, to be fitted with a Ferranti INAS, the inertial navigation and attack system. I know from talking to many Phantom navs that this was something of a pig to use. The equipment had been intended, possibly, for the long-dead TSR2; thus it didn't fit terribly well into the Phantom rear cockpit, some of the important digits having to be read through an adapting lens. It also took an age to insert the turning points and destinations – and of course the kit drifted. Nevertheless, navigator opinion was that a Phantom with INAS was better than one without.

As far as I recall the OCU had no INAS jets, so the first time I met one was on the squadron. But overall fleet availability was poor, with most INAS-equipped Phantoms being allocated to Germany; presumably the strike (nuclear) role held precedence. Thus we on 54 Squadron had only a couple. And at first those two were normally flown by our recce friends, so my own INAS experience amounted, in the early days, to just about zilch.

In the circumstances it made sense that the whole squadron's weapon-aiming practice was conducted solely with the basic, fixed sight for gunnery and bombing. This could be viewed as rather pathetic; we were dropping old bombs from this brave new aircraft using aiming systems inferior to those in the Hunter. We were also firing the amazing 6,000 rounds-per-minute Vulcan cannon using a fixed sight; one either slaugh-

A 54 Squadron Phantom armed with SNEB 68 mm rocket pods. On the centreline pylon is a recon-naissance pod. The two rear fuselage stations are occupied by Sparrow missiles, while the forward stations carry ballast rounds to keep the aircraft in balance. The aircraft, XV437, (later given the fleet letter 'F') was one of the squadron's few INAS jets. (Crown Copyright)

tered the target if one got it right, or wasted tons of lead if the aim was slightly off.

Later, when we acquired a couple more INAS-equipped aircraft, it became possible for a few crews to have a go with the more modern aiming system. On one occasion, when much of the squadron had been deployed on some exercise or other, I found myself at home base with my flight commander and an INAS jet. He had been a test nav during the Phantom's early acceptance days, and lost no time in giving me a full briefing on what the kit could provide and how to use it. Following which we spent a couple of sorties together over one of the east coast ranges 'having a go'.

When it comes to bomb delivery, second only in importance to aiming at the correct point is releasing the weapon at the correct distance from the target. Many different methods exist for arriving at that solution, but the INAS mode I learned that day was what is known as 'kinematic' ranging. For those with a mathematical turn of mind this meant that, as the target was tracked, the rate of rotation of the tracking line as the bomber approached would be integrated by the kit to give a distance from the target and, therefore, provide a bomb release cue. In fact it used similar methodology to 'ARBS' – the angle-rate bombing system – which the Americans later used on their AV-8Bs.

I didn't find this easy to work with during those sorties, but it was an interesting experience nevertheless. Clearly, it would have taken more practice to build expertise. And almost equally as clearly, kinematic ranging was no more than an interim answer. As I was to learn during my subsequent tours on Jaguar and Tornado, second and third generation aiming systems would provide far more user-friendly and accurate modes.

54 Squadron Phantoms over southern Germany. The photo was taken during a detachment to USAF air base Bitburg by the author using the forward-facing strike camera of a third aircraft.

The Phantom was a Mach 2 plus aircraft, although for us in the low-level ground-attack role the speed range from 420-600 knots (Mach 0.6 – 0.9) was the norm. Not only would higher speed have been pretty uncomfortable where we operated close to the ground, but would have been beyond the limits of the external stores we invariably carried.

The air defence squadrons must, more regularly, have got up into the higher Mach ranges. But maybe not as easily as they would have wished, for the UK versions of the Phantom were not as fast as they ought to have been. When we'd ordered the machine, opting to replace the well-proven General Electric J-79 engines with Rolls-Royce Speys, thrust was increased. Perhaps more importantly in those straitened times, the change had improved the balance of payments equation and brought work to Derby. But the modification brought significant limitations, quite apart from the teething difficulties we've already heard about. Yes, the engines were more powerful than the J-79s, but they also demanded far more air, so the airframe intakes had to be widened. This, naturally, increased drag, which more than negated the additional thrust. The UK Phantom was, therefore, disappointingly slower than the original.

I, like most of my contemporaries, had a 'need for speed'. For a mud mover, Mach 2 was somewhere out there but was, in most normal circumstances, unattainable. Then one day I saw my chance. I was sent by HS125 to RAF Aldergrove, near Belfast, to collect a newly serviced jet from the maintenance unit. There stood XT902 on the apron, glistening with pristine paint and with absolutely nothing hanging underneath to spoil its clean lines: no external tanks; and not even pylons or suspension equipment. My brief (our brief, I should say – my back seater that day was a lovely old gentleman we knew on the squadron as the 'silver fox') was simply to deliver the aircraft to Coningsby. Nobody had specified quite how we should achieve this objective, so the sky was ours.

Off we launched from Belfast, taking off in dry power to conserve fuel (with such a light aircraft reheat wasn't necessary to hop off the ground). Up the climb and pointing eastwards, our slippery jet soon arrived overhead Coningsby with plenty of fuel in hand. So now we aimed north-eastwards and changed frequency to high-level radar. In barely a couple of minutes we were over the North Sea and heading in the right direction. "Radar, are we cleared for high speed?" "On your present heading you are cleared high speed. Call complete."

Now we had to do it. Full burner, climb to the tropopause at about 36,000 feet, push to near-zero G to go supersonic and then ease the nose up – and up – and up. Then, topping out at about 48,000 feet, bunt over again and dive for speed. Mach 1.5 ... 1.7 ... 1.8. Was it my imagination or could we feel the heat of skin friction? Check the fuel and distance from base – by gum, we were far out and getting more distant at the rate of twenty miles a minute. The machmeter was now reading 1.9, but as our altitude decreased the airspeed was rising towards the 790 knot limit – and it was undoubtedly time to turn about. A pity to miss Mach 2, but it would have been even more of a pity to run out of fuel on the way home. We cruised gently inbound, our clean jet using negligible fuel in the descent. No regrets at missing our target, and I'd enjoyed the attempt. The silver fox remained unmoved.

The ground-attack Phantom was outstandingly equipped for self defence. As well as having the capability to carry Sidewinder missiles (although, in general, those wouldn't have been loaded on ground-attack missions because they occupied bomb stations) the aircraft had four semi-recessed fuselage mountings for Sparrow missiles. But, although we talked occasionally of Sparrow defence, I don't think it was taken very seriously at the time. Not until years later did I see some really imaginative work in this respect. That enlightenment came when I was attending a NATO tactical leadership course while flying Jaguars. By that time NATO had got around to the idea of 'big packages' – the idea being to overwhelm enemy defences with twenty or thirty bombers at a time. Embedded in one of those massive formations would, quite often, be a four-ship of USAF F-4E Phantoms, who would not only carry bombs but also, as they termed it, 'ride shotgun' with aggressive use of their radars and Sparrows. We'd often see those guys spearing off to deal with a threat, and with them around I always felt significantly safer. They were always back in place, too, to drop their bombs on the target at the allotted time.

On that same course I also met a couple of rather alarming RAF Phantom crews, who were by this time operating in the air defence role. They were from 19 Squadron and, as low-level interceptors, were tasked to oppose our large bomber formations.

Their head-on tactics appeared to be akin to playing chicken – break away if you dare. Whilst I would applaud the idea for real, I didn't appreciate on a peacetime training exercise having a face full of Phantom at quite such close range.

Although we may not have made optimum use of the Phantom's self-defence capability in my time, the squadron nevertheless had a go at a missile practice camp. There were six – or maybe eight – missiles to fire – I forget exactly how many. In fact the number hardly mattered; once the boss had opted to fire two himself, there were not many left for the rest of us, and certainly none for me. But never mind, the firings all went very well, and it turned out that 54 Squadron won the Aberporth trophy – for the best MPC results of the year. I remembered that much later when my own 31 Tornado Squadron had a similarly successful result. We should also, by rights, have been awarded the Aberporth. But by that time the powers that be had decreed that attack squadrons weren't eligible for the trophy; the poor old Tornado F3s were so short of success that, by then, the Aberporth had been reserved strictly for them! A great shame.

We used to do a fair number of practice interceptions on 54 Squadron. Although air defence was never, I think, declared as a secondary role – we were fully committed to NATO as a ground-attack force – it nevertheless appeared on the programme quite regularly. Mostly, I must say, during night-flying periods. Traditionally, attack squadrons had done the bulk of their work by day, only venturing airborne in the dark to keep current. The Phantom had some kind of night-attack capability, although it was usually our sister Coningsby squadron, rather than us, who did a little weapons delivery on the range under flares. Of course getting to a target at night at all would, in those days, have been somewhat problematical. We had an excellent radar which our trusty navs could have used in its ground-mapping mode, and we did practise radar navigation and simulated weapon release. But in doing so we were up at three or four thousand feet – in the altitude band most vulnerable to our opponents' surface-to-air missiles. So I'm not convinced that we ever had a credible night-attack capability. Anyway, rather than attack, we on 54 tended to do practice interceptions when we needed to fly at night. As mentioned earlier I enjoyed the maths involved, and PIs certainly beat the hell out of night high-level navexes or practice diversions to alternate airfields.

On one memorable occasion much later in my career I was able to turn the tables on a Phantom by dredging up nearly forgotten knowledge of how intercepts worked. While I was a flight commander on 6 Jaguar Squadron we set up a couple of air combat days with 74 Phantom Squadron. They were equipped with the twelve F-4Js which the UK had purchased in the early 1980s to pad out our interceptor force. Those were ex-US Navy aircraft, with the original General Electric engines, and the squadron was commanded by an old friend of mine. Needless to say they could easily out-perform us Jaguar boys in terms of both speed and manoeuvrability, and had the

54 Squadron Phantoms refuel from a Victor. (Crown Copyright)

inestimable advantage of a good air-to-air radar. So they were confidently looking forward to a series of easy kills.

The Jag had a radar warning receiver which gave a reasonable idea of the direction from which a radar threat was approaching. Knowing this, the Phantom crews wouldn't perform their interceptions with the radar continuously locked on. They'd take a quick squirt to establish their target's range, azimuth and altitude, and then switch to standby. They might take another peek later on but, to a great extent, they'd continue the intercept largely by using lots of their own mental arithmetic. Then, when approaching kill range they'd re-lock the radar and launch their missiles.

But I had a cunning plan – and armed with this, I launched off on trip one. The GCI controller split us outbound to about twenty-five miles and then pointed us roughly at each other. We'd been free to choose our altitudes and, going outbound, I'd staggered up as high as my poor old Jag could manage (that wasn't very high!) As we established on our inbound headings the RWR flashed up as expected as my opponent gathered data on me. Now was the time to put my plan into operation, and I rolled the Jag onto its back and pulled down steeply. If there was one thing a Jaguar was good at it was going down, and in two shakes of a cat's tail I was level a good 10,000 feet lower than I'd originally been. Now I knew where to look for the enemy: upwards. He, of course, knowing what my initial altitude had been, thought he knew where he needed to look. But I was no longer there, and quite soon I had the huge satisfaction of spotting my F-4J as he frantically weaved around searching. It wasn't too difficult, thereafter, to get myself into his low six o'clock, where his radar certainly wouldn't help him. And before too long I had a few seconds of juicy gunsight film as I tracked him through Sidewinder launch to guns kill. "Fox 2! Fox 3!" He bought the beers that evening.

Eventually, as the RAF's 1970s and 1980s game of musical squadrons moved towards its next stage, it became apparent that 54 Phantom Squadron was heading towards an air defence future. A couple of ex-Lightning pilots were posted in as flight

A 54 Squadron Phantom on final approach to land at Tengah air base, Singapore, in late 1972 during Exercise Bersato Padu.

commanders and we worked towards a date in 1974 when our Phantoms would be transformed into Treble-One Squadron in the air defence role. Many of the crews would move across. Those of us not destined to switch to that role awaited postings, and eventually there were only three or four of us left. We termed ourselves the 'ground-attack union', and laid down (light-hearted) laws as to what we would and would not do: no night flying; no PIs; only low-level flying, air tests, overseas jollies, and so on.

I would have liked to move to the Jaguar. Number 54's number plate was to go to the first of the squadrons equipped with the new jet, and indeed we'd met some of the replacement team. But they'd already selected most of those destined for the first two or three Jag squadrons, so for me it seemed that the natural progression would be to one of the remaining strike/attack Phantom squadrons in Germany. But for family reasons I preferred not to go overseas at that point. So what should I do? Against my instincts I applied for a QFI course. I mentioned earlier that most people posted to CFS were non-volunteers, and the powers that be must have thought that I was an outstanding candidate. Or, more likely, they were taken quite aback at actually hearing from a volunteer. Whichever the reason, they accepted me at once.

I awaited my posting notice in two minds. I didn't really want to go to CFS, but couldn't really see another way forward. But fate stepped in with a completely unexpected posting; I was to return to the Hunter as an instructor at the Chivenor TWU. For me, there couldn't possibly have been a better outcome.

CHAPTER 5
GROUND TESTED, NO FAULT FOUND

We all loved the techies because it was they who made the whole operation possible. But that doesn't mean that we didn't look sideways from time to time at them and the kit they serviced for us. Although many of our accidents could be put down to 'aircrew error', a significant proportion certainly had technical roots.

In all my forty-four years of flying I'm pleased to report that I only suffered one incident that was serious enough to be categorised as an accident. It wasn't my fault, but I'll stop short of blaming the techies – if only because conclusive evidence was lacking! It occurred on the venerable Hawker Hunter, and before going on to describe the event I'll first have to give you a brief run-down on the aircraft's wheel-braking system – which, incidentally, it shared with the Lightning.

Protruding from the front of the control column was an arrangement which resembled a bicycle brake lever. Squeezing it would apply hydraulic pressure to the main-wheel brakes, as determined by the position of the rudder pedals. With rudder neutral one could get anything up to maximum braking on both wheels. With rudder applied, less brake was available to the opposite wheel (but not more in the direction of the rudder) – up to the point where, for example, with full left rudder, one got zero brake on the right wheel. There was no direct steering system; the nose wheel simply castored, with differential braking on the main wheels providing directional impetus. You may easily see that, when landing in a strong crosswind with lots of rudder applied, one might have barely more than half braking available.

This was often a factor at RAF Chivenor with its single, short runway, and aircraft ran off the end quite regularly. I recall a particular incident during my tour there as an instructor when one of our foreign students landed on runway one-zero. Peculiarly, the far (eastern) end wasn't visible from the control tower (this is the 'old' Chivenor I'm talking about, before it closed in 1974 – they relocated the tower to a more prac- tical position when the station later reopened). So ATC lost sight of this chap as he disappeared behind the hangars about half-way down the runway. He failed to call 'clear complete' ('runway vacated' in today's terminology) and so, after a couple of unanswered enquiries and with aircraft queuing up to land, the local controller dispatched a Land Rover crew to investigate. They found the aircraft in the barrier net with its canopy open and the cockpit empty. After a little more investigation they located the pilot in the nearby officers' mess enjoying tea and toast – and denying that he had been airborne that afternoon.

At this point I feel a bit like Ronnie Corbett, sitting in his big chair and being continually side-tracked, because I now have to say that the foregoing story has very little to do with my own accident. I do admit to having had several close shaves at Chivenor on wet runways with strong crosswinds, but in every case I managed either to slither and judder to a halt just short of the barrier or to negotiate the turnoff in something of a three-wheel drift. And I know that many other Chivenor Hunter pilots will share such memories.

In fact my own story is set at RAF Brawdy, in Pembrokeshire, whence we decamped when Chiv closed. That move, by the way, came much to my wife's disappointment, for her family home was in north Devon; it was where we'd met, and we had very much enjoyed being back there.

Perched on a 350-foot high cliff and facing the Atlantic Ocean, with its main runway oriented far to the south of the prevailing westerly winds, Brawdy had possibly the worst weather factor in the UK. 'Gale force fog' was its speciality. Indeed I vividly recall the day (2 September 1974) set for our final fly-out from Chivenor to Brawdy. We had something like fifty jets to deliver, but at met brief we heard that Brawdy's weather was firmly 'red' and likely to remain so for the whole day. There was nothing for it, of course, but to adjourn to the bar. After an initial scare caused by the discovery that its stocks had been run down by the previous day's epic closing party, beer was magically found from somewhere and we passed another pleasant 'final' day at Chivenor before eventually making the transit on the 3rd. No wonder the Royal Navy had deserted Brawdy, and no wonder the RAF later passed it on to the army. No offence to the Welsh – the people and the surrounding countryside were delightful – but to me it seemed like no sensible place for an airfield.

Anyway, back to my accident story. Our new home was far from flat, and one day while taxiing out I found I was having trouble staying on the centreline. It transpired that the left brake was failing, and in the end I had no option but to heave to (correct terminology, Brawdy being an ex-RN station). Luckily I was heading uphill at the time, and managed to roll to a halt without taking to the grass. I applied the parking brake, asked for a tow, and shut down. Returning to the line hut I snagged the jet – and that, I thought, was that.

A little over an hour later I was programmed to fly again, and as sod would have it I was allocated the same aircraft. Impressively quick rectification, I thought. But on checking through the form 700 (the aircraft's technical record) my heart sank. There stood the dreaded words 'ground tested, no fault found'. My brief conversation in the line hut with the grizzled old chief technician was less than satisfactory. There most certainly had been a snag, I argued – but I got the unmistakable impression that he believed I'd imagined the whole episode. "We've had it up on jacks and can't fault it. Take it or leave it. Sir."

Faced with this challenge, I of course took it. You'll understand, though, that I came off the chocks pretty gingerly. The parking spot was on a slight downward slope so I rolled forward just a little, rudder pedals neutral, and gave a gentle squeeze on the brake lever to test both. There was an immediate swing to the right. I needed to stop this quickly, so applied full left rudder and a large yank on the lever. No result. Zero left brake. The castoring nose wheel had now established the machine in an arc to the right and it was inexorably heading for its neighbour on the line, so there was no option: I stop-cocked the engine and applied full brake, accepting the increased right turn but hoping that the aircraft would stop before hitting anything.

Luck wasn't with me, and the 'crunch' as my steed's nose buried itself into the fuselage side of the adjacent aircraft was impressive. I remember being staggered that such a low-speed collision could cause so much damage. The subsequent debrief in the line hut was interesting, to say the least, and I've no doubt that the accident caused plenty of work for the chaps in the hangar with their hammers and bodge tape.

To be fair, the Hunter was, by that time, a very old aircraft and was becoming difficult to maintain. Any snag which, in a more modern aircraft, could have been rectified by simply replacing a black box, would, on the Hunter, sometimes require endless hours of trouble shooting. Wiring looms were dusty and obscure, while fuel and hydraulic components were inaccessible. Although basically a simple aircraft, it must, towards the end of its life, have become something of an engineers' nightmare.

Anyway, things have changed now that aircraft have all that wonderful built-in test equipment. Or have they really? I'm not sure that some of that stuff isn't too clever for its own good. Operators of the Tornado in its early days will recall the 'CSAS test' which, at the push of a button, exercised the entire flight control and stability augmentation system. It used to be done, as I understand it, before each flight, but by the time I arrived on the 'fin' the requirement had been reduced to once per week or thereabouts. I certainly recall performing the test on occasions, sitting patiently for several minutes with the aircraft rocking as the control surfaces banged and thrashed around. And thereby lay the main reason why the 'once per sortie' test requirement had disappeared; all that thrashing and banging had, in turn, been causing all sorts of bits to break.

Then there was the nose-wheel steering self-test, which was performed automatically on the Tornado following each gear down selection. It quite regularly threw up a fault indication, following which it was necessary to make an approach-end cable engagement. Not surprisingly, the alleged fault was seldom found to be a real one, meaning that endless hours were wasted because of the BITE function itself.

It seems to be much the same with my relatively modern car. A year ago a warning light flashed up, accompanied by a power reduction. The traction control system (essentially a rather fancy, electronic differential) was indicated to be at fault; the associated computer was programmed to limit power available because the manufacturer had decided that the driver could not be trusted with full power following a traction control failure. I had little option but to take my car for a meeting with the main dealer's diagnostic equipment. Less than an hour later and with my wallet £100 lighter I was sitting across the desk from my 'technical consultant'.

"The test was inconclusive," said he, "but we recommend replacing widget X and digit Y, as well as reprogramming fidget Z as a precaution."

"How much?" said I.

"£800 plus VAT," said he – without the merest hint of embarrassment.

"Will that fix the snag?"

"Well, we can't really be sure."

"Err ... let me think about that for a while."

Over the weekend I recycled the system a couple of dozen times, the light eventually went out, and power was restored. Moreover, the problem has never recurred. So had it been a real snag or just an anomaly in the self-testing or monitoring system? I suppose techies would say that such gremlins are sometimes fiendishly difficult to pin down, whether they be oily, mechanical snags or geeky, computer-driven glitches. The difference is that computers don't look at you with the same knowing glance as an old-fashioned RAF chiefy. At least not so that we can see!

CHAPTER 6
VERY INSTRUCTIVE

The work at the TWU was marvellous. The hours were long and we found ourselves running from one debrief to the next brief, but the variety was absolutely terrific. It could be bombing in the morning, low-level navigation at lunchtime and air-to-air combat in the afternoon. We were also lucky enough to have an operational commitment in Gibraltar, which gave us three-week detachments a couple of times a year to relieve the instructional routine.

One of my aims on returning to the Hunter was to get myself a QWI qualification, and I was lucky enough to be selected just six months into the tour. It was an excellent course, long and thorough. Part of the reason for its length was because all our myriad weapon-aiming calculations had initially to be done by logarithmic tables and slide rules. Imagine that, in 1975! Calculators were well established on the market by then,

Hunter FGA9 of 234 Squadron passes a Soviet Kresta I class cruiser as it makes good speed near Gibraltar. The photo was taken in early 1976 using the starboard-facing F95 camera of a second Hunter flown by the author.

but the hierarchy was of a conservative mind set and took the view that what had been good for them must be good for us. With this in mind it won't surprise you to know that set-piece briefings sometimes had to be given using a blackboard and chalk, even though overhead projectors, acetate sheet and felt tip pens were, by then, commonplace.

One thing that hadn't yet become available was video recording of cockpit parameters, so we were stuck with wet film for the old gunsight cameras. This was a cumbersome system and prone to jamming, which made for some very long and laboured debriefs in the cine room. A painful process, not least because many of us were smokers and the air in the darkened room was a consistently thick fog. The worst offender in that respect was Buck, one of the instructors; he seemed to be able to

Hunter F6 of 234 Squadron reaches for the sky. (Crown Copyright)

get through a pack of twenty in an hour. On completing the course, we presented 79 Squadron with an extractor fan for the cine room, together with a plaque labelling it the 'Buck Buckingham memorial extractor fan'. Our little joke had both prescience and sad irony, for Buck died not many years later at a relatively early age.

I shall never forget my first dual instructional sortie on 234 Squadron following the course. It was an air-to-air gunnery trip and, after briefing it carefully, I stepped out with my student to fly. Off we launched to the south-west, contacted Hartland radar, and were vectored onto the old Meteor which was trolling up and down in the range towing the 'flag'. This hessian target, about twenty or thirty feet long and perhaps five or six feet high, and with a large bull's eye painted on it, was trailing on the end of a line roughly 300 yards long. Attached to its forward edge was a substantial iron bar with an even more hefty weight at the bottom – this to keep the flag flying vertically. The target sounds large, but from where I was sitting it looked tiny.

I set up parallel to the flag's track for my first demo pass, full of the expertise and patter I'd just been taught. "Here we are, Bloggs, abeam the target and a couple of thousand feet higher. Now, we turn in, drop the nose, pull below and behind the tug and flag, reverse the turn, point behind the flag and pull gently forward along its line of flight. Check the speed, adjust the power to maintain, call 'in hot', receive clearance, make the trigger live ... radar's green, that's 1,500 yards ... bring the pipper forward to the flag ... progressively increase the bank to maintain the line ... hold the G ... radar's amber at 350 yards ... pause ... fire ... cease ... roll in the opposite direction, maintaining G to go over the top of the flag ..."

CRASH

Christ, what the hell's going on? Everything's gone dark. We've hit the bloody flag!

"I have control." It's the student's voice. "No problem, all's well."

What had in fact happened is that my ejection seat, whose height adjustment was manually set by a lever with a thumb-plunger locking mechanism, had become unlatched under G, allowing the seat to crash down to its lowest position on the cockpit floor. I sorted myself out, making sure that the setting lever was well and truly ratcheted into position. Bloody thing!

"OK Bloggs, I have control. Now then, any questions on that pass?"

"No, all fine."

"Good, your turn now. Here we are, abeam the flag. You have control …"

Later, when I was in Norway flying the F-5, we used to do our air-to-air gunnery at 400 knots rather than the 300 we used on the Hunter. Given that the target was stooging at, perhaps, 180 knots, that greater closing speed was quite eye-watering. But teaching in the F-5B removed any pressure on the instructor to prove his expertise by scoring hits with his demo pass, for the two-seater had no gun. It was rather like teaching air-to-air refuelling in the Jaguar T2 – which had no probe.

Years later I did a very short Jaguar QWI course to convert my qualification to the new aircraft. It was only a week long, and majored on aspects of weapon aiming that were new, mainly the NAVWASS. By this time I had a couple of years on the Jag and was already back-seat qualified. It was a great aircraft to fly from the rear seat, by the way – offering a terrific view and with all the controls one needed. That course was nothing but enjoyable but, as it turned out, I never did an instructional tour on the Jag. Nevertheless, as a squadron supervisor, the qualification was useful.

The way in which I'd first moved, back in 1976, from Hunter to Jaguar, was a little curious. I'd not been expecting a posting away from the Brawdy instuctional staff for several months, but the Jaguar boys had apparently been experiencing a run of accidents and fatalities, chiefly to first-tourists, which had resulted in a demand for the force to be bolstered by a little experience. Thus it was that, one Thursday, I was warned to be at Lossiemouth the following Monday to start a Jaguar conversion. For domestic reasons that proved impossible and I negotiated a week's delay – which still made it tight but, at least, manageable.

Following the ground school phase, and once my wife had disentangled herself from her Welsh employment, I was picked up by a Brawdy T7 and taken south on what proved to be my last Hunter trip. Wife and I handed over the Welsh house and then motored north to take up residence in a small holiday cottage beside the River Spey. The winter of 1976 was harsh, and that cottage must have been one of the least well heated in Scotland. But we had a great time and, because of the urgency of the Jaguar situation, my short course was whistled through in just three months. Before we knew it, therefore, we were en route to 20 Squadron, which was in the process of forming at RAF Brüggen.

CHAPTER 7
NAVAL COOPERATION

We saw in an earlier chapter that soon after the Royal Flying Corps had merged with the Royal Naval Air Service to form the Royal Air Force, dedicated army cooperation squadrons had emerged. But although many squadrons displayed those 'AC' epithets, I don't think that the badges of any RAF squadrons ever boasted a 'naval cooperation' role description. Nevertheless many squadrons, notably most of the '200' series which had come from the RNAS, were dedicated to the maritime role, in my day flying Shackletons and, later, Nimrods.

The term 'naval cooperation' was in common usage within the ground-attack force for a long while, along with other acronyms such as 'TASMO' – tactical air support of maritime operations. Maybe both have come and gone over the years, but what I'm getting around to is simply to tell a few stories about working with our nautical cousins. "Hearts of oak have our men" as the navy says – "and heads to match" as the other services would routinely feel bound to retort!

But that's not fair, and anyway, I like the navy. Must be all that rum and ... er ... baccy. Maybe it's in the genes, for my late father was a wartime sailor. He saw much service in the Atlantic and the Bay of Bengal, but chiefly the Mediterranean. Luckily for him he never had to swim home.

I myself was very keen at one time to join the Fleet Air Arm before eventually settling for the light blue. Later, I got even closer to the RNAS when an offer came in 1974 of an exchange tour flying Phantoms on HMS *Ark Royal*. Not the recently decommissioned Harrier carrier, but the one before. The tour would have been on her last voyage, for Harold Wilson's government had announced the imminent end of naval fixed-wing flying. The trio of smaller aircraft carriers with their Sea Harriers came later after a much-needed rethink – driven partly by the Falklands experience.

It's extraordinary, isn't it, how history repeats itself? The hiatus in maritime capability of the 1970s/80s bears uncanny similarity to events following 2010's decision to do without naval air until the Queen Elizabeth class carriers enter service. One wonders, sometimes, how politicians can completely ignore the logical sequence: first, identify the threat they wish to counter; second, provide viable means to counter it. Did the threat magically disappear during those interludes? I think not.

Anyway, following the disbandment announcement back in 1974, the first sea lord had resigned and, not surprisingly, many of his aircrew had followed him. So the RN was having trouble manning its Phantoms and Buccaneers for the final cruise – hence the offer to us RAF types. I was newly married and it would have meant many months away from home, so I turned it down. Although not without lingering regrets about missing the chance of a lifetime. Those Phantoms and Buccaneers were bordering on being too large for the old *Ark,* and I understand that operating them on board was an incredibly exciting and challenging business. I know several who took the tour and had a fantastic time. They visited the Caribbean and New York, as well as firing and dropping every last weapon on board. And, as I heard it, they flew the aircraft so hard that the airframes had very little useful fatigue life remaining when they were eventually handed over to the RAF.

But there were many other times during my career when I got the chance to meet the RN, with Gibraltar proving to be an excellent rendezvous. In my visits to 'the rock' flying Hunters and Jaguars, the RAF and the RN had all sorts of adventures together. Firing at and bombing targets towed by ships was always fun, as was air-to-air combat with their fighters and exercises with RN helicopters. The latter habitually hid behind passing oil tankers, making for exciting chases which must have frightened the pants off those merchant ships' crews. Then there was the time when I nearly came to grief while working with the fleet a couple of hundred miles out into the Atlantic [for the full details of that near disaster, you need to read *Jaguar Boys*]. Why is it that fuel runs out more quickly when there's nothing but ocean below?

But it's the social memories that stand out. In any list of 'famous floating gin palaces', HMS *Penelope* would be near the top – even in these days of Roman Abramovich-type cruisers. The name sounds like a Gilbert and Sullivan creation – but no, she was a real ship. A Leander class frigate, she had become the trials vessel for a new guided missile. The weapon system, Sea Wolf, ultimately proved its pedigree during the Falklands conflict, but during the trial period the modifications to *Penelope* had some useful spin-offs. The ship's main gun turret and its equipment below had been removed to accommodate the new kit, leaving a vast space which had been converted into a wardroom big and opulent enough to grace a battleship. Kitted out with plush furnishings, fancy lighting and a magnificent sound system, it was the best nightclub in the western Med. And because the ship seemed to spend ninety-five per cent of her time moored alongside, she was a very desirable venue for the Gibraltar 'glitterati' – which of course included (in our estimation) the Hunter pilots. Yes, many an evening passed hazily away on board *Penelope.* I mean that, of course, in the nicest possible way.

It's best to say that loud and clear, for my wife proof reads these manuscripts for me! But as she reads this paragraph she'll recall accompanying me on a later Gib detachment, finding time for a little spot of naval cooperation herself. As a rule our working day (both on Hunters and Jaguars) started early out there, allowing us to fly a couple of sorties and get back in time for a few lunchtime beers on the patio of RAF North Front officers' mess – which overlooked the runway and bay. What a superb spot that was; it even had its own beach. My wife's routine during her visit was to lie in late until she heard us landing from the second trip, following which she'd join us for lunch. But one day she was persuaded by an invitation from the commander of the RAF marine craft unit to roust herself early for a sea trip. This was in the days, long gone, when the RAF still had such vessels based around the coasts, ostensibly for the search and rescue task which originated from the WWII need to rescue downed aircrew. The Gibraltar unit was one of the last, and its additional task was to monitor Spanish interference with Gib's territorial limits (that whole Spanish unpleasantness was, by the way, the core reason for our Hunter and Jaguar Gibdets). But on the day my wife was aboard the marine craft it was tasked with towing a splash target for us Jaguar pilots to bomb and strafe. This wooden target was streamed behind the launch on a long line and was constructed such that it threw up a huge water plume – or 'splash'. The plume was the aiming point, but naturally we sometimes thought it fun to shoot the target off. Which, when you think about it, was a bit silly, as that would immediately put an end to the exercise. I don't think it happened that day, which was the nearest my wife ever got to seeing me firing live ammunition. Altogether a lovely, sunny morning's work.

The aforementioned mess patio was a grandstand venue from which to watch the antics of other aircraft on Gibraltar's short runway. I recall on one occasion having my early evening cocktail rudely disturbed when an RAF Buccaneer burst both main-wheel tyres on touchdown, its pilot seemingly carrying out his aircraft carrier-style approach (with no flare) just a little too enthusiastically. The noise of those tyre bursts, re-echoed from the rock, was deafening.

Another time, in difficult wind conditions (which were often prevalent in Gib) we watched with interest as a Hastings transport on its landing run went barrelling past the mess heading westwards with its tail still in the air. The crew, undoubtedly antic-ipating a watery end to their roll-out, deployed the emergency dinghy from its wing stowage – but in the event the aircraft stopped with inches to spare. So close to the runway end, in fact, that it had to be pulled back to give the crew room to turn around and taxi to the apron!

Then there was the regular excitement of watching the daily British Airways Trident, which sometimes appeared to touch down with less than half the runway remaining – and almost invariably infringed Spanish airspace on departure. Tridents, to my eyes, never looked comfortable operating into Gibraltar.

Another task for us in Gib was to keep tabs on the Soviet naval units which used to transit through the straits and, quite often, loitered in sheltered anchorages just

'Yo ho ho!' The author 'jackstay transfers' between frigates of the Canadian Armed Forces off Halifax, Nova Scotia in 1987. Pennant number 236 is HMCS Gatineau.

off the Moroccan coast. I always relished seeing those impressive vessels, the Krestas and Kyndas for example. Generally they seemed to be enjoying a siesta in the sunshine, but occasionally they'd wake up and track us with their radars and missiles. If for any reason they had chosen to engage, I've no doubt they could have swatted us as one would an annoying fly, but it always felt more as though they welcomed our flypasts just as much as we enjoyed seeing them.

So that was Gib, but allied navies were good fun too, and an outstanding memory is, during a staff college day at sea, of being 'jackstay transferred' between two Canadian frigates off the Nova Scotia coast. They were belting along at what seemed like about twenty-five knots – in thickening fog – as I was hauled, hand over hand, by a bunch of jolly tars across a kind of aerial ropeway from one to the other. 'Yo ho ho' – I'm sure you can picture the routine – with the icy North Atlantic sloshing by just a couple of feet below. Having heard of 'accidental' dunkings which reputedly occurred to visitors being given this kind of treat, I was very grateful to reach the far side more or less dry. A stunningly exciting experience.

Returning to aircraft carriers, during the later time when I was the commander of Operation Jural, the RAF's contribution to the 'Southern Watch' policing of the southern Iraq no-fly zone, I spent a wonderful few days on board USS *Independence* in the Persian Gulf. 'Freedom's Flagship', she was known as, and whereas our ships tend to have mottos out of the classical Latin mould, hers at the time was, if I recall correctly, the very macho 'Don't Tread on Me'. The Yanks do have a lovely turn of

Aboard USS Independence in the Persian Gulf, Operation Southern Watch, December 1995. (All photos courtesy of the US Navy)

Welcome Aboard
USS Independence (CV 62)
Group Captain Ian Hall, RAF

October 3, 1995

'Philthy' briefs the author.

About to board the Tomcat.

DON'T TREAD ON ME

Don't Tread on Me! The pennant of USS Independence.

Ready to launch.

phrase! In fact that motto stemmed from a tradition that the oldest ship in the US Navy wore, at her bow, a pennant bearing a rattlesnake and the logo; the roots of the design stemmed from the earliest days of the fledgling United States.

I was accommodated in what was laughably known as a stateroom, a tin cell some six feet by three about fifteen decks down with no windows, and the ship had all the characteristics of a medium-sized town – even a McDonald's. There were something like 7,000 souls on board, and the vessel reputedly had no-go areas just like the Bronx. The US Navy is dry, of course, but the story was that a good deal of funny stuff was smoked in dark corners down below.

Up top, though, the operation was awesome to behold. The noise, the smell, the oil, the steam – it was all incredibly impressive. I was lucky enough to be given a trip in an F-14 Tomcat, which was a never-to-be-forgotten experience. You might recall from the film *Top Gun* that USN fighter aircrew have individual nicknames – and my personal chauffeur that day was known as 'Philthy'. He briefed me to brace hard during the catapult launch, and I anticipated an enormously powerful rocket thrust. But when it came, it was far from rocket-like. More akin to being shot from a gun – a hell of a bang. Having retrieved my teeth from the back of my throat, we proceeded to Kuwait for a training exercise. As a passenger I didn't have a map, but I had no trouble recognising one landmark as it zipped past and disappeared under the wing. It was the Iraqi border! Dear old Philthy was clearly lost without his regular fighter-gator, but after we'd discussed my position estimate he soon recovered his composure and headed back to friendly territory. And once he had locked on to 'mother's' TACAN he was OK. The arrested landing was the next highlight, rivalled only by my final departure for land aboard a C-2 'Provider' twin-prop transport. There must have been a dozen or so passengers in the back, mainly USN men heading for shore leave, and the screams of "Yeeeee – Haaaaah!" as we were shot off the bow were worthy of Disneyland's scariest ride.

My one and only visit to India was courtesy of the Royal Navy. At the time I was serving as a group captain in the MoD, and one of my tasks was to work on the 'navalisation' of the RAF Harrier force. That project came to fruition over subsequent years. Lucky Harrier people? I don't think the RAF boys widely shared that sentiment. Just imagine you were, say, an RAF chief technician with thirty years of service and you now found that you'd regularly be shovelled into a floating mess deck with dozens of others – many of whom would be going on shift while you were trying to sleep. Not what you'd signed up for at all! But now we're approaching the next iteration with the F-35 Lightning II, which, we assume, has been well prepared for, so perhaps the new norm will be more widely accepted.

At any rate, in 1998 we staff wallahs felt the need to pay a visit to see how 1 Squadron RAF was faring on board. Sadly, we were unable to find a suitable occasion while the ship was in cold, home waters, and so it was that two RAF officers, together with our oppos from the navy department, came to be poured off a British Airways Boeing in Abu Dhabi. We staggered aboard Her Majesty's luxury cruise liner *Illustrious* overloaded with kit for the four-day transit to India – carrying the eight or nine different types of uniform required by the ultra-formal Royal Navy even for a four-day voyage – including tropical mess kit last worn, in my case, twenty-seven years previously (it seemed to have shrunk!). It was a marvellous experience in brilliant weather and on mirror-like seas. Unfortunately there were no two-seat Harriers on board – they were too long for the deck lift and so were never taken to sea. So we had to be content with observing. And there was quite a lot to observe, especially on 'sports day'. In the middle of the Arabian Sea the ship's company took time off for football and volleyball on the flight deck, as well as sunbathing on the ski jump. And although nowadays it's very much the norm, at that time it seemed remarkable that a hundred or so of those matelots were somewhat unusually constructed – and wearing bikinis. I wonder whether they were known as 'matelottes'?

I had a few years earlier, by the way, enjoyed a trip in a two-seat Harrier off the ski jump at RNAS Yeovilton, and I still recall the bizarre sensation as the nozzles were rotated from full aft (max acceleration) to near vertical (lots of lift but very much reduced acceleration) as we reached the tip of the ski jump. I was, to my surprise, thrown violently forward in the straps at that point – it felt like engine failure. Later that morning, as part of my naval familiarisation, I'd also had a flight in a Hunter

T8M equipped witradar. Following all that I enjoyed the experience of 'splicing the mainbrace' as the entire station complement stopped work at lunchtime to celebrate. No, they weren't marking my visit. It just happened to be the day of Lieutenant Prince Andrew's engagement to Sarah Ferguson.

Anyway, back to the Arabian Sea, and perhaps shamed by not being able to offer me a Harrier ride, or maybe just anxious to get me off the deck for an hour or two, my hosts came up with the idea of launching me in a Sea King helicopter. Not just any old Sea King, mind you, but an AEW version – the type RN people

About to board HMS Illustrious in Abu Dhabi.

commonly call a 'bag'. Off we went with me in the left-hand seat to see what threats might be inbound to the fleet. But almost immediately after lift-off the machine's radar failed. I gathered from the intercom chat that this wasn't an entirely unknown event in the 'bag' world, and that they had already prepared a plan B for this crab's heli trip ('crab' is what the navy call RAF people). Their plan B involved staggering up to 10,000 feet and drifting around for a while.

Well, I'd had a go at various helicopters over the years – Wasp, Wessex, and so on – and had a working knowledge of how they functioned. To the extent, I suppose, that in the classic adventure-movie situation of the pilot dying and me having to land the machine, I reckoned I'd be able to make some sort of arrival. Probably not a tidy touchdown, but a survivable one. But I'd never been particularly comfortable in those rattling machines and, most certainly, this trip to 10,000 feet didn't do anything to make me love them more. There we were, high over the Arabian Sea in a pea soup of haze, with no land or horizon in sight and with absolutely no sensation of forward motion. The window beside me was wide open and there was only the incessant roaring vibration – together with the instruments in front of me – to tell me that we were 'ops normal'. Once we'd got back down to low level and had made a few approaches to both *Illustrious* and the other ships in the small flotilla I began to enjoy myself a little more. But if ever I'd needed confirmation that I preferred fixed to rotary wing, that sortie offered it in spades.

All too soon the cruise was over and we were approaching Goa, on India's south-western coast. But let me tell you, there's no finer way for a crab to arrive on the sub-continent than on the bridge of one of Britain's men'o'war, with a Royal Marine band doing its thing down on the deck and, by way of an encore, a lone piper skirling away on the tip of the bow. Yes, a carrier and its air wing certainly bring style to any arrival, and I cannot think otherwise than that we – the UK – should continue to maintain a maritime air capability by way of aircraft carriers.

As a postscript I should say that, these days, I spend part of my retirement time driving my own little cruiser around the Norfolk Broads. Shortly after I purchased this craft a naval friend suggested that I should go on a course to learn all about it. My natural RAF retort was that I didn't think that would be necessary; after all, I said, if the navy can do it then it can't really be all that difficult. But to balance that bit of inter-service frippery I would say that the captain of HMS *Illustrious* during my Indian trip was very much the sort of person whom one couldn't call anything but 'sir' – even though we wore equivalent ranks. He eventually became the first sea lord, and was undoubtedly the most impressive officer of any service that I met during my entire military career.

CHAPTER 8
BOUND TO LOSE A FEW....?

I lived through thirty-two years of RAF flying starting from 1967. And, although on my seven squadrons only two losses occurred, crashes were all around. Was that inevitable?

I often wonder whether there was still something of a Second World War attitude about the way the services saw things. At least during the earlier part of my career, there were many still around who had seen wartime service. 'You're bound to lose a few' was the watchword. Expressed flippantly? Perhaps, but I wonder whether some sort of belief might have been embedded in the minds of the higher echelons. My first Chipmunk instructor, Stan, with whom I really enjoyed flying, told me that during the Second World War he had shot down one enemy aircraft – but crashed four Spit-fires. His droll observation was that the war would have been over more quickly had he never joined up. He may have spoken tongue in cheek, but I've little doubt that there was more than a grain of substance in the sentiment. Training was so short and operational needs so pressing that literally thousands of air crashes, in both world wars, were attributable more to piloting inadequacy than to enemy action. Inciden-tally, I met Stan again many years later when I was flying Chipmunks on the air experience flight at Cambridge. He was still plying his trade forty years after the war and had had, to my knowledge, no peacetime accidents. But in my early days such was the expectation and acceptance of huge losses (at, incidentally, a time when no combat flying was going on) that extraordinarily high numbers of 'attrition' airframes were ordered at the same time as the initial batches – to fill the holes which were routinely expected to appear in the front line.

My generation had missed the war but, as the baby boomers, had grown up with a bomb site in every street. Thus we were immediately at home in an environment full of wartime legacies. That the squadron buildings and officers' messes at our flying training schools were wooden huts seemed quite natural. In fact I recall the luxurious feeling at RAF Chivenor of moving from a room in 'D' lines to one in 'E' lines. 'D' implied coke stoves and separate ablution huts – reached by running the gauntlet of wind and rain. 'E', by contrast, meant toilets and baths in the same hut in which one slept, as well as a gas fire in one's room. Unheard of luxury! In passing, dare I ask whether anyone then had heard of carbon monoxide poisoning?

It was often said that because military equipment was always stretching the technological boundaries there was no wonder that it failed. But I wonder whether that premise is entirely valid. Of course designers of military jet engines tried to extract every last ounce of thrust they could from their equipment. But airlines, too, have always demanded 'cutting edge' technology; they've needed minimum weight for the thrust required, minimum frontal area to minimise drag, and maximum fuel economy, so their requirements were, in their way, equally demanding. The military might cite the fact that civil jets had an easier time, operating as they do for long periods at cruise power, whereas military jets are banged repeatedly from idle to maximum. True, but if a jet is specified to work while being banged from idle to max then it should do so. If the designers and manufacturers can't meet that specification they should say so. Similarly, military hydraulic pumps need to work reliably under 6G or more; so they should be designed and built to do so.

What is undoubtedly true is that, during my time, we operated far more in the low-level regime than they do today. I don't think there was an option; it was firmly believed that opposition air defence systems were so effective that slipping in underneath their envelopes – and under their radar horizons – was the only way we stood a chance of being able to reach the targets we needed to attack. And the low-level arena was indisputably more dangerous than medium level: terrain was close, hard and unforgiving; weather was ever a factor; birds were plentiful; and, because air forces were huge, there were hundreds of others flying where we wished to fly. 'Big sky, little aeroplanes' was a dictum designed, perhaps, to comfort those who worried about mid-air collisions. Sadly, it proved not always to be true.

Was alcohol sometimes a factor? Other writers have, I know, gone to town on the amount that was consumed in the good old(?) bad old days, and I can certainly confirm that today's crews are infinitely more careful about the morning after than we were. That more or less mirrors, of course, the way that society's attitudes to drinking and driving have altered over time. In the civil aviation world the random breath test has also put in an appearance, and we occasionally read in the tabloid press that a passenger (or even a fellow crew member, perhaps bearing a grudge) has shopped a pilot on whose breath the whiff of alcohol was detected. It would be nice to think that drink-flying incidents could be brought to zero. But, as with drink-driving, where humans are involved there will always be those who stray. Simply put, though, the chances of alcohol-related incidents are much reduced nowadays.

I can't let the subject go, however, without relating one little story. Back in 1984 when I was a flight commander on 6 Jaguar Squadron we had been deployed to Denmark to undergo our tactical evaluation. Those events were doubly tough because, quite apart from the pain of the exercise during the day, we were accommodated overnight in primitive tents. And the campsite was bleak; the east coast of Jutland always seemed to lie prey to a cold, damp wind off the Baltic. After endex, and with a successful result under our belts, we went for it in a pretty big way with the grand-daddy of a beano on our muddy patch. The night's tented sleep that followed was short, but was nevertheless the sleep of the dead. The next morning several of us were lined up in the latrines relieving ourselves of many gallons of used beer. One of the young Jaguar pilots swayed slightly as he performed, steadying himself on a tent pole. By chance the squadron doctor happened to be standing next to him. "Bloggs," said the medic; "I hope you're not on the programme to fly a jet back this morning?" "Sure am, doc!" "Well take yourself off it now and go by Hercules. You're staggering all over the place." "Aw," retorted our hero. "That's not fair; all the pilots are staggering all over the place!"

It was small wonder that a whiff of oxygen was often welcomed by pilots on the early wave.

Sadly, many good friends died, and some accidents were complete mysteries. The first time I clapped eyes on Chris Haynes was when I, together with my fellow recruits on the new course, was wheeled into the barrack block at RAF South Cerney for our first day of officer training. He was already there; he'd been re-coursed from the previous intake because of some minor stumble or another. He was seated on his

bed reading a book, wearing the flying helmet with which he'd already been issued. I suspected that he was demonstrating to us brand new boys that he was something of a veteran and knew the ropes. But when I asked him why he was wearing a helmet in bed he answered that the idea was to keep out the noise of our jabbering so that he could concentrate on his book.

Notwithstanding this odd start I soon became best friends with Chris, and we stuck with each other right through flying training and beyond. Our families met, and we shared a car for part of our Jet Provost course at RAF Acklington, in Northumberland. What a marvellous station that was at which to train.

Chris Haynes, 1970, climbing into his 8 Squadron Hunter.

Close enough to the coast to give us sprog pilots infallible navigational pointers back to base (unlike Leeming, for example, or Syerston, both buried deep inland), it also had easy access to the most marvellous low-flying country in the Cheviots. It wasn't far from the humming city of Newcastle, with its Royal Victoria Infirmary offering ample numbers of young and lovely nurses. Plus there was Alnwick Teachers Training College close by, with its quota of equally luscious partners. Chris and I bought our old banger, a Morris Minor, for I forget how much – it wasn't expensive but, even so, neither of us could afford the complete vehicle. When we were awarded our wings at the end of the course we were granted two or three weeks leave before reporting to RAF Valley for the advanced phase. We tossed up for which of us should have the car over the leave period and I won.

Thus it was that, the morning after the final Acklington party, I threw all my kit into the Minor and set course southwards towards my parents' home in London. Now, Acklington was only twenty-five or so miles north of Newcastle, but by the time I reached the northern outskirts of the city I knew there was no chance of reaching my distant goal. An ominous knocking noise, increasing in intensity mile by mile and accompanied by clouds of smoke and a serious loss of power, told me that the big ends were going. What was to be done? I decided that selling the beast immediately was the best option. But this was a Sunday morning, so seemingly mission impossible. Not quite, though. By this time I knew the back streets of Newcastle well enough to know where the dodgy car dealers lived (we'd probably bought this heap from just such a place). And sure enough, before too long I found someone who would take it off my hands. "A fiver," he said. That wasn't enough. When I said I'd thrown my kit aboard I meant it. There might have been a couple of pieces of luggage involved, but most of my worldly goods were in a heap on the floor or in paper bags on the back seat. "A fiver plus a couple of suitcases," I countered. Disappearing into his loft, he returned with a couple of old holdalls. And thus the deal was sealed – with a lift to the station thrown in with the bargain. I completed the journey by train.

Ever afterwards, whenever I met Chris's mum she'd refer to the morning at their home in Lincolnshire when the postman had delivered my letter. "Dear Chris," it had begun; "disaster has struck." It went on to relate the sad tale before concluding: "I owe you a half share of the proceeds, which amounts to £2 10s plus an old holdall. See you at Valley next week."

Chris and I flew together many times during our holding period. Together we spent several months at Chivenor, mainly doing trivial tasks, but occasionally being let loose in a Chipmunk. Number 79 Squadron operated a couple of the little piston-engined trainers to train army forward air controllers, and during times when the aircraft were free Chris and I would loop and roll over the hills and beaches of north Devon. It was a glorious release for us during the interminable year waiting for our next stage of training. He and I were both posted to Bahrain for our first tours, he to 8 Squadron and I to 208. Then onwards to Phantoms together at Coningsby, to 6 and 54 Squadrons respectively.

The news of Chris's death, in 1972, came as a body blow to me. I was on a long detachment with 54 Squadron to Tengah, in Singapore. One Friday afternoon we were sat receiving the usual briefings, part ops, part parish notices. Towards the end the boss took the floor and said a few words. Among them was a brief mention that he'd had notification that our sister 6 Squadron had lost a jet. "The pilot was a young chap called Haynes," he said. "I can't say I knew him. Flew into a hill in the Lake District, I understand. Now, on to a couple of administrative matters …"

I sat, stunned. There was no practical way I could get back for the funeral, even if the squadron had been willing to release me. I was partly reassured by the knowledge that my wife, who by that time had got to know Chris very well, was able to represent me at the sad event.

What had caused the accident? We'll never know. The aircraft was alone, so there were no formation pressures – but equally, no witnesses. The weather was iffy; that might have encouraged a degree of pressing on in the hope of an improvement, but there was no particular demand on the sortie and one would have expected the crew to have pulled out from low level if things had got too difficult. There was civil airspace above, which would have made them careful with a pull-out, but nothing they couldn't cope with. There was no cockpit voice recorder or black box to tell us anything. The wreckage revealed no technical failure. Chris was, to my knowledge, pretty highly rated as a pilot, and his navigator was experienced, so who knows what happened in the cockpit on that day? All I know is that I miss him still.

It was sad and bizarre that Chris's brother, Stuart, also in the air force, was killed a year later almost to the day. This time it was in a road accident right outside the main gate of his base, RAF Scampton. But the hurt was no less for his parents. Who among us can imagine the loss of two sons in a year?

There is something of a happy ending to the story, though. I first knew the third brother, Lawrence, as a schoolboy when Chris and I were training. Lawrie, too, joined the RAF, and it was a huge pleasure for me to be able to get him airborne in Hunter T7 XL578 in 1975. At the time he was a junior technician on 41 Squadron at Coningsby, whence I was detached on exercise. I've always watched his subsequent career with huge admiration, taking it as some compensation for the loss of my great friend Chris. Lawrie, after completing his short engagement with the RAF, got himself a law degree and has subsequently achieved pretty well all that could be done in the upper echelons of business and industry. I'm proud to have made him, if only for one hour, a Hunter pilot.

Perhaps with some accidents we weren't clever enough about seeing the whole picture. To illustrate what I mean, let me tell of a young Hunter student who, in the mid 1970s, was having trouble delivering air-to-ground weapons. He wasn't hitting the target, had already had an extra dual sortie, and I was now programmed to have another go at getting the message across to him. Together we flew in the T7 and, sure enough, he wasn't getting the idea no matter what I tried. My write-up for the boss was fairly negative, and one of the areas I had to comment on was safety. I wrote that, although he appeared to have little aptitude for the job, he was at least safe, because his tendency was simply not to get close enough to the target.

I had nothing to do with subsequent discussions and decisions about whether or not he should be withdrawn from training. That wasn't, I know, something which would have been done lightly. On the odd occasion, perhaps for disciplinary or safety reasons, action had to be taken quickly, but this was one of those cases when there appeared to be time to progress matters in a more orderly fashion. Perhaps his particular aptitudes pointed him more towards air defence rather than ground attack?

A couple of days later the young man was flying a quite unrelated sortie. This was not unusual on the course; several phases would be run concurrently, primarily so that weather which might have put a stop to one event didn't bring the whole thing to a standstill. But he crashed, and was killed.

Well, I'd assessed him as 'safe' in the context of air-to-ground weapons delivery, but had I – had we – had the system – taken sufficient account of his state of mind? Fighter pilots, even trainee ones, are caricatured as being rough, tough, extrovert types, but under that veneer there still usually lurks a human being with the conventional range of sensitivities. Might he, even though he wasn't flying the event that was causing him particular trouble, have been worrying about his problems on the course and, indeed, his future, rather than concentrating on what he was doing?

Most pilots (even apparently outstanding candidates) must recall moments when they've had to grit their teeth and call on their reserves of determination to get them through sticky patches. I certainly didn't find my initial Hunter DFGA course easy, while I can confirm from personal experience much later in my career that all sorts of background issues begin to take un-wished for prominence when one is having trouble with a course. As I related in *Tornado Boys* I had a nasty personality clash with the staff of the TWCU when I was going through the second stage of Tornado conversion prior to taking up my squadron command. Quite apart from the flying, other concerns began to disturb my sleep when things got difficult. What would colleagues, friends and family think if I fell at this fence? Who would pay the mortgage if my employment suddenly ceased? All that provided, in my case, powerful incentive to force myself onwards. I wonder to this day whether that young chap had similar concerns. Might they have overpowered his powers of concentration? Sadly, we shall never know.

The navigator with whom I went through the F-4 OCU later had the most unfortunate of accidents. Dave Baker was an ex-Royal Navy trainee pilot; he had got as far as the Hunter tactical weapons course before he and the RN agreed he should go no further. At that point he'd applied to the RAF who had taken him on as a nav. He was a lovely chap and we got on well throughout our course. When the postings came I was happy to stay at Coningsby, while he proceeded to RAF Brüggen to join 17 Squadron.

The late Dave Baker. The picture is extracted from the photo of No. 11 Phantom course, May 1971. (Crown Copyright)

I never saw him again. Some time into his tour in Germany his aircraft had a problem which, in due course, became terminal. The pilot ordered ejection and out went Dave. The pilot, after counting the regulation 'one potato, two potatoes ...' from hearing the 'bang' of the rear seat, pulled his own handle. But no two people's 'potatoes' were ever going to be the same. It's also worth saying that the 'bang', when heard through a bone dome, could as easily have come from the rear canopy jettisoning (that would have happened first) as from the seat firing. So, in the heat of the moment and with the jet pointing earthwards, we can readily understand any error that might have been made. Anyway, Dave's seat was halfway up the rails when the pilot's canopy jettisoned as he initiated his own ejection. Dave received the front canopy full in the face and was killed.

What can be said about that one? Later, command ejection systems were invented, which sequenced the seats from cockpits, partly to reduce the risk of such events. Should the need for command ejection have been anticipated? Could it have been specified earlier – or was it, at the time, beyond the technology available? It's far from a clear-cut case anyway, as building sequencing into an ejection system implies delaying the second ejection. Which could, in certain cases, prove fatal in its own right. And, as chronicled in *Tornado Boys,* command ejection can have unwanted side effects, too. Is there ever any complete and perfect answer to these things?

Perhaps the most extraordinary accident story of all concerns my good friend John Mardon. He and I were on the same Jaguar course back in 1976, I as a fourth-tour attack pilot, he on crossing over from Wessex helicopters. He took to his new life like a duck to water, but I was posted to Germany while he went to Coltishall, so we didn't see much of each other over the following few years. Especially when I subsequently went on my Norwegian tour and he disappeared to the States to fly the F-16 with the USAF.

Following that he returned to the Jaguar as a flight commander. During that tour, he developed a serious complaint which resulted in his being grounded. To cut a long story short, after several years of serious pain, discomfort and disability he had a heart and lung transplant. Although he made a good recovery, no-one ever expected him to fly again – except John himself, for he was a determined man. Only the medics know how he managed to convince them, but he was able to demonstrate to them his fitness to fly. And one fine afternoon in 1991 he took to the air again in a two-seat Jaguar. Naturally, the press had a field day, and that flight made John very well known. He would never have flown solo in a jet again, but with an eye to his new-found future he had other irons in the fire. Meanwhile, he continued to fly periodically in two-seat Jaguars until, one day, he became a victim of a most unfortunate accident.

I remember exactly where I was at the time. I was converting to the Tornado on the TTTE at RAF Cottesmore, and was busy in the nav room planning a low-level trip. The clerk came in and plotted a point on the wall-sized map of the UK low-flying system. Around the datum was drawn a 10-mile radius circle, with the legend 'SAROPS'. Search and rescue operations. We knew what that meant; an aircraft had gone down. There was, at that time, no further information so we went on with our planning, ensuring that our routes avoided by a wide margin the temporary restricted area.

It wasn't until my wife phoned that evening that I learned it was John. His jet had collided with a light aircraft whose pilot had been busy photographing people's houses. The other pilot in John's two-seater had survived but John had left it too late. It was, as you would imagine, the most awful blow to everybody who knew him. On a personal note, his wife and mine were by this time very close friends – a friendship which, incidentally, endures to this day. But what was especially upsetting was the nature of the accident. Many years previously, in 1974, a couple of acquaintances of

mine had been killed in the fenland area when their Phantom had hit a crop sprayer. As a result of that accident the civil air notification procedure (CANP) had been initiated, which made it incumbent on civil pilots to notify the military of their intention to fly in the low-level arena. The idea was that military crews would receive this notification and be aware of civilians they might encounter en route. But the system clearly hadn't worked in John's case. It was a supreme irony that he'd survived so much and yet still succumbed to the perils of military aviation.

John Mardon with his wife Jeannie in 1991 prior to his first flight after his heart/lung transplant.

Truly, preventing military air accidents was a difficult task in those days. No matter how many measures were taken, accidents would still occur. Thankfully (and I hope I'm not tempting fate by saying this) today's crews seem to fly a lot more safely – notwithstanding the vastly increased number of combat operations in which they are involved. Quite apart from the human cost of accidents, it's just as well they're not throwing away aircraft at the rate we did, for not only do we now have very few aircraft, but each would cost a small fortune to replace.

CHAPTER 9
RUSHTON IS INNOCENT

This story relates to one of the most colourful Jaguar pilots, albeit one with among the shortest careers on the jet. His name is Phil Rushton, and I first encountered him when he was on 14 Squadron at Brüggen. I was on 20 Squadron, but everyone knew Phil; you couldn't miss him. He was a young first-tourist, a loud and boisterous character. There was nothing unusual in that; Jaguar pilots with spirit were ten a penny. But Phil always took things further. He was the one letting off a smoke flare in the officers' mess disco; the one being banned from RAF Wildenrath mess for anti-navigator activity; and the one being ordered to make a personal apology to the matron at Wegburg RAF hospital following alleged nocturnal adventures with her nurses. He was always on the carpet, but he never altered his modus operandi and was regarded by the rest of us as being slightly dangerous. We all secretly marvelled at how the conservative RAF training establishment had accommodated one who so evidently did not fit the conventional mould.

He regularly incensed Brüggen's station commander, the famous 'JR' Walker, who was known for his purple visage and throbbing temples when enraged – which was pretty often when Phil was around. Incidentally, JR reminded me later that his victims were often safe when the temples throbbed. In the inimitable words of his ADC when, many years later, JR was chief of Defence Intelligence, "You're OK until he starts talking slowly and softly". Anyway, he scared us all to death at the time.

There was never any question about Phil's piloting ability; indeed I understand that this is the only thing that persuaded the CO to keep him on for so long. And the upper echelons were well apprised of JR's views, as witnessed by this extract (circulated later by the HR department – arguably breaking the secret of the confessional) from one of Phil's annual appraisals: 'If he was shot down and incarcerated in a Soviet POW camp, he would make the commandant's life hell. Meanwhile he is practising on me.'

Phil's off-duty activities grew in outrageousness until the time came when JR accused him of setting fire to the nurses' quarters at Wegburg. This was actually one thing (perhaps the only thing) that he hadn't done, and on that basis OC 14 Squadron wanted to give him another chance. But JR was immovable. Normally, this sort of behaviour would have resulted in a posting away, but the upshot this time was that Phil merely moved across the airfield to 31 Squadron. Perhaps 31's boss, one Terry Nash, who was himself a somewhat larger-than-life character and went on to command RAF Coltishall, believed that he could tame Phil.

But our man continued on his unstoppable course. Things came to a head with a bout of firework throwing in the mess during a squadron detachment to the German base at Fassberg. Quite apart from an imprint of Rushton's bare backside appearing on the ante-room's high ceiling, there followed a bout of firework throwing. The story has it that Phil was ordered to bed, but returned with 'just one more' firework. This allegedly set fire to the boss's trousers – while 'Nashers' was wearing them. Nashers, nearly incoherent with rage, got on the phone to Brüggen to demand Rushton's instant court martial, with JR having to remind him that it was he who had only recently volunteered to sort out the problem. "So go ahead – bloody well sort it out!" But it was all too late, and that spelled the end of Phil's brief career on Thirty One.

He was banished to the headquarters at Rheindahlen to cool his heels while the appropriate administrative processes ground doggedly onwards. But before things had reached any conclusion Phil contracted some kind of infectious ailment – I forget what, but there was a minor epidemic underway across RAF Germany at the time and the medical authorities were dealing with it centrally. They had set up a dedicated isolation facility at – yes, you've guessed it – Brüggen. In the gymnasium, in fact, and it was to there that Phil was moved. Not for too long, as I recall; he recovered OK, leaving the station for what everybody believed would be the final time.

But wait – there was more. He was smuggled back to Brüggen in the back of a girlfriend's VW for a final dining-in night. Believe it or not his table place card was marked 'Flying Officer X' and, to prove it, he still has the card! For the latter part of this period Phil and his Jag mates had been wearing 'Rushton is Innocent' T-shirts, and it was after that dinner that the final atrocity was committed. The next morning we awoke to find a very public statement. In three-foot high letters, burned with weed killer into the lawn outside the Brüggen officers' mess, was the legend 'Who's Innocent?' We never officially found out 'whodunnit', but JR had reached the end of his tether and Rushton was hastened off the station – never to darken its doors again.

By all accounts Phil subsequently received a telex from Brüggen's new station commander (JR having moved on) asking him to pay for the lawn repair. The reply was: "Sir, with all due respect, Rushton is Innocent."

Phil was then posted to a 'bad boy' tour at RAF Finningley, training young navigators to find their way at low level. One can only wonder at the RAF's thinking, but after a year spent scattering his particular brand of stardust on ab-initio navs he was considered 'rehabilitated' and was posted back to Jags on 54 Squadron at RAF Coltishall. At his arrival interview the boss reputedly looked quite anxious. He proclaimed to Phil that he was very pleased to have him aboard, to which Phil replied: "I don't really believe that, sir … but we'll give it a try shall we?" Things went relatively uneventfully although, unaccountably, all the station commander's prize roses disappeared from his garden one evening. Also, perhaps equally unaccountably, Phil was appointed as mentor to two junior pilots.

After eight or ten months of this Phil applied for seconded service to the Sultan of Oman's Air Force, and 54's boss, probably with some relief, recommended the transfer. Phil then spent about eighteen months in Oman where, in his own words, "airborne hooliganism was an understated euphemism".

After that he moved into civil aviation, initially via all sorts of unusual routes: he obtained an ATPL and bought into a short-lived air charter operation around the Caribbean; he moved to the US and flew amphibians out of the Hackensack River; and he became an airship pilot, flying the Fuji dirigible.

He appeared on TV's *Krypton Factor*, representing the UK, and word is that he then got into the business of buying and selling Gulfstream executive jets in the States. His star ascended and folklore has it that he's now a millionaire. He's certainly been seen looking very prosperous (and larger) at the odd Jaguar reunion recently – where he's also renewed acquaintance with his old sparring partner, JR, now retired Air Marshal Sir John. Those two feisty characters have met, if not exactly on buddy-buddy terms, at least in an atmosphere of something approaching mutual respect. I believe that JR truly admires the way that Rushton has prospered. Certainly, they haven't come to blows, and Phil has, I understand, invited JR to stay at his house in Hollywood. The offer is still open!

CHAPTER 10
WORDS FROM THE 'FATHER' OF THE JAGUAR

Air Marshal Sir John Walker

More than three hundred people sat down to dinner at the 2017 Jaguar reunion, a number which, ten years after the aircraft left service, was an impressive tribute to the affection in which it is still held by its former operators. Most of the company waited with eager anticipation to see the resumption of the fixture between the afore-mentioned JR and Rushton, but they were to be shocked and disappointed by the receipt of some most unexpected news. Just a few days before the event, one of Phil's two little dogs had been attacked by a neighbour's Rottweiler. Phil had rushed to the rescue but, in doing so, had suffered a number of serious wounds to his arms. He was, we understood, making a good recovery, but he'd be unable to attend. A beast downed by a beast?

On the positive side, the story presented JR with heaven-sent opening lines when he stood up to speak after dinner. "Ladies and gentlemen," he said, "I want it to be

JR Walker (centre) celebrates a moment with 31 Squadron pilots. Second from the left is 'Nashers'.

clearly understood that it was not my dog. Moreover, I deny ever biting Phil's arm myself. If I had bitten any part of him it would have been somewhere much lower!" With that established, Sir John then regaled us with a host of insights and anecdotes surrounding the early days of the Jaguar force.

"My first flight in the aircraft, which occurred while I was with the Jaguar Conversion Team at Warton, was with BAC's chief test pilot, Paul Millet. Together we approached the machine and Paul made to climb aboard. As I set off to perform my customary walk-round inspection, Paul sprang back down the ladder. 'No,' he said, 'we don't do that here. It's not necessary. The ground crew have already done the external check.' 'But I always do a walk-round,' I countered. 'I've been doing one ever since I began pilot training. It's RAF routine.' 'Do that here,' said Paul, 'and we'll have the entire workforce out on strike. This is a civilian organisation and runs according to strict demarcation lines. Pilots do the flying and technicians do the servicing – which includes the final inspection.' He nodded towards a character in overalls who was lurking nearby. 'That chap's their shop steward, and he's watching you.'

"Well, I had no wish to provoke trouble with our primary supplier, but years of habit and training couldn't suddenly be jettisoned and I simply had to do my own walk-round. I went over to our friend with a smile. 'I do hope you won't object if I stroll around and glance at the aircraft before getting airborne.' My greeting wasn't returned. 'There's no need; I've inspected it already.' 'Yes,' I said, 'I realise that. But I hope you'll understand that when I return to an RAF station I'll be working with ground crew who aren't nearly so expert or highly qualified – or so good-looking – as you and your people. Therefore I must familiarise myself with what I'll need to be checking in the future.' 'But of course,' he came back, his expression relaxing into something which might have approached a smile. 'I fully understand. Please feel free to continue.' I trust that any of our marvellous and extremely competent RAF ground crews who might be reading this will understand why I had to say what I did."

"The new aircraft was great, but there were inevitably many aspects that needed attention. The staffs generally agreed with what had to be done, but in all too many cases weren't able to provide remedies within any sort of reasonable timescales. A good example was the paint scheme. The Jaguar wasn't a fighter, and wasn't going to survive if it got engaged too often by enemy interceptors. Its forte was its ability to hide: it was small; it was easy to fly low; and it merged nicely into the terrain background. But we quickly noticed that as soon as the aircraft turned it became very visible. Why? Well, the matt, grey/green drab of the upper surfaces was fine, but the undersides were finished in a light, silvery grey, which stood out like a sore thumb as soon as the bank came on. The solution was obvious: paint the aircraft grey/green all over.

"While the staffs agreed in principle, their answer on timescale was depressing: eighteen months to two years. The camouflage committee would have to meet and approve the change; the engineers and suppliers would have to prepare new patterns and adjust their orders for paint; and new contracts would have to be drawn up and approved.

"You won't be surprised to hear that we did it ourselves. And perhaps our action jogged the system, for quite soon afterwards all-over drab airframes began to appear off the production line."

"The Jaguar's cockpit could best be described as cosy, and this led to a strange glitch in one area of the aircraft's development programme. One of the test pilots who had been doing clearance work at Boscombe Down had been investigating a murky corner of the performance envelope and had encountered an apparent control restriction which could, in certain circumstances, prove dangerous. The boffins, after poring for hours over the data from the relevant test flight, concluded that his thighs had been inhibiting full stick movement; their proposed remedy was to redesign the stick and modify the entire fleet.

"Well, the problem was actually caused by his having a shortish back; this necessitated his positioning the seat unusually high up, which brought his thighs into play. Nobody else had encountered the problem, so we suggested that a cheaper and quicker solution than lengthening the stick would be for him to slim his thighs down a little. Or to be moved to testing 'heavies'. The boffins couldn't, of course, accept either line of reasoning without analysing the percentiles and satisfying themselves that there wasn't more than a statistically negligible number of Jaguar pilots with thighs wide enough to cause trouble. How, they wondered, could they do this? They settled on the idea of gathering empirical data from the sample readily available to them – which happened to be the pilots of the JCT who were with me at Warton.

"Thus it was that we were paraded in our flying underwear for measurement to much mirth amongst us. More than that, though, it generated even more mirth amongst what seemed like Warton's entire workforce. For the venue selected for the measurement was an annex to the main production hangar. So the workers were entertained by a panorama of a dozen Jaguar pilots in their shreddies having their thighs measured.

"Despite this, the 'stick lengthening' went ahead at huge expense. I often wonder, as did others, whether the longer stick, which had the side effect of partially obscuring some of the NAVWASS controls, was a factor in some later Jaguar accidents when pilots flew into the ground."

"It was time to design a 'Jaguar patch' for pilots to wear on their sleeves, and the JCT members sat down to turn their minds to this; we were aided by John Quarterman, OC 6 Squadron designate, who was something of an artist. The 3-Jag red white and blue logo they came up with has proved over the years to be one of the best of its kind. Anglo-French cooperation was always productive in the Jaguar area, and the 'patch' was no different. Later stories had it that the logo was a French invention but, on the contrary, it was they who came to us. Having seen our effort they used it, the only alteration being to reverse to 'blue-white-red' the colours of the three aircraft – reflecting the difference between our two national fin flashes."

"Returning to the theme of it being much preferable for the Jaguar to evade detection rather than having to fight its way through, we were becoming seriously concerned by the aircraft's give-away smoke trail. I brought this up with Rolls-Royce, who were adamant that the Adour met all the relevant specifications on the test bench – and was, as far as they were concerned, a particularly clean engine. Our growing experience bank, though, showed this not to be so in practice; when 'bounce' aircraft were intercepting a formation on training sorties, the first clue they got of the approach of the bombers was very often the smoke trails. So I determined to lay on a demonstration, and invited a couple of senior Rolls-Royce personages to Lossiemouth.

"My point was very quickly proved. Our visitors were installed at a suitable spot in the countryside over which a Jag formation was scheduled to fly. But we didn't have to wait for the overflight. In the beautiful, gin-clear Scottish air the smoke trails, heading straight towards us, were visible many miles away – and long before we could see the aircraft themselves.

"So our friends went away, scratching their heads and looking for the answer. Soon it emerged that, although each new Adour engine met the spec when it left the factory, it quickly became 'sooted up' in use and increasingly smoky. Give them their due, they found a relatively simple solution, and the first two modified engines soon arrived on the unit.

"To this day I don't know why, but fate decreed that I decided not to have both the engines installed in one airframe. Rather, I asked for two aircraft each to be fitted with one 'new' engine and one 'smoker'. Perhaps I wished to compare the two modification standards side by side. Whatever the reason, the decision proved fortuitous, for before long one of the 'new' engines flamed out as the pilot closed the throttle while breaking to land. The problem, again, proved relatively easy to fix. But I thank my lucky stars that I hadn't had the two modified engines flame out together in one aircraft – for there's nothing more certain than that the Jaguar was an extremely poor glider."

Having seen the Jaguar through the JCT stage and then getting 226 OCU up and running I was beginning to find time to enjoy the flying. I also knew that I had been earmarked to continue, in due course, the work by becoming RAF Brüggen's station commander as its strike/attack Phantoms were displaced by the new aircraft. Before moving, however, I got an early and unexpected taste of life at the top when Lossiemouth's CO was taken ill and rushed to hospital. As his nominated deputy I took over and, as it turned out, he wasn't able to return to post. It would take time for a new station commander to be selected and installed, so it was decided that I should remain at the helm for the interim. This precipitated hasty reorganisation all the way down the chain, with accompanying promotions.

"In fact the immediate changes were even more hasty, for the CO's departure occurred at extremely short notice and at a most inopportune moment. I received a telephone call at 1100 hours to be told that I was the new station commander. I hastened over to my new office to be met by the splendid PA. He held a substantial file in his hand. 'OK sergeant,' I began, 'tell me what's going on.' His reply was instructive. 'You have a whole platoon of AOCs, sir. Should we start with 38 Group? They, sort of, own us.' This was indeed the curious situation at Lossiemouth. While the Jaguars belonged to 38 Group, 8 Squadron's AEW Shackletons were owned by 11 Group and the SAR helicopters were 18 Group assets. The Gannets of 849 Squadron answered to a Royal Navy command chain. Two hours flew by while I absorbed all this.

"You may imagine the extra work this unusual arrangement brought with it. An AOC's annual formal inspection, for example, is a big event for a normal station to prepare for; so would we have five? Somewhat to my surprise, the powers that be recognised the problem and, on one occasion, two of my AOCs agreed to perform their inspections concurrently. Possibly a unique occasion.

"That though was for the future. More immediately, a potentially career-destroying event was fast approaching. It would occur on day one in about three hours time, when a formal VIP visit by a delegation from the Jugoslav government was to touch down to stay overnight. They would be accompanied by the deputy C-in-C STC, the AOC 38 Group and sundry other dignitaries. The big wheels were to be accommodated in the station commander's house, where there would be a formal dinner and after-dinner drinks; then, the following day they would be given a tour of the station. The problem was that, following the abrupt departure of the station commander and his wife, the house was now manned only by a cook and a steward.

"The scratch briefing from some high-ranking soul at Strike Command instructed me to get myself and my wife into the big house post haste, with a couple of suitcases, and to prepare to host the dinner, overnight stay and morning breakfast. Pre- and post-dinner drinks would be part of the package. We were not to let on to anyone what had happened. The line was to be that I was the station commander and that everything was normal.

"Silly me – I thought that 'cruel and unusual punishments' were banned these days. Or was this some special form of Taceval? It would require both skill and luck to carry it off; my wife and I didn't know where anything was in the house and feared opening any drawer, not knowing what might be inside. In fact it went off remarkably well, although there were two stressful moments. The first came when the Jugoslav air attaché asked me over sherry if it was customary in the RAF for a mere wing commander to command such a large base. Good spot by him – and it was a scramble to come up with a plausible answer. The second occurred at breakfast when my 'number one' AOC complained to my wife that there really ought have been a proper butter knife on the breakfast table. He doesn't know, to this day, how close he came at that moment to serious injury. Quietly, my lovely Barbara explained that we had not had time to locate the butter, let alone a butter knife; we'd been eating all we could find, which was margarine."

"At Brüggen we built up quite quickly to a strength of four squadrons, with sixty aircraft established but in fact sixty-eight on base. It was a formidable striking force and a key element in NATO's armoury. But despite its importance and our proximity to the front line, it was still difficult to push through essential upgrades. One such was the provision of active ECM equipment, for without such kit a unit's capability was limited; and importantly, it could not aspire to anything better than grade 2 in the 'operational effectiveness' field for Taceval.

"This, I thought, was unacceptable. Not only was it necessary for our crews to get through to their targets, but RAF stations had traditionally shone in Tacevals; Brüggen was not going to get grade 2s. The staffs agreed but couldn't offer better than two years for an upgrade programme. Once again we were going to have to do it ourselves.

"We were lucky enough to have RAF Germany's 431 Maintenance Unit co-located with us, equipped with all sorts of facilities, workshops and brainpower, and before too long we had, between us, the outline of a design. The Jaguar's brake parachute was seldom required on our 8,000-foot runway, so there in the aircraft's tail we had a usable space connected by linkages to a handle in the cockpit. And before long we had a prototype six-shot rotary chaff dispenser fabricated and operating. Its components included a motley collection of springs and sawn-up broom handles which would eject the chaff cartridges, and the time came to demonstrate it to the staffs. Thus a collection of very senior officers gathered one afternoon in a HAS to witness the fruits of our labours.

"The kit certainly made an impact on them – especially on the officer who was standing in the way of a piece of broom handle travelling at high speed and took it full on the chest. But it was a convincing display and we went into production with the mark one Jaguar chaff dispenser. Result? Tacevel grade ones across the board. And we were able to repeat that success for several more years."

"Returning to the subject of Phil Rushton, I do wish that he'd confined his fire-raising efforts to our Warsaw Pact targets rather than to our near allies. An incident at Weg-burg Hospital occurred when Rushton and a couple of his cronies (a gang which, these days, might be referred to as terrorists) gatecrashed their annual reception – the formal cocktail party at which an RAF unit acknowledges the help and cooperation it receives from its local neighbours. I received on the following Monday an irate call from the matron. Given that the welfare of my thousands of servicemen and depend-ents depended on good relations with our nearest hospital, we didn't need to make an enemy there. Thus I instructed the reprobates to go back and grovel. And in doing so I referred them specifically to the dictionary definition of the word 'grovel'.

"Brüggen was a vitally important front-line base, and one way I maintained the focus was by having a sign erected inside the main gate. It read: 'Your job in peace is to prepare for war. Don't you forget it.' Of course traffic through that gate comprised, as well as our service personnel, thousands of non-military characters – contractors, tradesmen, families and so on. The sign became infamous, with a few wives taking exception to it, saying that it frightened the children. On occasions I invited them to my office for a personal meeting, and I was generally able to convince them that, unpalatable though it might seem, deterring the opposition by demonstrating pre-paredness for war was the reason we were all there.

"The sign wasn't really aimed at wives, of course, but at the single-seat strike pilots at Brüggen who really did need to understand the seriousness of their responsibilities and the trust that was being placed in them. It was an outstanding fighter-bomber wing and it was a pleasure to serve with such great people. My association with the Jaguar was a highlight of my service career."

CHAPTER 11
NORWEGIANS WOULD...

They certainly would. They do things surprisingly differently up there, and I was about to find out – because we were off to Norway for three years. Many at my Jaguar station were of the opinion that I should never have taken the posting. It was a step backwards, they said; it would hold back promotion. I recall standing on the apron with Brüggen's station commander to greet my future Norwegian base commander (a brigadier) as he taxied in to meet me (or, as I subsequently found out, as he taxied in to visit the NAAFI with a view to replenishing his cellar!) Anyway, as he came onto the chocks in his F-5, my current boss mouthed to me that he didn't think I really ought to be heading off to fly such a basic aircraft.

But there's more to life than promotion, and in any case I was never threatening the top of the tree. I felt ready for the change of scenery, and in fact one of my best RAF friends would be handing over to me after his own three-year stint there. We'd already visited him and his wife on holiday and had heard their stories about the fun they'd had. So we trusted their judgement and accepted the tour. Not, however, without eyes wide open about possible pitfalls. I believe that the chap before my friend hadn't had an undilutedly great time – and nor am I sure that the man who followed me was totally happy.

The key, it seemed to me, would be to make a big effort with the language. In theory the Norwegian pilots, having all trained in the States, were fluent in English. And, working within NATO, supposedly, carried out all their routine chat in English. But of course it didn't work quite like that. Exciting operational moments would, unsurprisingly, cause them to revert to the vernacular, while crewroom banter went on, quite naturally, in Norwegian. Wives talked to their friends and children in Norwegian; many of the older generations had no English at all. So, my predecessor had argued, it would be necessary for both my wife and me to have language training prior to the tour.

And so it was. We did the course, took the basic exam and scored well – but on arrival we found that we understood virtually nothing spoken by real people. Indeed on our first social occasion I recall asking a statuesque Viking lady whether she'd like to dance. "Yes please," she said, "I'd love a drink." I assumed she hadn't understood; it surely couldn't have been that she didn't fancy dancing with me?!

Norway had only one TV channel in those days, but watching nevertheless helped us develop our language skills. Much of its content then was regarded as being a little staid but, just like the BBC, it was broadening its range all the time. Foreign programmes didn't always translate well, but I can assure you that *Fawlty Towers* with subtitles was, whether intentionally or not, even funnier than the original. In fact my new Norwegian pilot colleagues had a penchant for that type of humour, with the mere mention of the words 'Monty Python' sending them into paroxysms of laughter. In time I discovered that it wasn't so much the show's content that amused them as that their crewroom slang put a somewhat coarse interpretation on the word 'python'. It all added to my education – if not proving appropriate knowledge in subsequent formal language exams.

Speaking a foreign tongue is a tiring business. Both physically, because it uses muscle movements not natural, and mentally, for obvious reasons. On social occasions we thought we became more fluent up to a certain point. Perhaps it had something to do with the alcohol intake; curiously, the Norwegian word for 'fluent' is the same word they use for 'liquid'. So perhaps that's why our language ability seemed to take a dive towards the end of an evening. Anyway, by halfway through the tour we were truly comfortable with the lingo and I was a qualified interpreter. And the two of us were so pleased we'd made the effort. Never mind the flying or the place: it was the friends we made that we shall remember.

The conversion course was on 718 Skvadron at Sola, the military side of Stavanger Airport. We spent a pleasant six weeks there accommodated in a room in the mess, although my wife's sleep tended to be disturbed by nightmares after somebody told her that the building had been used by the Germans during the war as an interrogation centre. On completion of that course, in September, we drove to our permanent base at Rygge, south-east of Oslo, by the direct route over the high plateau of Hardangervidda. Climbing the three thousand plus feet from Stavanger's sunny autumn weather to find the landscape on top already in full, white, winter dress gave me an early insight into the climatic variations we would meet during the tour. In subsequent winters we would fit the marvellous *piggdekks* – studded tyres – but on this occasion we were pleased to return, as we descended on the eastern side, to the red and gold autumn.

My new jet proved fairly easy to fly. Although, with its sharp little wings, it resembled a small Phantom or Jaguar, it had none of the aerodynamic vices of either. In fact it flew like a supersonic Hunter, and it was quite possible to rudder it around in deep buffet with little fear of spinning. The small engines, of course, produced barely more power than a couple of good-sized vacuum cleaners, and had an alarming tendency to flame out from time to time – luckily, seldom both at once. But flame-outs proved, in any case, not too desperate a problem, as the engines almost always relit immediately on selection of reheat. That procedure took a bit of getting used to, but worked well.

An F-5 approaches Hardangervidda. Over such terrain the aircraft's natural silver finish provided excellent camouflage.

One surprise to me was that the Norwegians set so much store by procedural instrument flying. I soon found that this had its roots in their career pattern; a very high percentage of them would serve in the air force for at most a dozen years – many for less – before moving to a civil flight deck with SAS or one of the other large carriers. And things were organised such that a procedural instrument rating on the F-5 was fully valid on a commercial airliner. To one brought up on the non-procedural style of instrument flying practised by the RAF of the day, performing TACAN holds and the like was totally alien. But such fences are there to be jumped and I soon adapted.

All in all the F-5 was an absolute little sports car – with limited operational capability but enormous fun to zip around in. There were more advanced versions of the machine – the F-5E, for example, was equipped with more powerful engines and with radar – but Norway (and several other NATO forces of the day) had the F-5A. It was an extremely basic aircraft, but my operational unit got plenty out of it. Not only did 336 Skvadron hold down the traditional Hunter roles of day fighter and ground-attack, but also had a reconnaissance flight of RF-5As and a training role as the operational conversion unit. One could, perhaps, see this as a case of 'jack of all trades, master of none', but they undoubtedly had plenty to offer in all four roles. Indeed, they were adventurous to the extent that they flew visual, night low-level sorties, something I had never done in the RAF. Admittedly, it was generally on moonlit nights over snow-covered terrain, but those were nevertheless quite exciting trips. And the Norwegians were well and truly NATO orientated; I recall on one occasion leading a four-ship comprising a Brit, a Canadian exchange officer, and two Danish students.

A formation flown by 336 Skvadron over Drøbak on 9 April 1980 to mark the fortieth anniversary of the sinking of the German battleship Blücher. *Coincidentally, it also marked the fortieth anniversary of Norway's fall to German invading forces. The author is flying number three in the second four-ship.*

The squadron's multitude of roles gave me an opportunity to have a go at something I'd never done before, air defence, thereby getting a taste of a Lightning pilot's work. The way things were arranged in Norway was that F-104 Starfighters would hold northern quick reaction alert (QRA) from Bodø while the three F-5 squadrons would rotate southern QRA from their bases at Sola, Ørland and Rygge. So every now and then I'd 'hold Q' at Rygge – but only from 7.30 a.m. until 3.30 p.m., which was the extent of the F-5 commitment. You may ask what would have happened if the Soviets had chosen to attack out of hours, and I guess the answer is that some sort of overtime arrangement would have kicked in during any state of increased tension (one would hope so, anyway!). In fact 7.30 to 3.30 was the standard working day for the whole air force, which came as a very welcome change to me, allowing lots of family and leisure time. And those hours were very strictly adhered to; if one were standing by the camp gate at 3.29 p.m. there was a real danger of being trampled in the rush, and if not out by 3.31 one would very likely be locked in for the night.

Mention of organisational and cultural differences between the RNoAF and the RAF prompts me also to say that not only were the Norwegian forces heavily union-ised – which was something new to me – but a year or two before my arrival had undergone an upheaval to their rank structure. 'Democratisation' had resulted in the regular, senior non-commissioned officers becoming officers overnight. Sergeants became lieutenants; flight sergeants became captains; and warrant officers became majors. There were no longer officers' and sergeants' messes, with the single group now sharing establishments known as 'befals' messes'. Aspects of this system naturally took a while to get used to – for example it wasn't uncommon to be marshalled in by a major – but it nevertheless appeared to work very happily.

Returning to the QRA thread, because of the pattern of Soviet flying the situation of being surprised by an intruder virtually never occurred in south Norway. A 'Bear' or suchlike would set course from the Murmansk area and would be tracked by radar and intercepted by a northern Q aircraft as soon as it entered Norwegian airspace. Messages would be sent to prepare southern Q in case it should be required; meanwhile, northern Q would shadow the stranger as he proceeded. Thus we in the south would have at least a couple of hours warning, and there was seldom any need for a speedy getaway.

I had not been scrambled by the time I entered the third year of my tour, which was a disappointment as I'd been looking forward to seeing my first Soviet aircraft. But one fine summer's day my chance came. I was on duty when an intruder trundled around North Cape, and the controllers opted to launch the Rygge Q forward to Ørland (near Trondheim). Off I shot with my number two, and within the hour we were refuelling on the ground at Ørland. We plugged in the telebrief and waited. Eventually, the message came: "Scramble southern QRA." At this point my wingman's aircraft had a technical failure, so I headed alone north-westwards out over the North Sea.

It was a long chase, and by the time I was getting close to the bogey he was approaching the western edge of Norway's area of responsibility. I knew that I'd be called off soon, not least because I could see in the middle distance a couple of RAF Phantoms approaching from the west to take over the shadowing. Lest I was ordered home before achieving my objective there was nothing for it but to have some kind of tactical radio failure. "Radar, I'm sorry, your transmissions are breaking up. Continuing with the intercept visually." And continue I did, to draw alongside the massive 'Bison' recce/bomber. It was an awesome sight for one who was basically a mud-mover. Sadly, of course, there was no wingman there to photograph me, but I nevertheless had the satisfaction of knowing I was no longer an air defence virgin.

There were all sorts of good memories from that Norwegian tour. One was of trips to the far north, to the wild, wide expanse of Finnmarkvidda stretching towards the Soviet border. Ordinarily, this was beyond the geographical limit set by Norway for visiting Brits, but the exchange officer was allowed right up to the border. It was an odd feeling to arc over Kirkenes and to look out eastwards over to the other side. There was just more of the same white, empty vastness – but somehow it had a threatening aura about it. It was the same feeling I'd had all those years earlier when I'd looked over another sector of that same border

High over the North Sea, my Bison.

during my transit in a Hunter from Tehran, via Turkey to Cyprus. That was thousands of miles south of Finnmark, which brought home the vastness of the Soviet empire. Both views offered nothing to see except wilderness – yet in both cases just being there was full of hidden meaning.

My first trip to the far edge of Norway was in mid winter, and emphasised to me both the huge length of the land and its peculiar shape. I landed at 3 p.m. at Banak air base in pitch darkness, which didn't surprise me at all. It's December, I thought; we're way north and of course the days are very short. I went to bed anticipating that the following morning would begin very late, but was surprised to be woken at 7 a.m. with the sun streaming in on me. It took just a glance at the map to tell me what I'd failed to note up until then. Not only is Norway enormously long from south to north but its northern stretch curls right around and extends far to the east. The place where I had spent the night could, with justification, have been a couple of time zones ahead – hence the unexpectedly early daylight.

For just one week during the tour I was able to pitch the F-5A against the more up-market F-5E when my squadron put me in for the 'air combat manoeuvring course'. This was run by a couple of guys from the USAF's 527 Squadron, the aggressors based at Ramstein in Germany. They put on a series of lectures and seminars, as well as flying exercises in which, with their F-5Es, they simulated Soviet tactics. Very good stuff, with course participants including both Starfighter and F-16 pilots as well as ground radar fighter controllers – and it was great fun.

In common with all who flew fighters I was well used to the standard air-to-air combat set-ups of one v one, two v two, four v two and so on. But that course introduced a couple of innovative scenarios. For example a couple of sorties were set up as a one v one v one v one – in other words with four mutually hostile aircraft. As always, keeping tabs on the opposition was the key, and finding the little F-5 in a big sky was always a problem. In this particular scenario our naked F-5As were clearly at a disadvantage against the radar-equipped F-5Es and F-16s. But in my early Hunter days we had always paid particular attention to the altitude at which condensation trails formed on any particular day, for in the times before radar-equipped fighters those 'scratches' could be something of a giveaway. So here I resurrected that knowledge, and found that an effective trick during one v one v one v one was to pop up briefly into contrail level and then quickly descend – to disappear again. Then, from a safe distance, I'd watch as the other three converged on the little contrail they'd spotted, thinking they'd find a jet in the vicinity. With all of the other three now in sight, I'd be well placed to set up for a kill or two.

Another memory was of the time an RAF Phantom squadron visited Rygge on detachment, when it was a pleasure to fly together with a couple of former colleagues in a two-seat F-5. The visiting crews certainly enjoyed themselves that week, and

we'll not dwell on the squadron's unfortunate loss of the outboard motor from the station's boat in the middle of a lake. Better move quickly on to the party the visitors put on for their hosts. Being from Leuchars, they'd brought haggis for the event. For reasons lost in the mists of time there were no tatties or neeps available

When you get a spot of luck just lie back and enjoy it! Our apartment block is just above the centre of the picture, near the edge of the Oslofjord. The picture was taken by an RF-5A of 336 Skvadron's recce flight.

– so they substituted salad. Imagine hot haggis and cold salad on cold plates! The Noggies eat some pretty strange things themselves, but even they turned up their noses at this congealed mess. And I couldn't blame them.

One minor disappointment in my assignment was that, when I'd initially been posted, I'd been led to believe that I'd transfer to the new F-16 aircraft at some point during the tour. But as with many things in the military the timescales slipped. F-16 deliveries were delayed and, by the time my duty came to an end, the RNoAF still only had three or four of the new jets. I did have one memorable trip in a two-seat F-16B, folllowing which I was left with the slightly surreal impression that one just had to wish the aircraft onto the desired vector and it would turn there. Lean that way and you go that way; tremendous. But that was the closest I got to the F-16. If only …

My successor flew the F-16 and no doubt had great fun doing so. But on the other hand, rather than continue at the relatively civilised Rygge air base, enjoying the same lovely apartment I had with its breathtaking views over the Oslofjord, he made the case that the exchange should be relocated further north to a more operational location. And so it was that he spent the second half of his tour at Ørland, the base on a windswept island an hour's ferry trip offshore from Trondheim. As far as I recall from my visits there, the air station was practically the only habitation on the island – whose landscape boasted not more than a couple of stunted trees, both bent double by the prevailing gales. Many Norwegians would, given their love of the wilderness, be happy living at a place like that. But all I could say of it was good luck to my successor.

CHAPTER 12
SCATTERING IRONMONGERY

You'll forgive me, I hope, for returning to the subject of accidents and incidents, but they do occupy such a large part of my military memory bank. This started early; while I was at Chivenor awaiting my Hunter course, one of my jobs was to assist the chap who compiled the station's operational record, the form 540. I was fascinated, from time to time, to delve back through earlier volumes, and was always struck by the incredible frequency of accidents during, for example, the 1950s F-86 Sabre era. Each pilot's death (almost always student pilots) would be marked by a period of two or three days when the station RAF ensign would be flown at half mast and his comrades would wear black armbands. In some months it seemed that the flag never reached the mast-head – while clothing stores must surely have had a standing order for black crepe.

Thankfully, things had improved a lot by my day, but accidents were still a huge aspect of our lives during the 1960s and 70s. Each RAF command published its own monthly flight safety magazine full of stories of crashes and near-accidents, while the RAF's central flight safety organisation published the glossy *Air Clues*. We would avidly read about and discuss the 'accident of the month'.

There were, of course, always lessons to be learned from those lurid tales. But what everybody really wanted was the ability to foresee the likelihood of an accident and to put in place measures which would prevent it. The trouble lay in proving the need; it was always very difficult to extract money from 'the system' to fund measures which might or might not prove useful.

In *Jaguar Boys* several of my storytellers wrote eloquently about the hazard posed by the truly awful layout of the controls for the navigation and attack system. This problem was much talked about in the Jaguar force, for we were all convinced that fiddling with 'the kit', components of which were located deep down behind and below the control column, had caused the deaths of several of our friends. Indeed, I can't think of any of those who survived who couldn't recount at least one near miss of his own. But could we get anything changed? No, could we hell. Because we couldn't actually demonstrate the consequences of the problem; all those who had, most probably, encountered it in a really serious way were dead, leaving no proof. It wasn't until the original NAVWASS was replaced by FIN1064 in 1984 (the aircraft having been in service since 1973) that the Jag force got, as well as enhanced navigational performance, controls that were ergonomically designed.

Those with their hands on the purse strings seemed to us to treat the whole thing as something of an intellectual discussion. In a way I see the problem, and an analogy might be drawn by posing the theoretical question of whether it's worth spending money on flu jabs. Let's say, for example, that I have a jab and don't catch flu. My friend has no jab and is flu free. Another has a jab and does catch flu. Clearly there are elements of probability and statistics to be analysed before we draw any sensible conclusions on the cost-effectiveness of the flu jab. Not least, was flu more prevalent this winter than in other years? But could there ever be an absolute answer? Perhaps not. That's why it was easy for HM Treasury and the MoD civil service to ask questions about proposed new expenditure on flight safety-related modifications, questions which were often very hard to answer.

In similar vein I always found the airline attitude to spending money on safety to be somewhat accountant-led. For example an airline might be haemorrhaging pilots to competitors offering better prospects, and the pilot union would argue that salaries should be increased to help retention. The HR department would counter that there were any number of young pilots queuing up to take the places of those who were leaving. The bean counters would like that, because new entrants come in on the lowest salary scale, replacing those on higher rates who had left.

"But," would argue the union, "you're replacing experienced pilots with people newly out of training. Flight safety will suffer."

"Show me," would say the accountant; "the newcomers meet the mandated standard."

"There will be accidents and incidents caused by loss of corporate experience," says the union.

"Let me know when one occurs," says the accountant. "It hasn't happened yet."

Of course something was learned from every accident, and sometimes remedial measures were put in place. In 1973 a friend of mine had an engine failure in a Phantom. He shut down the engine but, unfortunately, it turned out to be the wrong one. Now he effectively had two dead engines, and a Phantom in that condition is only heading in one direction; my friend and his nav had no option but to step over the side. They got away with it but, sad to relate, two Danish civilians found themselves in the path of the stricken aircraft – and were less lucky.

My friend was found guilty of negligence for shutting down the wrong engine. He didn't, I think, dispute the facts. But in evidence it was pointed out that all the Phantom's warning lights were on one side of the instrument panel – including both the 'left engine fire' and 'right engine fire' lights. Soon after this accident the really important warnings were relocated to the appropriate side. Should this obvious measure have been foreseen? Whether or not, until an accident happens it's very difficult to squeeze money out of the 'system' for such preventative measures. And, of course, where humans are involved there will never be a solution which covers every eventuality, as witnessed by the Boeing 737 accident at Kegworth in 1989. Regardless of advances in cockpit design, the wrong engine still got shut down.

That Phantom accident was, I think, classified as a 'pilot error' event, and my friend certainly paid the price. Not least, he lost a very nice Canadian exchange posting for which he had been destined. But there wasn't a pilot on the squadron who didn't sympathise with his predicament when faced, immediately after take-off, with a confusing battery of warning lights. And although the hierarchy dealt out its justice, the notion that pilot error is very often consequent on some kind of 'system error' was perhaps recognised by my friend's receiving, after a suitable cooling-off period, a new and at least equally attractive exchange posting to Florida.

Continuing with systemic causes of incidents, for a long time it was the practice, when making simulated attacks on ground targets, to leave all the weapons switches in the safe position. Later, there grew up a belief that if we were in the habit of 'attack-ing' with switches safe there would be a chance of forgetting to make them live in the real case – through sheer force of habit. So we were directed to change our pro-cedure to making most of the switches live on simulated attacks, leaving only the final safety break in place. The new practice demanded the utmost care, of course, especially if the sortie was also going to include a range detail with practice weapons. Even so, Murphy's famous law says that 'if it can happen, it will'.

And it did – to a friend of mine on 6 Phantom Squadron. As he was on his attack run to a firing range he made the switches live ready to release his practice bomb. And then he thought, "Oh gawd, I've already done this today". Thirty minutes earlier he had carried out a simulated attack on an unsuspecting road-over-river bridge on the outskirts of a village in Scotland and had, in accordance with procedure, made the switches live. Well, almost in accordance with procedure. He'd actually made all the switches live, so when he made his simulated 'pickle' a small practice bomb would have dropped. Nothing was ever found of the offending weapon and the bridge survived unscathed; the assumption was that his aiming had been less than perfect and the bomb had plopped harmlessly into the river. Lucky for him that he wasn't the hottest of weaponeers!

The ultimate expression of this sort of cock-up came when a Phantom pilot shot down a friend of mine who was flying a Jaguar. I'm very pleased to say that my friend survived, and if you'd like to read the full story of that debacle you'll find it in *Jaguar Boys*.

Weapons switchery was ever a potential source of trouble. Those of us who flew smallish aircraft tended to look enviously, when travelling away, at those Buccaneers and Canberras whose ample bomb bays offered lavish accommodation for baggage. But even there, occasional problems lurked. A very well known Buccaneer man was heading away for a night stop at an RAF station where he was attending some kind of formal event – one which required his best uniform bib and tucker. All was safely stowed in the bomb bay but, eager to make something useful out of the sortie rather than just purely transiting, our hero opted to drop a couple of practice bombs at one of the east coast ranges; I believe it was Cowden, in Yorkshire. Running in towards the target the crew performed their final weapons switchery which, on this occasion, included rolling the bomb-bay door open. Not being all that familiar with the Bucc I'm not sure whether this was absolutely necessary, for I believe they generally carried their practice bombs externally under the wings. But at any rate it was done on this occasion and you may easily guess the result. The tumbling bag of overnight kit received the assessment traditionally given by the range safety officer in such events: 'unscoreable at six'o'clock'.

In fact such procedural mistakes happened occasionally with most aircraft types. They were, rather disgracefully, all too common on the Jaguar, generally as a result of the pilot's failure to select the auto/manual switch to 'auto' prior to an attack when the pickle button would need to function as a 'commit' button. This would be the situation when one wished to use the NAVWASS-generated target position to provide the release cue; if 'manual' were left selected for an automatic attack, the bomb would drop as soon as one pressed what should have become the commit button. I've no idea why, amongst all the switches we routinely managed to select to the correct position, the auto/manual switch so regularly got misplaced. Perhaps I could comment that the switchery shouldn't have been that complicated in the first place (there was a hell of a lot to do on the run in towards a target). On the other hand, there must have been a bit of carelessness around.

Some events make it difficult to get all the flight-safety decisions right. Back in 1978 I was leading a four-ship of Jaguars from Brüggen on a practice toss-bombing mission on one of the Dutch coastal ranges. Nobody liked those ranges much; they were on islands which were little more than sandbanks, and the tide washing in and out would sometimes make the targets difficult to pick up even on the best of days. But worse than that, the best of days were few and far between, and there was often a glassy sea, no horizon and a fair amount of cloud. Jets had crashed there over the years, and extreme care had to be taken.

On this particular day the weather was marginal. Maybe even sub-marginal, for the habit in RAF Germany (apparently accepted by the authorities, perhaps because we'd never have got anything done if we'd interpreted the published limits too literally) was to be liberal in our judgements. Our 'toss' manoeuvres took us into cloud after bomb release, following which we'd pull around the corner on instruments (using the head-up display) onto the outbound leg, descending back to low level in readiness to turn inbound again for our next bomb run. Somewhere on that recovery we'd regain visual (sort of) flight conditions. With four aircraft in the pattern it was imperative we made our radio position calls at the correct points, as we would rarely see each other.

I mentally clocked the calls of blue 3 and blue 4 as they called 'downwind' abeam the target outbound. I followed but, as my bomb released and I started my recovery, the next call I heard was 'blue 2 downwind'. I immediately stopped my turn and queried him; "Yes," he came back; "sorry, a bit late with the call." This didn't tell us enough; was he well past the downwind position and just late with his call – or was he out of sequence in the pattern and really in the downwind position? We were all moving at 450 knots and couldn't see each other so there was nothing for it but to call the event off and regroup in an orderly fashion. This we did and lived to fight another day, but the debrief was interesting.

It emerged that my young friend had lost it on his recovery and had spent a minute or so gyrating in cloud before getting things back under control. Understandably, he'd been too busy at the time to let anybody else know of his predicament, but the fact remained that two other aircraft had somehow passed him in cloud. Not a comfortable thought, and the debrief was sharp and pointed.

I mulled this over during the following twenty-four hours. He hadn't had the easiest of starts on the squadron and I decided to have a heart-to-heart with him over a beer. We discussed whether he did, in fact, feel entirely at home on the jet, or whether he might be better off doing something else. We had always got on very well together and he knew that my main object wasn't to get rid of him; but he'd had a nasty fright and I needed to ensure that his pride shouldn't drive him to continue along a path on which he wasn't really comfortable. I would hate for that to have led him into a smoking hole in the ground, and it was a good, constructive conversation. I was tempted, drawing on my previous experience, to take the cautious approach and report the whole story. But I judged that he was a sensible chap and deserved the chance to influence his own future. He opted to continue, and I was pleased to see that he gradually worked his way onwards and upwards, remaining safe throughout his fast-jet time. His RAF career wasn't particularly long because, in the end, he chose to move to the airlines. And he's now a very senior captain with a major carrier.

So was the course of action I took the right one? No lives were lost so it's difficult to know either way. But might there have been a better course which was even safer? Such dilemmas will always arise.

Some pilots seemed to have nine lives. I knew one who ejected four times, twice from Jet Provosts and twice from Jaguars. His spine must have been something special for, in general, each ejection took something out of one's back. He was a very well respected and popular character, but there's no escaping the fact that at least one of those accidents was pure pilot error. Or was it? Put simply, he failed to lower the undercarriage before landing. That seems pretty cut and dried – although later thinking tends to look more closely at systemic failings which might have led the pilot to make the ultimate error.

A friend of mine managed to survive not just one but two air-to-air Jaguar/Tornado collisions. The first was, partly at least, a consequence of radio difficulties (radio equipments, year after year, seemed to be the Achilles heel of RAF aircraft). The Jaguar formation was warned of the presence of a Tornado – but for various reasons not all the formation members were on the frequency. There were other factors, though; importantly, the Tornado was tracking inbound to Honington through the Coltishall outbound route.

All sorts of lessons were learned, not least that stations' visual inbound/outbound routes were unofficial and not normally publicised to others. But rather than labour the reasons, let's switch to the lighter side. The Jaguar pilot had seen nothing and had no idea what had caused his jet's loss of control. He was in no doubt, though, that he had to eject. Having parachuted down he was soon reassured to see a yellow RAF rescue helicopter approaching. Up he went on the winch, and as he appeared over the lip of the chopper's doorway he spied a face he'd known from years ago. "Hi, B-H." he said; "I didn't know you were on helis now." "I'm not, you silly bugger," replied his oppo; "I've just ejected from the Tornado you crashed into!"

His second collision, not all that long after the first, occurred up in the Newcastle/Durham area. This time, although the Tornado crewmen were forced to eject, he managed to wrestle his broken Jag back onto the ground at Leeming. More consequences followed, although whether as a direct result of this accident I can't say. One was the introduction of flow errors through choke points in the low-flying areas, making them one-way.

To have two head-on collisions was both unlucky and, in the sense that they were both survivable, remarkably lucky. To misquote Ian Fleming's *Goldfinger,* "Once is happenstance, Mr Bond. Twice is coincidence." What a good job my friend didn't get to test out Goldfinger's premise that "Three times is enemy action".

CHAPTER 13
CRAZY VIKING

Here's a good story which originates from an old friend of mine, Martin Selves, who had a flying career as varied as, if not more varied than, mine. His first four operational tours were, in order: Javelins in Singapore; Hunters in Bahrain; Phantoms in Germany; and Jaguars in the UK. Not a bad selection. This tale stems from short visits he paid to Norway but, as I'll explain later, touches on my own experiences to a remarkable extent.

"So there I was sitting in an F-5B at Rygge with a Norwegian aerobatic pilot in command. Brakes off, burner in, and we were off on a memorable one hour and a bit flight. I knew him quite well already, that's why I was sitting on this particular bang seat. He was also a winter survival instructor. We had met the year before in a five-star hotel in the mountains north of Oslo. Yes, survival in a five-star hotel! Rooms were in short supply, so our instructor was living in the linen cupboard, and he invited the three Brits on the course around for a drink. His billet was narrow, was stuffed full of lots of sheets and duvets, and a kettle was boiling near the sink at the far end. A pint of what tasted like hot Ribena turned up. This was unexpected because your average Norwegian can sink vast amounts of beer and whisky. Clearly this one was a health addict, but a very pleasant fellow nonetheless. We agreed to have another one to be polite, and started on the second just as the first kicked in. Yes, it was half a pint of moonshine (over 100% proof, he later admitted) topped up with juice and hot water. We

An F-5 over Børja firing range, just north-east of Oslo.

were determined to remain upright, and continued drinking in the bar. This was a survival course in more ways than one.

"And now my Jaguar squadron was on exchange with his, and my friend and instructor was taking me on a very unusual flight in his F-5, one I would always remember. We were going to start by overflying Torp, an airfield on the other side of the fjord from Rygge. After returning from a mission over there last year he had been arrested and court-martialled. He'd spent a week in jail for doing something very bad. He'd been authorised to perform an aerobatic display in front of a large crowd at that very airfield. The final part of his routine had been to dive at the crowd line and pull up over the spectators (a manoeuvre not permitted at UK air shows). He'd tracked with his gunsight a spot just in front of the crowd, and admitted to having pressed the 'pickle' button for some reason. A Sidewinder missile had come off the rail; it had impacted and broken up in front of the crowd, but (probably because it was launched at too close a range, missiles having anti-self damage safety breaks built into their arming sequences) hadn't exploded.

"This F-5 had previously been pulled off QRA, hence the live Sidewinders on board; the armament switches had been left live for this trip, but he hadn't registered this. Our friend had had to wait several months for a jail cell to become available in the guardroom at Rygge. But now he'd paid his penance and all had been forgiven; he was back as the aerobatic pilot, and I was his passenger.

"So here I was racing down the runway at 150 knots with a mad Norwegian, and we set off across the fjord to Torp. The weather was poor, with visibility and cloud base both marginal. As an instructor myself I knew this was well below student limits, but I was content to concentrate and watch – with fingers crossed. My friend's full aerobatic routine just wasn't on, so he had a go at his 'flat show' instead. I felt very uncomfortable and was relieved when he aborted out – undoubtedly not before time. Surrounded by mountains, and in cloud, we climbed away to get visual on top. We broke out at around 8,000 feet, where my friend decided to show me his display at medium level. He said he always started with a low-speed 'confidence manoeuvre', which in this case was a pull to the vertical, watch the speed bleed off to around 150 knots, and then apply full pro-spin controls. Well, the aircraft flicked as expected and, as all pilots know, if one centres the controls at that point the aircraft usually forgives and normality returns (in most types, at least). It did in this case, except that both engines had now flamed out. All I heard was 'It's never done that before,' and we descended in and out of cloud, with mountains all around, with my friend busily attempting to relight both engines. The alarm bells were going off – in the cockpit and in my head – but

336 Skvadron F-5s over the wilderness.

the engines quickly relit and we climbed out once more to regain visual on top. He then flew his aerobatic sequence, by which time I was feeling queasy – or was it just anxiety for my own safety? For the second time I was learning that this guy, my moonshine friend from the winter survival school, was dangerous.

"Now he wanted to show me Norway at low level. That was more like it. Being a mud mover myself, this would be bread and butter to me. After flying northwards for a while my pilot eventually found a few holes in the undercast and, after one aborted dirty dart, managed to get us down below.

"Now, 420 knots at 250 feet is good fun at any time, and we were flying a lot lower than that in beautiful countryside. But did he know where we were? We were heading east, and the mountains had flattened out quite a bit. It looked a lot different from Scotland – and from Norway for that matter. As an instructor you sometimes get a feeling the guy in the other cockpit has run out of ideas or doesn't know what he is doing – and I now had that feeling loud and clear. He had given the game away because he had stopped talking and was doing a lot of thinking. A turn westwards was long overdue, and I was about to communicate my feeling to him when he made that turn.

"A glance at the fuel gauge showed the needle to be so far around that I could see we were now very low on motion lotion. It was time to climb to a level where our range would be greater and we could pick up some navigation aids. As if he was a mind reader, my friend did both. We climbed and he started to tune TACAN frequencies. After a short while he calmly announced: 'We are in Sweden'. At least he was being honest with me.

"With the fuel gauge needles at an amazing angle and the fuel-low lights burning brightly, we were a long way north of where we had started an hour ago. Could we make it back? I didn't think we could, so suggested we should land at Oslo and pick up some fuel. This option would of course have given the game away and, with his history, he probably preferred to take a chance on the fuel rather than do this. I tightened my ejection seat straps because I could see only one ending to this mission.

"But as soon as you close the throttles of a jet engine the fuel consumption falls to near zero, and my friend made a cruise descent with the fuel gauges very, very close to zero. At this point 'instrument error' came to mind, as I remembered an incident with a Hunter many years before at RAF Muharraq when the engine had flamed out from fuel starvation with 400 pounds still on the clock. At last, though, we were high downwind and made the base turn to line up with the runway. I wondered whether, as soon as he applied power, both engines would stop for the second time that day. But they didn't, and we taxied back and shut down as if nothing had happened. My knees were weak as I climbed out – but my crazy friend was smiling!"

As I hinted earlier, several aspects of this tale rang bells with me – indeed some have entered RNoAF folklore. I too did a similar winter survival course, and could almost write a book on that aspect itself. Downhill skiing on NATO 'planks' (the heavy, military version of cross-country skis, firmly attached to standard-issue army boots at the toes, with only a bungee around the heels) was one of the most hazardous occupations known to man, and how no course member broke an ankle I'll never know. Sleeping overnight in a snow cave we'd hollowed out by taking great banana-shaped slices of snow off the walls with two-handled, flexible saws was memorable, too. The sleeping shelf in the cave was supposed to be warmer than the ambient temperature, but it was still around -4°C!

But more relevantly, I can certainly vouch for the craziness of Martin's friend – because I knew him well. In fact I shared an office with him on my own Norwegian exchange tour. Unbelievably, during my time there this character was the squadron training officer. He had a heart of gold, and in fact did have quite a lot to offer, even though his talents were often misdirected.

Torp airfield is, these days, a civil airport, known variously as Sandefjord, Oslo/ Torp and Oslo South – according to the whims of the airlines that fly in there. Although it lies a good distance from the capital, low-cost operators do have a tendency to prefer the last option. I myself have landed there several times in F-5s. Indeed my first two trips from Rygge both resulted in diversions to Torp because of fog at the main base – followed by ferryboat journeys back across the Oslofjord with flying helmet in one hand and parachute pack under the other arm.

Martin's mention of overflying Sweden prompts me to say that Rygge itself was not so far from the Swedish border. There was a Swedish air force base in the vicinity and it made sense for us and them to nominate each other as alternate destinations in case of weather or other problems at home base. But because of the politics – Sweden's strict neutrality and Norway's membership of NATO – that was only permitted in the most dire of emergencies. Nevertheless the two air wings did have a relationship, expressed through occasional social visits. Thus one afternoon I found myself, in company with a couple of dozen already-well-oiled Noggie pilots, on a 'practice diversion' to Såtenäs in a military bus. With more crates of beer on board it was the equivalent of the 'jolly boys outing'. We were royally entertained, the highlight of the evening being a trip up the tower of the old stone mess to drink akvavit on the roof. The tradition, we were told, was to make a swift 'skål' before downing the firebrew in one, followed by throwing the glasses over the parapet. We needed, apparently, several refills before we were able to perform the ritual to our hosts' satisfaction. Gawd help anybody who happened to be standing down below – or perhaps the locals were wise enough to carry umbrellas while traversing the area during happy hour.

The following morning we witnessed the hairiest display of low-level aerobatics I have ever seen, as one of our friends from the night before put the SAAB Viggen through its paces for our benefit at zero feet. The Swedes may not exactly have been on our side, but I'm certainly glad they weren't on the opposition's.

I should explain why the F-5 weapon switches were live on the trip on which the 'crazy Viking' disgraced himself. At the end of an air defence QRA shift it was the practice for the ground crew to check with an IR lamp the tracking of the Sidewinder missile heads. During this procedure the cockpit switches had to be made live. And who, forgetfully, had left them so on the fateful day? It was the squadron commander! A man who, I think I'm right in saying, later rose to be the chief of the Royal Norwegian Air Force. As always, 'it's the rich wot gets the gravy and the poor wot gets the blame'.

Our friend's delayed jail time wasn't, in fact, unusual in Norway. Many who were sentenced opted to serve their time during their annual holidays, thereby concealing their enforced absence from their friends. I don't know whether postcards got sent, but if so the sender would have had to find a greeting other than 'weather fine, wish you were here'. I believe that, during the jail term of the central character in this tale, the squadron happened to be short of pilots – so he was let out during the day to fly.

The last time I saw him was around the turn of the century when we bumped into each other in the briefing room of a major European airline. I won't tell you which, for fear you'll take fright. Although, come to think of it, he's probably retired by now – so you may relax. But I will say it wasn't a Norwegian company; I guess they would have had his number. And, to be fair, I'm sure he was fine in the airline world. Many extremely responsible and competent airline pilots have had somewhat chequered military careers in their younger days.

CHAPTER 14
BOOZE AND BABY JETS

Outwitting the taxman was a national hobby in Norway. I'm not saying that the locals are (were – of course I'm talking of thirty-five years ago) any more dishonest than other nationalities, but they were certainly unusually open about it. And nowhere was that more apparent than in the area of booze. Most readers will be aware that alcohol in Norway is extraordinarily expensive, so it's not surprising that getting around it was something of an industry. The obvious way was to distil one's own. Although this practice was strictly illegal, the tacit acceptance of it by the authorities was visible in any supermarket. Whereas our UK shops display in the home-baking aisles little bottles of food colourings, almond essences and so on, the equivalent Norwegian shelves offered flavourings for the neat alcohol their customers had bubbling away in their bathrooms: tiny shots of concentrated flavourings for gin, whisky, vodka and brandy.

For pilots, though, an opportunity existed for duty-free stocks to be brought in – and this might not just have applied to the military. I heard tell that the civil pilots' union had negotiated similar chances for its members flying for the national airline. The word was that each pilot was entitled to a set number of flights during each roster period that would fly in from overseas to somewhere up-country Norway, before returning to Oslo as an inland service. The crew would then be able to come through the domestic channel, untroubled by the attention of customs.

I can't verify that story, of course, but I did see and hear a good deal of the way the military fighter pilots played the system. It seemed to me that by the time they retired from the air force they could have amassed sufficient hooch to last for much of their remaining lives. Depending, of course, on their personal rate of intake!

Each year pilots were entitled to a couple of overseas training flights. These were, ostensibly, for the purpose of broadening experience and increasing familiarity with NATO procedures. It fact it wasn't only the pilots who took advantage of this opportunity; because the engineers knew exactly what was going on, their own union had negotiated a share of the cake. Thus each OTF would usually comprise two F-5s, a single-seater together with a two-seater containing a pilot and a technician. They would normally head for a NATO base, and while you might have expected that the boys would choose to visit somewhere hot and sunny, the choice normally fell on a

1982, and a well-earned beer after what the Norwegians termed the 'last famous'. On the left is the Canadian exchange officer on the squadron, Brent Anderson. Next left is the squadron commander, Tor Strand, with whom I made great friends. Later, when I was flying airliners into Stavanger, he was the airport manager. (Photo courtesy of the RNoAF)

USAF or RAF base somewhere in Germany. Why? Because those were the places which had the duty-free liquor stores. And I can assure you that a standard-sized shopping trolley rarely proved adequate for what each of those Norwegians needed to purchase.

Now the F-5 was not a large aircraft, but the boys had this drawback taped. On a pylon designed to carry external fuel tanks or weapons they would mount a 'baggage pod', a fuel tank modified with the addition of easily opened hatches. But that was not the end of the story. Firstly because the crew's overnight bags would take up quite a lot of the space in it. Secondly, because any customs officer worth his salt who was sent to meet the incoming flight would know very well the potential for squirrelling illicit booze into the baggage pod. So the further measure practised by our resourceful crews was to carry an additional, rather more cunningly designed device. As I recall it, this was a fuel tank which had no giveaway doors and which looked exactly like the real thing. But not only did this 'tank' have a secret access panel, it was in no way connected to the aircraft's fuel system. Therefore it offered the required dry, secure stowage for the contraband.

On the belt-and-braces principle, yet more precautions were taken. In those days Rygge, being mainly a domestic base, didn't have a permanent customs officer. A man would be summoned from the nearby port by ATC to meet an incoming flight from overseas, the call being triggered by receipt of the flight plan. So the crews' trick was to file the flight plan at the last permissable minute, thereby virtually guaranteeing that the F-5s would have landed and the booze dispersed before Mr Customs arrived on the scene. Of course that system wasn't foolproof, and I did hear of half a squadron being caught laden with grog at another base on return from a NATO exchange exercise. They were on board a Hercules aircraft, so perhaps they'd neglected to allow for the transport's longer flight time.

With all that as background I can now relate a story I was told. A colleague was, one day, flying one of a pair of F-5s back from Germany. Indeed he was in the machine fitted with the clandestine tank, which was groaning with hundreds of kroners' worth of bottles. For whatever reason the 'flight plan' wheeze must have misfired, for the customs man was on the base as they approached to land. But never fear, there was yet one further back-stop plan ready to swing smoothly into action. ATC notified the pilot to expect a non-standard taxi route after landing, while squadron engineers rushed to a thickly wooded corner of the airfield. The F-5 landed and was directed around the peri-track towards this area, where a technician magically sprung out and marshalled the pilot onto a secluded track. He was brought to a halt, a weapon-loading trolley appeared from the undergrowth, and in no time flat his dangerous cargo was winched down and spirited away into the forest. The F-5 was sent on its way to rejoin the other aircraft at a nearby junction in the taxi track, before the two of them pro-ceeded to the usual squadron parking area – where the customs man was waiting.

Later, when the dust had settled, the booty was recovered and distributed to its owners. Minus a little, I've no doubt, which would have had to be paid to ATC and the engineering team. I often wonder whether similar goings-on still occur.

For a short while the skies of Britain were graced by a low-cost airline called BMI Baby. To me that was a strange title, seeming to lack the reassuring overtone of com-petence and safety that the travelling public generally likes. It was catchy, though, so perhaps the marketing gurus knew what they were doing. Or maybe they didn't; it only lasted for a few years. They weren't the first aviators with a 'baby' connection, though, and here's another tale of the baby jet I used to enjoy flying.

My own Norwegian base was situated in a part of the country where my wife and I experienced our share of 'bracing' winter weather, offset by generally fine summers. But we did make a number of trips to the frozen north to experience the real thing. Bodø (a bit over 67° north) was a fairly regular destination for me; as a change from our usual squadron role the main task for a week up there was usually to tow an air-to-air gunnery target for the resident Starfighter squadrons. As the working day was short and we had friends there, my wife and family would come up by airliner and join me. Marvellous. We saw the Northern Lights in winter and the midnight sun in summer. Well, sometimes. Some arctic summers are brilliant but others are dank, and in the poor years the locals refer to having two winters – a white one and a green one. I recall

...IT DIDN'T DECREASE THE ENJOYMENT OF THE TRADITIONAL AKQUAVIT...

being taken up a nearby mountain one summer solstice to view the midnight – err – cloud. Ah well, it didn't decrease the enjoyment of the traditional *akvavit. Skål!*

Flying in the north was terrific, and colleagues and I often engaged in their favourite pastime of just floating around and admiring the scenery. The mountains; the islands; the red and gold autumns; the huge glaciers tumbling down to the sea in turquoise ice-falls; the spectacular winter weather; and the ever-changing sea. Norwegians are inordinately proud of their country, especially its scenery, to the extent that they find it hard to believe there can be anywhere else quite so lovely in the world. Thus it was a huge pleasure for me on one occasion to be able to turn the tables. I took three of them in our little jets for a night stop at RAF Lossiemouth in Morayshire and, as luck would have it, it turned out to be one of those gin-clear spells of weather when Scotland basks in million-mile visibility. As we popped down through some broken cloud to the south-west of Glasgow the whole of the highlands opened out before us and it seemed as though we could see all the way to John o'Groats. The sun shone over the purple heather, the rowan trees glowed like red beacons in the moorland, and we just cruised along at a couple of thousand feet drinking in the vistas. My Norwegian friends simply couldn't believe it.

Just as in Scotland, though, there were catches to flying in Norway. The weather could close in fast, and even ground operations could be difficult. Of course the Norwegians were well equipped for the winter and appeared to make light of clearing the snow from their runways. This contrasted with the dog's dinner we often made of it in the RAF. At home it was always the responsibility of OC operations wing to supervise an airfield's 'snow plan', and I'm eternally grateful I never held that post – for the thing invariably turned into a shambles. To be fair, we in the UK were poorly placed by Norwegian standards for a couple of reasons. First, arctic snow tends to be of the dry, powdery variety which makes it relatively easy to clear even when it's deep, whereas ours is of the wet type that turns to slush during the day and freezes solid overnight. Second, the volumes they have to deal with make it worthwhile investing in lots of the very best equipment, whereas we (and even Heathrow has been found wanting) are sometimes caught out by having insufficient and inadequate equipment.

When conditions were right they'd simply press grit into deep, rolled, dry snow, which made quite a sure-footed surface for the little F-5. Once the F-16 began to arrive, though, they found that its low-set air intake sucked up the grit; unsurprisingly, this turned out to be a diet its engine didn't relish. The simple solution? Just grit one half of the runway, allowing the F-5s to use the left side and F-16s the right.

One of the biggest hazards in Norway was (still is, probably) the colossal spans of electricity cables which stretched across valleys. They were regularly struck by the unwary, and I must say the Norwegians had only themselves to blame. They themselves relied very much on local knowledge, for not all the spans were marked on maps. So it was often foreigners and visitors who ran into trouble, and I recall a German Phantom crew spending Easter in jail after putting out the lights on the population of an entire valley one Maundy Thursday. Whether prison was the automatic penalty or whether this crew were jailed just because they were German (memories were long) was never clear to me. Then there was the famous photo, displayed in every RNoAF briefing room, of a small Swedish aircraft suspended upside down by its floats from a span some thousand feet above the surface of a fjord. Now that's really what you'd call an arrested landing!

I myself came close to falling into the trap one day, having set off southwards from Bodø with a friend. In our two *frihetsjægere*, we headed down a long sea-fjord between the mainland and the row of high, rocky islands which lay just offshore. Cloud was lowering ahead, and my colleague decided to alter course and fly to seaward of the islands. I was content to continue for the time being, but he eventually suggested I ought to join him. Bowing to his local knowledge, I turned westwards to cut between two islands. But something had been lost in the translation; he had not intended that I should take the shortest route to join him, but rather that I should head back north until I was clear of the islands before turning south-westwards. And the reason pretty soon became clear, for as I headed between the two massive rocks my windscreen was suddenly filled with the biggest span I had ever seen. There was no time to climb above, and plenty of room below, so I pushed under. Time stood still as the endless rows of cable zipped past above me. An added and unexpected hazard turned out to be the anchor lines which hung vertically down – they're affixed to some particularly large spans to reduce movement in gales. Wow – what a good job the little jet was manoeuvrable. It wasn't an experience I'd care to repeat.

The picture, displayed in the author's time on every RnoAF briefing room wall, of the famous 1976 'wire strike'.

…UNLOADED HIS CARGO OF DISPOSABLE NAPPIES…

I should not, of course, continue much further with this chapter without clarifying its title. Yes, the F-5 was diminutive – but there's more to the 'baby' epithet. Travelling by airliner with an infant isn't easy at the best of times, so when my wife flew to Bodø I would generally help out by transporting some of the paraphernalia in the F-5. Most combat aircraft, however small, have a sizable space available when the gun ammo tanks are empty, and the Freedom Fighter was no exception. The stowage was a bit grimy, but was ideal for crushing in plastic bags full of all the stuff our infant son apparently needed in the arctic. I'll never forget the incredulous expression on the face of the Norwegian ground crew who marshalled me in at Bodø that time, as the English fighter pilot unloaded his cargo of – wait for it – disposable nappies!

Finally, a story which neatly links the 'crazy Viking' and 'baby jet' tales. On my own winter survival course I met a Norwegian instructor who, one day, set out to show his NATO students how 'real men' dealt with the problem of obtaining food. Well up in the high, wild, snow-covered hills he set up a snare and, before too long, had himself a grouse. "First we need to kill it," he said – "like this." And he took a great bite at the unfortunate bird's breast. Spitting out feathers and wiping the blood from his chin he continued to chomp away; "There you are," he roared, "real Vikings start by eating out the heart!" We were all relieved to hear that he recommended cooking what remained.

Despite this unpromising start he proved to be a very pleasant and cultured chap, and my wife, who was spending the week in the mountain hotel while I came and went on course activities, later made friends with him in the bar – and we stayed in touch. This came in very useful some months later when, for reasons lost in the mists of time, my wife needed urgently to get back to the UK. This character's day job was flying the RNoAF's DA20 Jet Falcon aircraft on a squadron based at Gardemoen (that base now being the new Oslo Airport). The DA20's role was electronic warfare training for the fighter force, as well as a little light communications and transport duties. Hearing of my wife's need and knowing that one of his aircraft was due to partake in an exercise with UK air defence forces, he kindly offered wife and baby a seat. Not only a seat, but he'd slip in an extra sector from RAF Lossiemouth, the originally planned landing site, to RAF Coltishall, which is where she needed to get to. So she was treated to an exciting trip inbound to Lossie, being intercepted by RAF Phantoms.

God Jul
Godt Nytt År

Entering into the spirit of the tour in 1981, posing in Norwegian jumpers (long before they became fashionable in the UK!) with wife Jacqueline and son Matt. The greeting is, of course, 'Happy Christmas and Happy New Year'.

Not only that, but their arrival at Coltishall proved to be one of even higher drama – surrounded by fire engines because they'd had to declare an emergency after some of their on-board electronics started to smoke. It was always nice to involve my wife where possible in the excitement of a military flying career!

After the end of the Cold War things changed a lot in Norway. Only two operational fighter bases now remain, both in the north. Rygge air base moved more towards civil operations, becoming known as Moss/Rygge Airport – although as I write in 2017 I learn that its major low-cost carrier is pulling out and the airport will close. But I often look back on that wonderful exchange tour, with memories overwhelmingly dominated by friendships made with lovely Norwegian people – with many of whom we're still in touch. I remember diving in midwinter in the Oslofjord for mussels, and of sharing hot chocolate and fresh oranges during a pause in a sunlit Easter cross-country ski trip. Of picking wild raspberries on Rygge air base. And of the wonderful flying.

CHAPTER 15
WATCH THE ALPHA, CHINA

Many jets (I'm talking about my generation of aircraft – they're almost certainly designed more cleverly these days) had nasty characteristics when their angle of attack limits were exceeded. So why would anyone exceed those limits? Well, a fighter aircraft has to be flown right up to the edges of its flight envelope if one is to get the maximum out of it. However, once in the top corner there's occasionally an upset which pushes the aircraft over the edge. The commonest such event, in air-to-air combat, is hitting somebody else's slipstream. It might be from the element leader or it could be from the target one is chasing. Sometimes jet wake appears in the air like an oscillating, liquid trail. But it's not always visible, even from a smoky aircraft like the Jag. And, whichever way, it's occasionally impossible to avoid when the heat's on. As a rule, when there's an excursion beyond the limit there's a heart-stopping moment as the aircraft goes its own way with little reference to the pilot's control inputs, before training kicks in and the pilot centralises everything. This normally results in the situation returning to calm stability. But on the odd occasion, things go horribly further.

Because of this we were all taught from early training days to recognise and recover from a spin. The incipient phase was relatively easy; just centralise and all would be well. Provided there was sufficient height available, that is; even an incipient flick could be deadly at low level. A fully-developed spin was something else, and we were drilled to recognise its characteristics, identify its direction, and take the correct recovery action – and, with most aircraft types, only the precisely correct action would work. The direction of the spin might seem obvious but, because one could spin straight into cloud, it was necessary to confirm via the instruments. Also, an inverted spin could produce misleading sensations of direction. We also had to acknowledge that a canned set-up, although the best-available training, might not prepare one fully for an inadvertent spin.

We never practised spinning the Gnat; it wouldn't readily recover, so we just learned the drill in case the unexpected happened. But we spun Chipmunks, Jet Provosts and Hawks until our eyes popped. It was an exercise I never much enjoyed; I always felt faintly uneasy, perhaps envisaging the enormous stresses and strains on the airframe as it gyrated and flicked around. I swear I could sometimes almost hear it groaning, so I just got on as quickly as possible with what had to be done.

I related in *Jaguar Boys* the tale of Jim Froud, the elderly QFI who had preached the mantra of "watch the alpha, china", before one day finding himself on the end of a parachute after not 'watching the alpha' – or perhaps after becoming a victim of the slipstream I mentioned. 'Alpha', by the way, is one expression for measuring the aircraft's angle of attack (AOA) in degrees – too much angle, plus a spot of unwanted yaw, would bring the aircraft into spinning territory. Different aircraft configurations would render the basic machine more or less susceptible. In that book I also suggested that the Jaguar had a recommended spin-recovery technique which we all committed to memory. But reciting it in the briefing room is one thing; putting the actions into effect in the disorientating heat of the moment could be a different proposition. And in any case those actions had never been known to work in practice. One who was unfortunate enough to confirm this at first hand was my old friend David Milne-Smith, with whom I've shared many happy experiences on Hunters, F-5s and Jaguars. Here's his 'alpha' story:

"Our four-ship's mission was to carry out basic fighter manoeuvres in the training airspace adjacent to RAF Gütersloh. This was for the benefit of two newly arrived junior pilots (JPs). Prior to walking we found we were down one aircraft due to unserviceability, while mine was configured with an unusual centre-line carrier for practice bombs. This imposed a different AOA limitation on my aircraft; I also noted that my AOA warner was (not unusually) inoperative.

"We launched as a three-ship and soon reached the training airspace at 20,000 feet. The original number three and I took it in turns to fly as target, calling in the JP to practise visual attacks upon us. Halfway through our sortie I was the target and, as the JP approached to within a mile, I started a turn towards him, forcing him to overshoot and enter a high-speed yo-yo manoeuvre.

"I pulled back on the stick, while looking over my shoulder to judge his closure rate and angle; at that point my aircraft flicked violently. Centralise the controls to restore normality? No chance! The Jag instantly entered what can only be described as a seriously disorientating pitching, yawing and rolling manoeuvre. Both engines blew out, and although the gyrations appeared to proceed in extremely slow motion, cockpit instruments were impossible to focus. But still I knew that I'd never seen an altimeter unwind so quickly, even in my worst simulator ride. My number three started to broadcast heights to me, which was a godsend as I tried to take in what was happening. Vivid memories from ground school of Jaguar spinning tales flashed before me, the most significant being that, although a Jaguar two-seater had once been recovered from a spin, no single-seater ever had without the use of a special (test) spin parachute. I did not have one of those but the recollection still prompted me to deploy my brake parachute – which immediately streamed above me and disappeared like a cloud of chaff. As "10,000 feet" was shouted at me, I felt that the rotation had slowed a little, and even believed that I might recover, but within a nano-second "8,000 feet" came, so I gritted my teeth and pulled the ejector seat handle.

"Following an almighty roar and an incapacitating G force, my next recollection was of a tremendous jerk about my shoulders and I was looking down at farm land and open fields in a stable, if somewhat rapid descent. After attempting to steer my chute away from some menacing power lines, I struck the ground with some force, hitting my nose on the laces of my right boot – and that was flexibility I had not demonstrated since I was one year old!"

Terrifying to imagine. As it happened, my wife and I were staying with DMS and his wife at the time of the accident. The two of us were having lunch with Sue in the back garden when we spied, striding across the grass towards us, the station commander. He was clearly on a mission, and as he hopped over the garden fence it crossed my mind that something serious was up; station commanders just didn't act like that. It's strange the thoughts that whiz through one's mind at times like these; I noted that there was no padré in tow, so felt confident that it couldn't be the ultimate bad news.

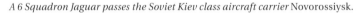
A 6 Squadron Jaguar passes the Soviet Kiev class aircraft carrier Novorossiysk.

A pair of Jaguars pass a Soviet Kresta II cruiser.

With some ejections there's time to prepare and plan. Running out of fuel might be one situation; having a Lightning main-wheel leg fail to lower could be another. With time to prepare it would be possible to adopt the correct ejection posture (back straight, legs forward, thighs on the seat, elbows in). But I wonder whether preparation time is completely helpful; just imagine knowing that, within five minutes, you're going to have to pull that black and yellow handle.

Anyway, as we've just seen, more often there's very little warning, and we'll follow up with a story which offered zero thinking time. It comes from another friend, Rick Lea, with whom I did the Hunter QWI course and the Jaguar OCU. By coincidence, the above-mentioned DMS was also on that same QWI course. Later, Rick moved to Oman to fly the Jag, and on this particular day he was carrying out a fire-power demonstration for VIPs at a range near Thumrait. He takes up the story as he pickled off the fourth bomb:

> "I felt the thud as the ERU pushed off the bomb; almost immediately my whole body was hit by a tremendous force and I was being shaken violently. I was surrounded by intense white light and incredibly loud noise. I felt severe pain on my face; I shut my eyes but could still see the light. I knew the bomb had exploded prematurely and I was being burnt. I seemed to be turned to the right, vibrating and shaking horrendously; my right arm was somewhere above me, flapping wildly. I also knew I had to find the ejection handle to survive.
>
> "I could only move my left arm. Blindly I fumbled around with my left hand and found the ejection handle. I pulled it very hard (luckily I'm left-handed). Strangely, instantly, the control column was really close by the left side of my

head, I must have opened my eyes because I was looking at the cockpit floor, again very close, my body bent double. The shaking and noise stopped. I rose swiftly, my head pressed onto my chest. It was a vision I will never forget: the cockpit floor rushing away; a diminishing black hole in a huge orange fireball that was rolling forwards beneath me; black pieces of something falling away on either side. Then the chute opened and there was just a thin line of sky in front of me. My body was shuddering; it felt like I was freezing for a few seconds. The silence was uncanny. I felt profoundly deaf and my vision was now also blocked by the helmet that had rotated forward over my head."

The bomb had detonated 15 feet below the port wing. The faulty weapon (the safety and arming and fuzing mechanisms had malfunctioned) was an elderly 500-pound bomb which the Omanis had acquired from the Pakistan air force. Rick was extremely badly burned, indeed he was lucky to survive. I'm pleased to say that he made a complete recovery.

Returning to alpha, the Phantom was the first aircraft I flew that used alpha to guide flying. To use an example, with earlier aircraft we calculated the final approach and landing speeds based on the aircraft's weight; the heavier it was, the higher the speed would have to be. In practice we used fairly broad-brush figures, adding, say, '5 knots for each 500 pounds of fuel above 800 pounds'. For maximum-rate turns we simply used feel, transferred from the buffeting of the airflow over the wings to our little pink backsides.

Phantom landing performance on aircraft carriers was, I'm sure, much more finely judged, and it was necessary to get the speed right to the very knot. And that had to be done by the pilot while looking out ahead at the pitching deck and also to the signals of the landing officer. Therefore the manufacturers had installed an angle-of-attack gauge in the cockpit, together with an almost-head-up little gizmo indicating regimes from 'too much angle' through 'just right' to 'too little angle'. Just right would always imply the right speed for the weight. The AOA gauge would also be useful in combat, for the Phantom buffeted so much (in common with many other jets of its era) that it was very hard to 'feel' the point of maximum lift. Thus we were drilled to pull to '19.2 units' for optimum turn performance. I don't know whether I ever knew what a unit represented, nor why they chose units rather than degrees, but if I did I've certainly forgotten now.

As an aside, that buffeting and the high G attainable made combat in the Phantom quite an uncomfortable experience. The stick was located unusually low down, and I found I'd often land from a one-v-one sortie with quite a painful right arm. The G resistance of one's head and body was, as usual, improved by the provision of an anti-G suit worn on the legs and stomach, but this did nothing for the arms. The result in the Phantom was, quite commonly, a mass of blood blisters (thankfully, short-lived) on the forearm.

The Jaguar took the alpha process one step further by displaying the AOA in the head-up display, and alpha quickly became one of our primary flight parameters – especially on final approach and landing. As far as I know, very few pilots had any difficulty learning this new way of flying, despite the QFIs trying to complicate matters by insisting that 'power controlled alpha and stick controlled speed'. I'm sure they were right in theory, but the majority of us either did it instinctively or believed that 'stick controlled alpha and throttle controlled speed'. There's nothing like a QFI to confuse an issue!

'Slippers' can also be extremely dangerous in situations far removed from combat manoeuvring. One of the biggest no-nos in the operational world is drifting too high when air-to-air refuelling; the vortices generated by the refueller's wing are, at that close range, absolutely horrendous. And another example is when, on final approach to land, one encounters the jet-wake left by an aircraft landing ahead. This turbulent trail generally disperses quite quickly, especially when, as is usual, there's any sort of crosswind. But one of my abiding memories of Phantom detachments to the NATO air weapons training base at Decimomannu, in Sardinia, is that the wind was often extremely light, so slipstream from the aircraft ahead in the landing pattern tended to linger. And perhaps the Phantom's wake was particularly 'dirty', for I don't recall the problem being so marked with other types. But I certainly remember having a healthy dislike of being the tail-end charlie in a Phantom formation, for I invariably seemed to end up being thrown on my ear on short finals.

This problem isn't limited to the fighter world, and minimum spacing between landing airliners is strictly regulated according to the size of both the leading and the following types – and hence the propensity to produce nasty jet wake or the ability to resist the wake of the type ahead. I do recall having to go around at Schiphol in my little Fokker 50 having encountered ferocious jet wake from a preceding jumbo. "You were the prescribed distance behind," said air traffic control, cross that their landing flow had been disrupted. Yes, thought I; but prescribed distances are a guide, and on this day and in these conditions they didn't work for me, so I felt a go-around to be necessary on safety grounds. Nobody ever questioned that sort of decision.

CHAPTER 16
TORNADO TIMES

The first time I saw a Tornado was in Norway. The year, I would guess, was 1982, and I watched from Rygge air base as this exciting new machine did a low approach and then disappeared to from whence it had come – presumably its squadron was on exercise elsewhere in Norway. My overwhelming first thought was how ugly it was – it appeared to be so short, and the impression left by the massive fin was overwhelming. The nickname given by the Americans to the A-7 Corsair came immediately to mind – the SLUF – 'short little ugly fella' (fella being the most polite form).

Other similarly proportioned aircraft had proved successful in the past, though, most notably the early Soviet MiG-15 Fagot and MiG-17 Fresco. The simple fact is that directional stability is dependent on the moment provided by the fin, and the shorter the rear fuselage the larger must be the fin area. Sometimes, (as with F-15 and F-18) the solution has been to fit more than one fin.

Another aspect of the Tornado's geometry was that, for reasons of centre of gravity, it wasn't permitted to sweep the wings on the ground. That didn't apply to the F3, which had a longer nose to balance it, but it was a pity in the case of the GR1/GR4 that we couldn't store them in pairs in hardened shelters, à la Jaguar.

Of course C of G problems on the ground weren't confined to fighter types. Much later, I remember seeing ground crew sitting on turboprop nose wheels in an effort to avert disaster when too much baggage had been stowed in the rear hold before sufficient passengers had boarded to balance things up. And I also recall an RAF VC10 settling onto its tail while being defuelled prior to servicing. As I remember it, the team had emptied the wing tanks while the fin tank was still full, which proved an expensive mistake; the damage was either unrepairable or, at the very least, not economically repairable.

Later I flew the Tornado GR1, and one of my most memorable trips was when my squadron was tasked to escort four MiG-21s of the Hungarian air force across Europe. They were en route to the international air tattoo at Fairford, and their refuelling stop at Brüggen would be the first visit of former Warsaw Pact aircraft to an RAF Germany station. They had, we were told, very limited radio coverage, and in any case they

The author with 31 Squadron, 1992. (Crown Copyright)

The author in a Tornado GR1.

A 31 Squadron Tornado GR1 with wings fully swept.

Tornado GR1 firing an AIM-9G Sidewinder on missile practice camp.

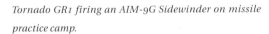

The author – with the luxury limo provided by the company.

couldn't speak English. So our briefing for the rendezvous was through a third party interpreter – and anything could happen.

And it did! Our two Tornados launched from Brüggen on a good weather forecast and headed south-eastwards towards the Czech border. We made the RV and turned back homewards. I was enjoying seeing these former 'enemy' aircraft at close quarters, and we seemed, even without a mutual language, to be getting on famously. But as we approached Brüggen it became apparent that the weather forecast had been hopelessly wrong, and thunderstorms were raging across the area. We had no precise knowledge of the MiGs' remaining endurance but suspected that it wasn't much, so we took the safe option and headed for the nearby German base at Nörvenich, whose weather was usable.

As all six of us headed in along the centreline at 1,000 feet and 300 knots for a standard NATO break and landing (intending to space up in the circuit) I looked over my shoulder at the nearest couple of MiG pilots and gave the standard international signal for 'land here' by pointing down towards the runway ahead. To my huge surprise, rather than following me around the circuit, all four made a dirty dart straight down towards the runway. How they managed to lose in the remaining three miles all that speed and height, while getting configured for landing, I'll never know. But none of them ran off the end, so it seemed to work out.

I learned later that they'd had five minutes fuel remaining when they'd landed, and the Germans didn't blink an eye at the arrival of this odd, mixed formation. They happily gave us lunch and even produced a couple of MiG-qualified engineers from the former DDR to turn around the Hungarian jets.

Then it was time to proceed onwards, and a new briefing was required. By now the heavy cloud had come the way of Nörvenich, and it would be necessary for us to perform what we knew as a 'snake climb'. In other words we'd all roll at specified time intervals, take up roughly one-mile trail positions through the cloud, and re-form on top. The Hungarians appeared to understand this briefing, indicating that they'd use their radars to look after the spacing. But on popping out on top I was taken aback to find that they were now well ahead, having overtaken us in cloud. There would clearly be no opportunity to debrief it, so we waved goodbye and handed them onwards as they proceeded into UK airspace. They hadn't hit us, although we were uncertain whether to be impressed by their close-range radar work or grateful for our good luck.

Some days later on their return trip following the air show we were able to enjoy kinder weather conditions and entertain our Hungarian friends to lunch at Brüggen. And that, for us, truly marked the end of the Cold War.

The Tornado units at Brüggen had their idiosyncrasies. 14 Squadron had a snake called Eric, a python who lived in a tank in the crew room. It used to, I was told, eat

Top: Tornado of the author's squadron escorting MiG-21s of the Hungarian air force, July 1993. Bottom: The author meeting the MiG pilots after landing. (Crown Copyright)

live rabbits – at least until the local pet shops began to rumble the regular orders and refused to supply any more. 14 Squadron's boss and I never got on particularly well, and I do recall one particular incident following a fly-past performed by his squadron at Rheindahlen HQ. I forget what the occasion was but I, together with the other three squadron commanders, were on the ground in our best uniforms amongst the crowd. It was a glorious day and the fly-past took place as advertised, on track and on time.

Afterwards I congratulated Frank. "Nice fly-past," I said, "Well done. You were lucky with the weather." "Ah," he said, "you make your own luck." "The weather, I'm talking about," I repeated; "you were lucky." "Yes, he said, you make your own luck." No, I was never on his wavelength.

17 Squadron had an old East German Trabant car, one of those notoriously smoky old rust buckets. Across the top of the windscreen it had one of those stickers naming the occupants; in this case it was 'Dusty and Lesley', who were then the boss and wife. It was a machine full of character, and on Friday nights it wasn't unusual for one of the other squadrons to steal the Trabbi and take it for a trip around the peri-track. Following one of these episodes, OC 17 felt he had to make a point at Monday morning's station execs' meeting. "You can't steal our car and drive it around," he said; "it's only insured for my squadron." "You mean," we said, "that if we got it insured for our squadrons we could steal it and drive it around?"

I can't remember what IX Squadron did. They were, I know, very taken up with a long-standing argument with Marham-based 617 Squadron over which of them had actually sunk the *Tirpitz*. There was a bit of memorabilia involved which, periodically, they used to steal from each other, so perhaps they were too preoccupied with that to trouble the rest of Brüggen. Anyway, I don't recall any particular incidents with them.

The author hands over 31 Squadron in 1994 to Steve Parkinson following their flight together. Wally the goat is disinterested. (Crown Copyright)

As for us on 31, we had no pets or gimmicks until a bunch of our young aircrew clubbed together to buy us, as their leaving present, a goat. At the time a common saying in the RAF was that an event was 'a complete goat', meaning a shambles or a cock-up. Whether or not that influenced the youngsters in their choice of gift I can't say. Although I anticipated that he would be more trouble than anything else, 'Wally' turned out to be a very cute little chap. We sent him to lodge with the local shepherd, the intention being that we'd bring him out on parade for significant occasions. The shepherd, by the way, grazed his flocks on Brüggen's broad acres; it suited all parties, not least ensuring that the station's grass-cutting bill was kept down. Amazingly, the sheep never seemed to blink an eye at the appalling noise of Tornados taking off and landing. Nor, apparently, did they blink an eye at Wally, who seemed to get on well with his new friends; to my knowledge no 'geep' or 'shoats' were produced. But it seems that, sometime after I departed, Wally was captured by one of the other squadrons and fed with too much grass, or something else that didn't suit him. I understand that he swelled up and died, so that was the end of that.

CHAPTER 17
OTHER BOYS' TOYS

One cannot serve for thirty-two years in the RAF without coming up against many types other than those on which one qualified. Although I only checked out on Hunter, Phantom, Jaguar, F-5 and Tornado, I can't resist telling a few tales of how some of the others struck me. Let's start with that interceptor icon, the Lightning. When I picked up a copy of *Lightning Boys* to read I expected that many of the stories would involve aircraft either catching fire or running out of fuel. The tales would, I guessed, have one of two endings: either the writer would fight the aircraft back onto the ground by the skin of his teeth; or he'd eject into the cold North Sea and swim home. Those scenarios seemed, to the rest of the air force, to be pretty well routine in the Lightning world. And I wasn't far wrong – which made the book an exciting read.

In fact the first meeting with a Lightning for me and for many of my course mates at our Jet Provost base at RAF Acklington tended to reinforce our preconceptions. One fine summer evening came a message over the tannoy: "All students to report to their flying squadrons immediately." So we put down our pints and trotted off to work, wondering what was afoot. It turned out that a Lightning had diverted in; the pilot had shut down and the aircraft was now stranded at the turn-off from the runway to the taxiway. He had, it seems, found himself in one of the afore-mentioned emergency situations, and must have been in dire trouble to have chosen Acklington rather than heading for Leuchars, Leeming or Leconfield – which could only have been marginally more distant from his operating area. For our flying-training station had a runway that was too short for Lightnings, as well as taxiway surfaces that couldn't bear the weight of a fighter.

So there he was, up to his axles in soft and broken tarmac, surrounded by a small army of cranes, fire engines and assorted other vehicles. The job for us students that evening was to provide extra muscle for lifting and pushing. It provided an amusing interlude for us – and confirmed in our minds that the life of a Lightning pilot often involved drama of one sort or another.

At any rate, like any red-blooded pilot I remained curious to 'have a go' in a Lightning, and my opportunity eventually came a couple of years later at RAF Gütersloh. Before going on to relate the story of the flight I had better first explain how and why I came to be there.

In common with most trainee RAF pilots of my time I hit something of a log jam at the end of the Valley advanced flying phase. I have to admit sympathy for those who are responsible for manning the force – for organising the recruiting, scheduling the training and training the trainers. No sooner do they think they have everything running on rails than there's a change of government, the new team bringing with it an entirely new defence policy. Either that or operational requirements alter or equipments suddenly fail (for example the Valiant, as well as the long hiatus in Buccaneer ops, both following unforeseen metal fatigue problems.) Or perhaps industry falls behind with equipment deliveries. It's rather like the traffic on the M25; rather than proceeding at an orderly pace, recruitment and flying training bunches up and comes to a halt, followed for no apparent reason by a clearance and a spell of tearing along. There's either a surfeit or a shortage of pilots.

Unfortunately I happened to be part of a surfeit, my particular 'hold' being, I think, caused by a rapid succession of equipment orders and subsequent cancellations. TSR2 disappeared, followed by an order for F-111K and then, fairly soon afterwards, by its cancellation and replacement by the Phantom. P1154 (the supersonic Harrier) went west, as did the AFVG (Anglo-French Variable Geometry), both before metal had been cut. All in all, the upshot was that dozens of pilots were recruited too early and would have to have their training delayed. Some sort of employment had to be found for them during their wait.

My particular snarl up was to last for over a year, and the first job found for me was on what was termed the 'wide speed range trial'. This was mounted by the Central Trials and Tactics Organisation in support of equipment procurement related to the coming Harrier's dispersed operating plans. The premise was that the new aircraft's remote sites might be located by enemy reconnaissance aircraft, but how easily would depend partly on how low and fast the recce chaps flew. The faster and lower, the more survivable would be the bad guys but the less chance they'd have of finding the sites. One would have thought that all this would be self-evident but, as I found much later, unlocking money for new equipment depends on being able to produce empirical evidence – which would often be obtained from scientific trials. I also learned, when later serving in the MoD, that to get the results one wanted from trials, the parameters needed to be set with a degree of cunning – but that's by the by!

Anyway, the first part of this trial was held in Northern Ireland and, together with several of my ex-Valley buddies, I was shipped over the water. There, we spent a very pleasant couple of weeks in the countryside with troops of army Saracen armoured personnel carriers hiding in woods, while Hunters flying at various heights at both 240 and 420 knots, as well as helicopters flying at 90 knots, tried to locate us. We, meanwhile, having spotted them, would record how long they were exposed to our simulated surface-to-air missiles.

Throughout, we were accommodated at an almost deserted beachside army establishment called Magilligan, a spot later to achieve notoriety as an internment camp during the troubles. During our time it was run by a pleasant old territorial army colonel whose day's work appeared to consist of supplying the mess kitchen by fishing off the beach and shooting game.

Driving those armoured vehicles around in the sunshine was great fun, and part two of the trial was to take place in West Germany during the winter. This time camouflaged, plywood, mock-up Harriers were to be placed in the woods, while recce forces tried to locate them. On arrival by air at RAF Brüggen (my first ever trip away from the UK) I found I would have to move around a bit, and my first stop was the driving school. There, I was presented with a manual of German road signs together with a list of rules and regulations, and told that I'd sit the 'tick test' in a couple of hours. I did, I passed, and I was then taken by a sergeant for a trip around the block in a left-hand-drive Land Rover. I'd never driven any sort of Land Rover before, let alone a left-hand-drive version, but within ten minutes I was signed off. Notwithstanding, I might add, all the embarrassing graunching noises as I fumbled with the four-wheel drive selector after having mistaken it for the gear lever. That afternoon I was issued with my own Land Rover and a map – and told to report to RAF Gütersloh. That base lay 100 miles to the east, the route lying through the most densely populated part of the Federal Republic. Gulp!

Despite my fears I made it there safely, and settled happily at Gütersloh for a couple of weeks. The trial took up some of my attention, but left plenty of time to make friends and enjoy myself. One of those friends was Phil, a 19 Squadron Lightning pilot, who undertook to fix me a trip in their T-bird. And so it was that, one morning, I found myself at the foot of the ladder gazing up at the awesome bulk of Lightning T4 XM991.

The rain was sheeting down and the cloudbase was not far off the deck. No improvement was forecast. Thus the aircraft's already short endurance was going to be further reduced by our having to be back on the landing approach with sufficient fuel to divert to a distant field if we couldn't land at base. And we were going to have to do all our work at high altitude, above the thick layer of clag. Nevertheless, Phil was determined to show me as many of the aircraft's party tricks as he could squeeze into the brief time we'd have available.

We strapped in and leaned towards each other as the canopy came down; the cockpit of the dual-seat Lightning could best be described as an intimate space. The first excitement on the agenda was to be a rotation take-off. This would involve holding it low after lift-off until about 250 knots, then whipping the stick back and standing the beast on its tail. Clearance for vertical departure having been received, we shot off, spray and scud flying as we raced towards unstick speed. Now we were airborne, followed by a hefty check forward on the stick to hold it low. Gear was selected up;

rain was slashing back up the windshield and it was hard to see what the hell was going on. "OK," shouted Phil, "we give it one!" He snatched the stick back into his stomach and we disappeared into cloud; now we had only instruments to tell us that the jet was heading vertically upwards. Amidst the commotion there had been reassuring thumps as the wheels had locked up. But, regrettably, only partly reassuring; there had only been two thumps, and on the instrument panel now glowed an accusing red light to tell us that the nose wheel was unlocked. "Oh bugger," Phil muttered, "we're going to have to sort this." He cancelled reheat and pushed forward to regain some sort of sensible climb attitude, meanwhile telling ATC of the change of plan.

What had happened wasn't, it seemed, uncommon. The Lightning's nose wheel retracted forwards, so if the speed got too high the resistance of the airflow prevented it retracting fully. Hence the need to select 'up' only a nanosecond after the wheels left the ground. Now, there was no option but to reselect undercarriage down and then raise it again at a more controlled speed, and this we did. Phil then requested a new clearance to climb and, with this approved, went once again for reheat and the vertical. For all this time we had, of course, been in thick cloud, and would be for a further 30,000 feet, so the impressive majesty of this vertical climb was somewhat lost. But as soon as we'd popped out into the sunshine on top I certainly had no difficulty appreciating the aircraft's ability to guzzle fuel. We had only enough left now to make a brief supersonic excursion before we'd have to commence our recovery.

This we did, achieving Mach 1.1 in dry power, but up there one gets no sensation of speed so it hardly mattered. Even that speed would, though, have trailed a sonic boom across the ground below, which is an interesting reflection on how things were in those days. It was absolutely prohibited to go supersonic over the UK land mass (except in cases of operational necessity), with high speed runs having to be radar monitored over the sea on headings pointing away from the coast. But not so in Germany. Whether that was a legacy from the days when the allies were occupying powers I can't say. Perhaps not, for I feel sure that, in the 1960s and 70s Luftwaffe pilots were themselves well used to dropping booms over their homeland.

Anyway, so much for my one and only Lightning trip, but I spoke earlier of the fact that many of us at training school hadn't much fancied flying the jet because of our impression that air defence work was boring. So I'll just slip in one more story to counter that by illustrating the scale of the job those Lightning pilots were doing. After training with me, a friend of mine departed for his first tour, which was on 74 Squadron in Singapore. I understand he enjoyed a fabulous time. Of course; would it be possible not to relish that scenario? Following the UK's withdrawal from its far-eastern commitments in 1971 he was posted to RAF Leuchars, but I soon got wind that things were not going altogether well there. I saw him at one point when he was attending a nearby hospital for, he said, attention to some kind of physical complaint. But over a couple of beers he also got round to relating how the Leuchars work had been affecting him. He told me of QRA scrambles in appalling weather. Of course, when the Soviets came visiting the UK air defence region the interceptors had to go and investigate, come fair wind or foul. He understood that well, but he'd experienced recoveries to Leuchars in the middle of the night, on the wing of another Lightning, in weather well below limits – and with no fuel left to go anywhere else.

The whole thing had, it seemed, been getting to him, and not long afterwards he gave up flying completely. He was (is – I still see him occasionally) a good guy, and he made a very successful second career in another branch of the RAF. It just shows that we should never underestimate the pressures that exist in some jobs. And now that I know better, I take my hat off to those Lightning boys.

Later, when they had been relieved by Phantoms of the primary air defence task, the last two Lightning squadrons adopted a more close-in, low-level pattern of work. They were repainted in low-level camouflage and had lots of fun racing around at low level. They partook in the 'dial-a-Lightning' scheme whereby we mud movers could phone up and book some opposition for our simulated attack missions. My very last Jaguar trip from Brüggen saw me leading a four-ship against a pair of Lightnings, and at that stage I could happily have volunteered for a tour doing what they were doing. I know they were enjoying themselves.

Although many of the navigators with whom I joined the RAF in 1966 went on to fly Canberras, we pilots were, by and large, too late for the old bomber. This was because of the longer pilot training process as well as the hold to which we were subjected. Of course the Canberra PR9, as well as target-facilities versions, went on for many more years, but here I'm really talking about the basic bomber and tactical recce variants.

None of us from my advanced flying course at Valley were posted to the venerable machine. The Canberra OCU had closed, and new and exciting things were about to happen. In fact my course was the first from which graduate pilots were posted to the latest generation of jets, with two of my friends sent to the Buccaneer and one to the Phantom. As so often happens in the RAF, though, things changed because of slippage. Although the Buccaneer boys continued on their destined course, our Phantom chap had his posting changed during the holding period and he finished up on Lightnings. And there was another consequence: because of the delay to the Phantom, the Canberra OCU had to be re-opened to sustain the front line. And so it was that two of our number had their postings switched across to the old bomber.

It was, therefore, a terrible irony that both of them died during their first tours as Canberra pilots. One crashed during a mishandled practice bombing manoeuvre in Germany, while the other was particularly unlucky. On temporary detachment from his German base to Cyprus he suffered an engine failure. Unable to land the aircraft immediately, he lost control during a go-around. Asymmetric flying was well known to be a tricky business in the Canberra but, even following a loss of control, the crew should have been able to eject. In this case, though, the complication was that they had an airman passenger aboard – who had no ejector seat. We'll never know for certain, but it seems likely that the pilot stayed at the controls in an effort to save the passenger.

He was Roger Ellis, a very popular man and a great friend of mine, and indeed of many of us on our training course. On the day after we finished at Valley he had been married to Hilary, a most lovely lady, and most of us had been guests at their wedding. He'd originally been posted to Hunters before things had been changed, and it's hard not to think 'if only ...'

As for my own personal, tiny sliver of Canberra experience, it came during the same detachment to Germany which gave me my Lightning flight. As well as Brüggen, Gütersloh and Rheindahlen, my work on that wide speed range trial took me to RAF Wildenrath (the place which, nowadays, has a high-speed rail track built around the perimeter which is used for testing newly built German trains). There I ran into a chap who had had the next bedspace to mine in the barrack block during our initial officer training. Together we had suffered the agonies of making bed-packs, scouring the latrines and polishing the floors, as well as hiking up the Brecon Beacons carrying telegraph poles.

In 1969 I was a mere holding pilot, while Rod Hawkins (the alphabetical proximity of our surnames explains why we had been together in the block) was already an operational bomber navigator on 14 Squadron. Needless to say he did his best to arrange a trip for me, and what came out of the hat was a weekend ranger to Gibraltar. In our Canberra B(I)8 we cruised southwards at high level. That variant had no dual controls, so en route I had to be content with sightseeing, but compensation came in being able to witness my first landing on 'the rock' from a prone position in the glass-nosed bomb-aimer's position.

The much-missed Roger Ellis is on the left of this picture, with the author on the right. In the centre is Ian 'Mac' McIvor, a New Zealander who went on to fly Lightnings. The picture is an extract from the No. 40 Gnat course photo, August 1968. (Crown Copyright)

Jaguar GR1 and Buccaneer S2B of 16 Squadron over Scotland. The Buccaneer must have been specially painted for the occasion, for 16 Squadron had been equipped with Tornados in between Buccs and Jags. (Crown Copyright)

It was a truly exciting experience. I probably ought to have been strapped into the rumble seat, but never mind, we were a long way from home!

We spent the weekend doing what one does in Gib: climbing to the top of the rock; peering at the apes; exploring the tunnels and caves; and eating and drinking in the many marvellous little pubs and bars. When it came to Monday morning it seemed that this last activity had taken up too much of my time. I was feeling somewhat jaded, and on the cruise home this showed up in the only attack of 'the bends' I've ever experienced. The Canberra's pressurisation wasn't, I gather, particularly powerful, which always resulted in a cabin altitude which was unusually high for a jet. Nor did the heating system seem to be up to the job; it was freezing cold up there. So it was a pretty uncomfortable flight, but no long-term harm was done. And I'm pleased I was able to get an insight, however brief, into what it was like to be on Canberras.

I knew many Buccaneer operators and, to a man, they were loyal to their machine – even following the catastrophic metal fatigue accident of 1980 and its aftermath. The Bucc had by no means been the RAF's first choice when it was procured, but it was adopted with relish and almost, it seemed, with love. I never flew in one, although I did come close. In the intense period in Germany during which exercises to test war preparedness ruled the calendar, aircrew from one base would commonly be co-opted as evaluators at another. So it was that, for a couple of days during 1978, I found myself at RAF Laarbruch as part of the 'maxeval' team. Watching the exercise scenario unfold in their 'hard' – the protected briefing facility – was enlightening, as it was useful to pick up tips from another unit. And relaxing while the victims struggled in gas masks and charcoal suits was always amusing.

But airborne evaluation was a part of the game, too, and what I really fancied was a Buccaneer trip. Thus I was delighted when I was programmed to sit in the back seat of number four of a four-ship on a simulated attack mission. But the weather intervened. It was poor across northern Germany, which meant that the formation would have to fly a high-low-high profile to a distant target area where conditions were usable. For the climb through cloud it was usual for Buccaneer crews to use their radar to maintain formation station. This was deemed to require the services of one who knew how to work the kit, and I was turfed out in favour of an expert. A rather weak excuse, I thought, but not one with which I was qualified to argue. So that was the nearest I came to a Buccaneer flight.

The Harrier was the one I had always wanted to fly, and in the end I had several opportunities. All came while I was in staff appointments, and as anybody who has done that sort of work will confirm, it makes a marvellous break to get out of the office and visit an operational station. Fresh air and the sight, smell and sound of jets do wonders for one's motivation, so I was always happy to find a reason to make a 'staff visit'.

I've already related the story of my Harrier trip with the Royal Navy, and that one came while I was lecturing at the Department of Air Warfare. A couple of naval officers had been on a course I was running, and it was easy to find an excuse to make a reciprocal visit to them at Yeovilton. The next time I flew a Harrier was while I was working in the MoD. My job had to do with future plans for RAF equipment – for me, specifically, that meant Harrier, Jaguar, EFA (at the time a paper aeroplane, but much later to become the Typhoon), and their weapons. One of the hot topics was the imminent introduction of the Harrier GR5, which needed a two-seat version. The assumption at the time was that a number of T4s would be given GR5 avionics and re-issued as the T6. There was, though, a problem. The GR5 looked like a Harrier, but its airframe and especially its wings, were so different from the GR3 that it really deserved a new name. The development was positive in that the GR5 was much easier to fly than the GR3. But that made it doubly odd that, with the T6 in the fleet, students would have to learn in the bad old airframe to fly the brand new jet.

Readers might puzzle over the reason for this strange situation, but the answer lay, as with so many things military, in affordability. Putting new avionics into the existing fleet of T4s would have been expensive, but that cost would pale into insignificance compared with designing and building a new two-seater based on the GR5. Although, given that McDonnell Douglas already had their TAV-8B equivalent in the air, I'm not sure that BAe had quite as much work to do as they made out. But anyway, all the Harrier pilots I knew, ranging from flying officer to air chief marshal, agreed that the existing plan was seriously flawed, but there was no consensus on how it could be rectified. My job was somehow to find an affordable way of changing course.

Well, we did it, and the Harrier T10 was born. But not without some serious pains in the labour ward. For a start, there was no new money available, so the fourteen T10s had to replace a larger number (I forget how many) of the GR5s that were on order. Those T10s would, therefore, have to count as operational as well as training machines if overall combat-capable numbers were not to be reduced too drastically. This wasn't as simple as it sounds. The T10, with its second cockpit, would be much heavier than the GR5 but would use the same engine; this would not only have a huge impact on hover performance but would reduce the useful range and/or pay-load. On the positive side, I know it to be true (although you wouldn't catch many Harrier pilots admitting it) that a two-seater could be very useful for leading the big, mixed formations that were coming into vogue in NATO – with two people in the cockpit, one could fly the jet while the other could look after the big formation.

All concerned recognised that the revised plan had its limitations, but agreed that on balance it was an improvement on the original assumption. Meanwhile I, wiping a staff officer's sweat from my brow after battling the change through the massed civil service defences of the MoD and Treasury, needed to smell jet fuel again.

So to my Harrier flying. Finding time and excuses for three separate staff visits to RAF Wittering between 1988 and 1990, I flew the T4 (still the only two-seater in service) on each occasion. The experience was just as thrilling as I'd expected, with of course hovering the beast a must. I'd previously 'had a go' in helicopters several times and had, as expected, found it hard to hold the machines steady; each control movement seemed to induce, as well as the desired movement, some additional, totally unexpected reaction. It was similar with the Harrier, although I got the impression that there was one significant difference. This is hard to explain without the aid of pencil and paper but, if you could visualise somebody suspended under a parachute you could perhaps see a certain stability there; the person is hanging and therefore tends to stabilise towards the centre point of any oscillation. That, in my mind, equates to a helicopter 'hanging' below its rotor. Now visualise a ping-pong ball balancing on the top of a jet of water; it's very unstable, and that, to me, seems more to resemble a Harrier on its column of jet thrust. Harrier boys will no doubt correct me if this analogy is invalid. But I never-theless think that those first chaps who converted to the jet back in 1969 – without the benefit of T-bird or simulator – did the most extraordinary job. They must be excused the occasional 'dead ants' they left scattered around their practice areas.

The other factor I found with my own hovering efforts was that there's so little time to practise. One can't begin until the fuel has reduced to 'hover weight', and such is the enormous fuel consumption at the high power levels required that the time from that point to minimums can be very short. Just think of that when, for example, planning a recovery to an aircraft carrier. Margin for error equals zilch!

Anyway, my instructor deemed me to have successfully hovered and landed vertically. Whether I actually did (I'm absolutely sure I wouldn't have been sent solo after any of those trips) or whether they simply wanted to see this staff officer drink the 'hover pot' in the bar afterwards I leave you to guess. I forget exactly what the drink comprised, but I feel sure that it would have been a typical RAF concoction on such occasions – ice-cold beer compounded with something else both strong and indigestible. And maybe a couple of raw eggs, too. Such things just have to be done.

Then in 1996 I managed to scrounge a flight in the fruits of my earlier labours, the T10. It was all I could possibly have hoped for and provided a fitting end to my Harrier flying. I envy and respect the pilots who flew the jet for a living, and I've read their books avidly. I still think that, for chaps trained for short-range close air support trips from dispersed sites in Europe, 1 Squadron's 8,000-mile trip down to the South Atlantic to land on a little platform bobbing in the ocean, and then their operations from a deck (incidentally being unable to properly align their primary navigation and weapon-aiming system) in a shooting war, must amount to one of aviation's epic achievements.

I have had only minimal contact with the V bombers. The Valiant had gone before I arrived, while I knew the Victor only as an airborne petrol station. I know it did outstanding work for many years, most notably during the Falklands and Gulf campaigns, but it was without doubt my least favourite of the six refuelling types with which I operated. Its wings flapped in anything other than the calmest of air, which used to make the hoses snake horribly. And I suspect that its old autopilot wasn't the best, for the aircraft seemed to continually wander in both heading and altitude.

I had little AAR experience with the Vulcan, but it did appear to offer a more stable platform. And of course one couldn't but appreciate its awe-inspiring presence up close. I had the honour, on 21 March 1984, of participating in the type's final sortie in service, refuelling in a Jaguar from a Vulcan over the North Sea. I understand that the AOC 1 Group was in the co-pilot's seat that day.

The TriStar was OK and the KC-135 great fun (I also flew in both types while fighters were refuelling), but for stability it was hard to match the VC10 and KC-10. I hear stories that the RAF's new refueller, the A330 Voyager, has wings that flap like a Victor's. That's progress for you!

I did, by the way, have the pleasure of flying the VC10 a couple of times while I was at the helm of Operation Jural; as well as the Tornados at Dhahran I also had a VC10 or two at Bahrain. Great fun.

The author with the Operation Jural VC10 detachment at Muharraq, 1995.

While on the subject of refuelling I could mention that the taught process for a receiver is that, when making contact, the pilot shouldn't look at the probe or basket. The tanker is well marked up with guidelines and cues, and those should be used exclusively while closing up and in position. Not least because, as one gets closer, the fighter's 'bow wave' tends to move the basket. And of course, if it's turbulent and hose and basket are riding up and down, trying to follow them can prove a dicey business. But in some cases it was tempting to watch the probe and basket. On the Jaguar, for example, the probe was well within vision and it was often possible to help the contact with a last-minute squeeze of rudder. With the Phantom, on the other hand, the probe tip was somewhere up above the pilot's right ear, and therefore well out of sight. That would sometimes tempt the nav to do the 'looking at the probe and basket' routine and to ply the pilot with 'helpful' advice. I never found that particularly useful, with a typical commentary seeming to go along the lines of: "Up a bit … steady … right a bit … steady … looking good … keep coming … excellent … missed completely."

My generation was largely too late to fly the Meteor, although the navs not by much; they were, at the advanced training stage, on only the second or third course after withdrawal of the Meteor nav trainer. The only contact I personally ever had with the old jet was to fire against a flag towed by a 'meat box' from Chivenor or Brawdy. 'Sir Winston', our venerable F8, was the usual tug, and a fine sight he always made. And a fine sound, too; although the Hunter was well known for its 'blue note', the Meteor's voice at high speed was quite similar.

One member of my advanced flying course did, though, have a go. I mentioned earlier that we all had to hold for a year or so between advanced training and our

OCU courses. For Bill Cope, that meant a posting to RAF Binbrook. That Lincolnshire airfield was a bleak spot and he might have expected something of a non job. But wait – there was the prospect of a little flying. Bill is a member of our Norfolk old flying codgers lunch club, and here he tells his tale:

"On leaving Valley in 1968 I was allocated to the Buccaneer, but that would be a year or more in the future. However, I was lucky enough in the meantime to be posted to RAF Binbrook to temporarily join 85 Squadron, which operated the Meteor T7s and F8s which provided training for the school of radar controllers at Bawdsey.

"Even to one brought up on the Jet Provost the Meteor T7 was somewhat rudimentary. The cockpit had no pressurisation and little heating. However, the single-seat F8 was an enjoyable ride. My conversion was naturally fitted in when time and T7s were available, and it took some five months. Nevertheless it was great fun.

"The Meteor taught me a great deal about twin-engined flight. The rudder pedals had to be set precisely such that, if one engine failed, a stiff leg on the appropriate side kept the aircraft flying quite straight. I vividly remember a check-ride on return from leave. Chunky Gundry, whose knowledge of the Meteor was encyclopaedic, pulled the port engine to idle at about 200 feet on climb-out after take-off – whereupon I pushed my right leg forward to keep the aircraft in balance. My leg remained in this position for some fifty minutes, until Chunky allowed us to land. Following which the ground crew had great fun watching my impersonation of Long John Silver (without a crutch) as I painfully staggered back to the hangar!

"At the time, the cold war was in full freeze, and we knew that the Soviets were watching and listening to our every move. We were very careful about communication security, and each unit changed its callsigns every fortnight or so. We never announced our aircraft type over the radio, instead using thinly disguised descriptions such as 'single-jet trainer' or 'four-prop transport' as appropriate. Whether that sort of thing ever fooled the armies of listeners in the many so-called trawlers that inhabited the North Sea must be doubtful, but the procedure did give me a little fun. When I had completed my practice intercepts and was contacting Eastern Radar on the way home I would be asked for 'aircraft type, please'. The main occupants of Binbrook were its two Lightning squadrons, and my answer of 'twin-jet fighter' wasn't exactly a lie. It might not have thrown the 'listeners' for more than a minute or two, but it kept me happy.

"All in all I amassed seventy-eight hours on Meteors and learned a great deal from my more senior colleagues on 85 Squadron. I never had any difficulty with asymmetric flight with the Buccaneer – it was a piece of cake after the Meteor."

Returning to the Canberra, I did have a connection with it in my later life when I was deputy director of air ops in the MoD. One of my responsibilities was the Canberra PR9, and I was endlessly amazed by the extraordinary capabilities of the aircraft. It had all sorts of secret kit fitted, and I recall one day being shown a picture of Big Ben which had apparently been taken when the aircraft was vastly distant. The clock face was as clear as though it had been seen from Parliament Square. I wondered what we would do to replace the Canberra when it eventually became life-expired. No direct successor had been planned or identified, and I guessed that a combination of Nimrod's successor, Sentinel, unmanned air systems and satellites would, between them, do the job. I left before all that was decided, and I have no idea what the eventual answer was.

The Nimrod was another of my responsibilities in my MoD job – in both 'MR' and 'R' forms. I had a couple of most enjoyable flights in MR2s from Kinloss, and at one point travelled down to Bournemouth to witness the first four MR2 fuselages being stripped in preparation for conversion to MRA4 standard. But, in view of what happened following the 2010 election, the least said about that project the better. As for the Nimrod R1, I had just one trip in that amazing machine. If I said where we went I would have to be taken out and shot, but I do recall much talk en route about the limited fatigue life remaining on the three airframes. The co-pilot, who was flying the sortie, then impressed me by roaring into home base and doing a run and break, à la fighter. It turned out that he was an ex-Phantom pilot!

Finally from Whitehall, a little story of the complex way in which the military interacts with its political masters. Back in 1998 there was a series of devastating forest fires in Indonesia. Wildlife was dying and the smoke was drifting across Sumatra and the Malayan peninsula, darkening cities as far away as Kuala Lumpur; the Indonesian government had appealed to the international community for help. Now, we in air ops knew that our Canberra PR9s had sensors which would be very useful; they could pinpoint the seat of the fires from far off. They were available and could have been out there within a couple of days. Time went by, which we eventually found was being occupied by discussions between the Department for International Development and the MoD over who would pay the bill for any deployment. The MoD, pretty reasonably, said that it wasn't their responsibility – and the argument went on for some time. Part of the case concerned how much account would have to be taken of training bills which would routinely have accumulated if the aircraft weren't away on ops. Eventually the questions were settled and the government made the offer of assistance. The fires were, by now, pretty well out and the smoke had dispersed, but the Indonesians nevertheless made a public and gracious acknowledgement of our offer. So everybody was happy: the minister for International Development had received a nice response; the MoD had offered, thereby demonstrating the RAF's useful capability; and the Treasury had incurred no costs. The saga would have made an excellent episode of *Yes Minister*.

CHAPTER 18
SIMULATING IT

Flight simulators are strange beasts, and there can be few pilots who truly enjoyed all their simulator sessions. When we first moved to a new aircraft it was a teaching tool, and most people prefer to get beyond that and on to the 'qualified' stage as soon as possible. Then, once on a squadron, the periodic sim sessions seemed always to bring with them an element of criticism and testing. Granted, there would be learning included, but on balance the sim slots were largely to be endured.

My first brush with the genre was with the 'link trainer', a cockpit perched on a wobbly pole at my flying training school. It was staffed by a couple of well-nigh unintelligible Polish master pilots of Second World War vintage. The object, by and large, was cockpit familiarisation and procedures training, and the machine fulfilled its purpose.

I have vivid memories of the Hunter simulator. The cockpit was bolted to the floor, its canopy whitewashed. But what sticks in my mind was the little square up in the top front corner of the screen which was left clear. The reason for that would become apparent during each student's 'final evaluation' sortie. Then, he would be briefed to attack a target deep into enemy territory. En route he would be cued from time to time by the instructor to look up at the clear patch. And there he'd spy a picture of an aircraft cut out from a magazine, pressed there by the instructor's palm. An instant decision was required: "Hostile!" if it was a MiG, whereupon the student would have to make the gun switches live and enter an evasive manoeuvre; or "Friendly!" if it was a Lightning or similar, when the student ought to continue en route. Thrilling stuff! Of course, given no visual or motion, and with only dead reckoning navigation, the actual operational profile over 'enemy territory' was limited. But the mission invariably ended with a catastrophic emergency known as a 'turret drive failure', at which point both hydraulics and electrics failed. The simulator, which at the best of times was a pig to fly, now became next to impossible. Occasionally it could be wrestled onto the ground from this hopeless state but, more usually, there would be an ejection. Following which one would clamber out and be asked difficult questions about escape and evasion – and so on.

Do you know, I can hardly remember anything about the Phantom simulator. Except for one peripheral incident. Halfway through my tour at Coningsby, Princess Margaret was due to visit the unit. For one reason or another I was nominated by my squadron to be the station's assistant project officer. On the big day I would escort and marshal the press, but during the run up there were mundane duties to attend to. One of these related to the simulator, which HRH was due to visit. She was to be escorted to the side of the cockpit, from whence she would observe a crew in action – and maybe even ask them some questions. The cockpit was high up, and a problem was identified by the protocol people: the platform and the steps to it were made of perforated metal. When the princess ascended, they said, there would be a danger of disrespectful people peeping up the royal skirt. So a replacement piece of access furniture was commissioned – made of solid wood, and I had to check on its progress and installation. I regret to report that I have no recollection of the success of the arrangement – or, indeed, of the royal visit.

Early simulator visual systems were crude, but nevertheless expensive and complex. The basis was one – or several – terrain models, above which 'flew' cameras in response to the pilot's inputs from the sim cockpit. The pictures were transmitted to a screen in front of the pilot. The model was the size of a hangar floor, and the lights required to provide good pictures needed electricity in quantities which could only be provided by a small power station. But those early visuals were a good step forward, permitting ground attacks to be practised against somewhat lifelike targets.

After the Phantom switched to the air defence role its visual system was deemed superfluous, and the model in the RAF Germany Phantom simulator was dismantled. I hope it found a good home – perhaps at a model railway club. The space in which it had been installed was converted into a wing briefing room which could accommodate one hundred pilots – which gives an idea of its vastness. Incidentally, this was at Brüggen, the Jaguar base which had previously hosted Phantoms. The latter had now moved to Wildenrath, but their simulator (minus visual) remained at Brüggen. The Jaguar simulator had always been at Wildenrath, even though Jags had never been based there. Harriers had moved from Wildenrath, via Gütersloh to Laarbruch, and I've no idea where their simulator was. But it's a fair bet that, at least some of the time, the Harrier completed the RAF Germany set of no simulator being at the same base as its parent aircraft.

The Jaguar simulator is the one I recall most fondly. Perhaps it was something to do with my age, my experience, or where I was in my career at the time, but I felt truly on top of it. The missions set were tough, but I was always confident of keeping one step ahead of whatever the instructors threw at me. It was a good feeling, never to be repeated.

One of the simulator types, I forget which, could be upset. With a spot of judicious over-controlling, the motion system would trip and cause the cockpit to fall onto its left side. Not very comfortable for the crew, but a useful ten minutes of the sortie would be spent relaxing while the technicians reset the system.

In the book *Jaguar Boys* I told stories of japes played by the instructors on students. A favourite was to place a large spider or two onto the terrain model which, when viewed by the travelling cameras and relayed to the screen, would appear as monsters. If the staff were really lucky the spiders wouldn't be fried by the overhead lights and would still be alive. Truly mobile targets!

Civil simulators were something different, and I never felt comfortable in them. There could have been many reasons. In the RAF I flew a sim trip roughly once a month, so was generally current. With airlines the general practice was to do a block of three or four trips semi-annually. So I, personally, always began the block feeling out of touch. In commercial life time is money, and simulators are used on a twenty-four-hour basis. I never found it easy to give of my best when the briefing was at midnight and the sim slot was from 2 a.m. until 6 a.m. "It's just like the real thing," I hear you cry. "You train like you fight!" OK, you've got a point. But the debrief, lasting until, perhaps, 7.30 a.m., was nevertheless sometimes hard to take.

The other reason for feeling uncomfortable is perhaps more difficult to rationalise, but I think it possible that I was past my best by the time I was reaching the end of my civil flying. Certainly, I regularly disappointed myself by my performances in airline simulators.

It was nevertheless fascinating to enter the 'simulator hall' of the training establishment, to be greeted by a panorama of, perhaps, half a dozen separate machines moving gently around on the top of their hydraulic legs in response to the inputs of the crews inside. There was always something vaguely alien about the sight – as though several space monsters were dancing together. And I should also add that, depending on the instructor, there was occasionally time for a little fun in them. It was good, for example, to have a go at one's aerobatic sequence in a twin-turboprop transport – although it did tend to crash the hydraulics if one wasn't careful. And such was the scope of the library of destination airfields buried in the machine's computer that it was sometimes possible to find the USS *Nimitz* or the like. Landing an airliner on the carrier's deck without the benefit of an arrestor hook took some doing.

I haven't mentioned the Tornado simulator yet, and that's because I've saved it to open a discussion on motion and visual systems. Years after the Phantom and Jaguar had visuals I found it strange, when moving to the 'fin', to find that the Tornado GR1 simulator had no such refinement. Perhaps those who specified and designed it had stressed the 'night, all-weather' aspect of the new aircraft and decided that, although a visual system would have been useful, it wasn't essential. More likely, though, the bean counters got in on the act and decided that money had to be saved.

The advantage offered by motion and visual systems is obvious: the more the crew believe that they are really flying, the more they get out of the training. That both aren't always of equal importance is self evident; if one is practising instrument flying, for example, there is less need of a picture. But what's not perhaps so obvious is that comprehensive instrumentation, although in theory telling the pilot all he needs to know, might not be entirely sufficient. Because much of one's sense of which way is up comes from the balance organs, motion can be extremely significant when there is no visual.

This is more in the negative sense than the positive. When it comes to orientation, eyes generally give the very best information. The visual clues can come from the eyes scanning the instruments. But motion can induce erroneous sensory inputs that a pilot needs to guard against and to train to ignore. Just as a sloping cloud layer can easily present a pilot with a false horizon (an erroneous visual input), the balance organs in the ears can, in combination with motion, give powerfully wrong impressions of one's attitude. So it's essential to train to believe the instruments, and all aircrew are taught from an early stage of the insidious dangers in this area.

The best example I can give of the problem is the 'leans'. In common with pretty well all aircrew, I've experienced many times the dangers of this phenomenon. The feeling can come in a long, sustained turn in cloud; after a while one can get the impression that the aircraft has returned to straight and level flight, despite the evidence of the instruments. I personally found that the sensation was most strongly apparent when flying in formation in cloud; I've regularly been subjected to powerful impressions, given no other reference than the formation leader's wings (it's more or less impossible to include the instruments in one's scan in such circumstances), of being banked well past the vertical. In a two-seater, it was very reassuring to be able to talk to the navigator about what I was feeling and to have him read from the instruments the correct (and invariably safe) bank angle. Pilots sometimes experience those disconcerting leans when air-to-air refuelling, which of course is a type of formation flying.

Another common type of spatial disorientation is the feeling that a sustained acceleration is in fact a climb. Pilots have been known to correct for this powerful, false impression by diving, despite their instruments indicating straight and level. On several well-documented occasions in airliners, this has cost much loss of life.

So all this says that, in general, simulators ought to have both motion and visual. Or so I thought, but the following little story sheds a slightly different light on the case. Some twenty years after I left the Jaguar, and seven years into my civilian career, I needed to return a favour owed to a friend. He was madly interested in jets and, since I knew the chap running the local Jag simulator, I was able to fix a ride for him. Things had certainly changed since my last visit to Coltishall. The old Jaguar GR1 had been usurped by the GR3, and with the new model had come a much-changed simulator. Much to my surprise I found that, whereas the original had boasted visual and motion, the new version was fixed to the floor. Quite a step backwards, I thought; another example of cheese-paring. But while my friend was having his trip I was permitted to sit on the surrounding platform. And boy, I soon saw why motion wasn't necessary. The new visual was of such high fidelity that the sensory effect was staggeringly real. I needed to hold on to the platform, even though it wasn't moving.

Anybody who has been on a virtual ride in one of Orlando's fabulous theme parks could have told me that this would be the case, for those rides give the most extraordinary effect of motion – derived purely from visual sense. I believe the final version of the Harrier simulator did something similar. Almost all-round vision was provided within its 'dome' to permit even peripheral vision – all adding to the realistic training in the hovering regime. So a simulator without motion is now quite the norm, if its primary purpose is to simulate a mainly visual flight regime.

Returning to the Jaguar, after my friend had completed his flight I was of course invited to have my go. The mission was to originate from RAF Valley, and soon after take-off I set myself up for a flash past the Menai Bridge. Underneath it, of course – who, given a pleasure trip in a simulator, would ever dream of flying over the bridge?! Then into Snowdonia, where an enemy aircraft carrier happened to be operating on Lake Bala. No problem; I dealt with it first by bombing and then, on a second pass, with cannon. Soon it was no more than a stream of bubbles rising from the bottom of the lake. But wait – now I needed more fuel to get me back to base. No problem with that either, for I could see in the distance behind Cader Idris a VC10 tanker. A quick RV and I was soon plugged in and filling up – following which I was able to make a swift transit back to Valley and a greaser of a landing. Yes! I could still do it after all those years.

Seriously, though, it was marvellous to experience the fidelity of a modern simulator. It's just as well, I suppose, that they are so good, for as time goes by the ferocious cost of live flying makes them more vital than ever before. Not only can they truly replicate the sensation of being airborne (after decades of promises that this might be possible) but they can, in many cases, exceed the value of live flying. By feeding in realistic hostile threats and scenarios, for example, which can't be replicated over home territory in peacetime – and by networking connections to the simulators of other allied systems. They'll be doubly important, too, with the F-35, for it will have no dual-control version. A pilot's first trip in the aircraft will also be his first solo.

CHAPTER 19
TORNADO OPS

I arrived in 1992 for my seventh flying tour with a chest bare of medals, a situation that was quite normal for a 'cold war warrior'. A few, either the exceptional ones or those specially favoured, had picked up the odd AFC or MBE along the way but, by and large, we hadn't been decorated. We had seen no live operations; our job had primarily been to deter, to show the certainty that we would retaliate if attacked by demonstrating our superlative equipment, capability and readiness. And, given that there had been no conflagration between the superpowers since the Second World War, I suppose we could be judged to have been successful. Of course, much to everybody's surprise, there had been the Falklands conflict, but apart from the Harrier squadrons the RAF fast-jet types had missed out.

All in all, given that the aircraft I was going to for my command tour was basically a cold war machine, the prospects of breaking my operational duck didn't seem great. The Tornado GR1 had been procured as very much a part of the UK's nuclear deterrent force, and had proved wholly adequate in the role.

But a couple of things had changed. First, the world's political and strategic geography: QRA readiness had been relaxed from 15 minutes to 12 hours in 1986; the Berlin Wall had fallen in 1989; and both the Warsaw Pact and the Soviet Union had dissolved in 1991. Second, just a year before I arrived at Brüggen to take over 31 Squadron, my future team had taken their jets to war against Iraqi forces. Based in Dhahran,

Tornado GR1 refuels from a TriStar in 1995 en route from Eielson air force base, Alaska, to Goose Bay, Labrador.

Saudi Arabia, both men and machines had acquitted themselves brilliantly. So on the day the new boss took command, he was the only one amongst the aircrew not to have a medal.

Was there, at the time, any expectation that operations would continue and broaden over the coming years? No, probably not. Certainly we could see that it would have been better if the Iraq business had been pushed towards a conclusion, but I don't think that we (or, more importantly, the world's leaders and politicians) had really foreseen quite how things would develop.

Anyway, I had been in the chair for just a few months when Saddam Hussein began to rear his head again. His forces began seriously to harass minority groups, the Marsh Arabs in the south and the Kurds in the north. Coalition forces moved to their defence and I deployed for the first of my three desert detachments just after Christmas 1992. At last, my operational flying was off and running.

I will not pretend that I played a big part; I didn't drop a bomb or fire a missile in anger. And, although the missions were long and wearisome, my only moment of real excitement came when an engine blew up some hundred miles north of the Iraqi border. The Tornado flies very well on one, so there was no immediate drama as I turned tail and headed for Kuwait, but the engine had gone off with quite a bang and, in that circumstance, I couldn't be sure that no damage had been done to the remaining motor. While the coalition had an excellent combat search and rescue organisation in theatre, I had no wish to test it out by having to eject into Iraqi territory. Anyway, before too long the buildings of Kuwait City hove into view, and soon the wheels were safely on the ground. It was interesting to see, as I taxied in, that there were still signs, in the form of wrecked and rusting equipment, of the original 1990 Iraqi attack.

I did, by the way, finish up receiving a gong, albeit just a humble General Service Medal designated for 'Air Operations Iraq'. I forget, now, what the criteria were for the award; was it time in theatre or number of operational missions? One thing's for sure; the presentation couldn't exactly have been described as a glittering occasion. The decoration arrived by post, addressed to me by the wrong rank. I could embellish the story by saying that it was by second-class post, but in all honesty I can't recall whether that was the case. What I can say is that the medal retains a wholly appropriate place in its cardboard box, tucked deep in a dusty drawer in my den.

But one great spin-off from my time out there was my chance to see again Bahrain, the place I'd known so well on my first tour. The Hunter hangar was still there, albeit now occupied by an international parcels delivery organisation. The mess was now occupied by a department of the Bahrain government, so was out of bounds. And its marvellous old swimming pool appeared to be derelict. But on the bright side, for a brief period my wife was able to join me for a spot of R & R. Twenty-five years after she'd heard all those stories of my first flying tour she was able to hitch a ride on a

VC10 heading eastwards. It was just great for her to be able to soak up a little of the atmosphere of a place I'd once known so well.

Those Operation Southern Watch detachments in 1992-1995 formed part of an extraordinary series of Tornado GR1 (later GR4) operational deployments over the second half of the aircraft's life, and it's safe to say that no-one could have foreseen the future employment of the 'fin' when it was specified, procured and introduced. Iraq, Kosovo, Afghanistan and Iraq again followed in quick succession, and the pace of ops for the boys (and girls) may be judged by the list of my own squadron's calendar. Starting with the build-up to the Gulf conflict in 1990, there had been seventeen operational detachments to the Middle East in as many years, each for an average of three months. First of course there had been Operations Desert Shield and Desert Storm. Then Operation Jural, policing the southern no-fly zone from Dhahran as part of the coalition's Operation Southern Watch, had continued unchanged until, in 1997, the mounting base had moved to Al Kharj, Saudi Arabia. In 1998 the task had meta-morphosised into Operation Bolton and moved to Ali al Salem in Kuwait. Another re-naming to Operation Resinate (South) until the Iraq War, which had prompted a further redesignation as Operation Telic. And this, with a further move to Al Udeid, Qatar, is how it had remained until the end of the work to restore stability and infra-structure to Iraq. Interspersed had been Kosovo, as well as a couple of detachments during 1997 and 1998 to Incirlik in Turkey for Operation Warden – the UK's contribu-tion to policing the northern Iraq no-fly zone. The coalition effort there was originally known as Operation Provide Comfort, but later Operation Northern Watch.

Then there had been four detachments to Afghanistan (Operation Herrick) between 2010 and 2014, followed immediately by Operation Shader, the resumption of Iraq ops in response to Islamic State (ISIS or ISIL) aggression. And that's where we stand at present. My goodness, the fast-jet people who succeeded me have certainly deserved all the medals they've been awarded.

All these episodes have been well documented in the book *Tornado Boys* and there's little point in going over the detail once again. But it's instructive to contrast how we saw events as they unfolded with how they're seen in retrospect – and of course there's no finer example of that than the endless discussion of political decisions surrounding the Iraq War, colloquially known as Gulf War Two. A good way of doing so would be to look back at some of my own writings.

For sixteen years, starting in 1999, I edited *Star News*, the newsletter of the 31 Squadron association. This 400-strong organisation is a thriving entity, and finding articles to entertain the membership proved an enduring challenge. Naturally, most of the jottings were on the lighter side, but we were supporting an active Tornado squadron which was pretty well constantly involved with operations. And, of course,

The author at Dhahran, Saudi Arabia, in 1995 on Operation Jural with the C-in-C Strike Command, Air Chief Marshal Sir William Wratton and the Hon Nicholas Soames MP, Minister of State for the Armed Forces. Briefing the party is Wing Commander James Kirkpatrick, the CO of 17 Squadron.

The author while commander of British Forces Jural.

The author escorts HRH the Princess Royal in 1995 during her visit to the Operation Jural VC10 detachment in Bahrain. In the background is the old Hunter hangar which the author remembers from 1970.

Each one of the RAF's then Tornado squadrons was represented in this line-up at RAF Marham to mark the seventy-fifth anniversary of the formation of the Royal Air Force. Visible in this picture are GR1s from, nearest first, II, 14, 17, 27, 31, 617 and XV Squadrons. Then come F3s from eight squadrons.

every one of those currently serving had family members who waited anxiously at home for them. So it's not surprising that, now and then, editorials took on a more thoughtful tone.

I've little doubt, by the way, that other operational Tornado squadrons were wrestling with similar questions. But let's start with what the Goldstars' editorial had to say at the end of 2002 about the developing situation in Iraq:

"'We need traffic calming measures,' cry the people, 'to slow the mad flow of vehicles through our village.' 'There is no evidence,' says the district council, 'that such measures would be cost-effective.' 'So just how many deaths would it take to convince you?' retort the frustrated villagers. Meanwhile, the freedom party threatens to go to the court of human rights if anybody should infringe their right to drive as fast as they bloody well like. And village shopkeepers aren't so sure, either; anything which might deter through traffic would likely harm trade. In matters such as these, it's impossible to satisfy everybody. I'm glad I'm not a parish councillor.

"Right now the global village is facing a similar but much more serious question. In this case it's the policeman who is convinced, and he's trying to persuade the council and the villagers of the need for action. Hence the following from the *Daily Telegraph* of 21 August 2002: 'America cannot afford to wait for proof that Saddam Hussein is building weapons of mass destruction,' US Defence Secretary Donald Rumsfeld has declared. 'Think of the prelude to WWII,' Mr Rumsfeld said. 'Think of all the countries that said, well, we don't have enough evidence.' But the UN Security Council has had difficulty in agreeing the measures to be taken. For security isn't the only issue; it's widely suspected that some members' vested interests – trade with Iraq, for example – make them less than enthusiastic about altering the status quo. And the anti-war factions seem, despite the lessons of history, to prefer keeping their heads in the sand.

"Even though our neighbourhood bobby knows that the local ne'er-do-well has a gun, he has difficulty arresting him on the grounds that he *might* use it. The *capability* to commit a crime does not prove the *intention*. Nevertheless, the global policeman has, essentially, argued for a pre-emptive strike. The authority has come up with a resolution, but not one going that far. Although it's legally framed, world opinion is still troubled. From *The Independent:* '... International law and political morality just don't seem to figure at all in the calculations ...'

"Now this last comment prompted me to dig out my old staff college notes on the ethics and morality of war. A subject I had found of only passing interest during the course. After all, in most of our historical case studies, it had seemed relatively easy to discern who was the enemy. Provided they could clearly have been shown to have committed hostile acts against us and our allies, we had been fully entitled to use all proportionate force to defeat them. So why did we students have to agonise for a week over moral philosophy – over the ethical use of force – over the 'justness' of wars? Perhaps I can now see why.

"Case studies focused on conflicts where right and wrong weren't always obvious. Vietnam, for example; and the 1986 US punitive strikes against Libya with the F-111 attacks on Tripoli. In both, public opinion had a great impact on the political decisions which affected the conflicts. And so it did in 1991. It's often said that we should have pursued Saddam Hussein to the logical conclusion at the end of the Gulf conflict. If we had, the argument goes, we would not now be in our present difficulty with him. But I remember that situation well. The Iraqi army was defeated and, as it straggled back towards Baghdad, presented a target described by at least one American A-10 pilot as a 'turkey shoot'. In the face of international clamour to stop, the allies had no choice but to cease fire immediately. In any case, we hadn't actually declared war against Iraq; the stated mission was solely to liberate Kuwait from Iraqi forces. Since then, there's been continual debate as to whether international sanctions against Iraq have been effective against the regime – or have merely brought misery to underprivileged elements of the population. And it hasn't only been the media and the liberal left who have had doubts. Indeed, while I was playing my part in Operation Southern Watch, one of my own flight commanders went as far as to question openly what exactly we were supposed to achieve by being there.

"Of course we're now in the realms of terrorism rather than pure international conflict, and terrorists are not protected by the law of war. The staff college notes are disappointingly light, though, on state-sponsored terrorism, on the culpability of states which harbour terrorists, and on state terrorism itself. Generally, those aspects have come to the fore in the time following my course. But it's also noteworthy that most of the philosophical material I found was written according to the Judeo-Christian ethic of warfare. There's nothing on Islam. Experience now teaches us that other cultures have different understandings of right and wrong. Not necessarily superior ethics and moralities – or indeed inferior ones. But definitely different. Even our own churchmen struggle, as reported in *The Times* on 25 September: 'The Bishop of London endorsed the principle of a pre-emptive strike against Iraq. His surprising move split the highest ranks of the Church of England. Bishop Chartres said that there was nothing in Christian doctrine to prevent a country from taking

direct action to preserve world peace. His comments are in stark contrast to
the opposition to war of the Archbishop of Canterbury designate.'

"So, all in all, none of this is terribly helpful in the current situation on Iraq.
And now, to add to the confusion, try this for size: 'There are reported to be
over a hundred militants with links to al-Qaeda in areas of Iraq controlled by
Kurdish groups *opposed* to Saddam' (*The Telegraph*, 22 August). So who, exactly,
is the enemy, and just what is the justification for doing what and to whom?

"'What weighty questions these are. Just as with the traffic calming measures,
I'm glad I'm not the one responsible for finding the answers. But still, the village
bobby's job is to carry out the tasks determined by higher authority, and our
squadron is heading into eastern skies in a couple of months. Our thoughts will
be very much with the team should things come to a head during their watch."

Whew! Reading that again brings home to me how much more politically minded
are military people now than was the case when, for example, the young me served
in Bahrain in 1970. But the fact is that the military, in the end, does what the politicians ask it to do, and the Iraq War went ahead. Afterwards, here's what the newsletter
had to say in its summer 2003 edition:

"They're back! Marvellous news. 29 April was the day the main Goldstar party
returned, safe and sound, to Marham. A day late owing to a technical problem
with the TriStar (the truckies' embarrassment was well documented by the
local media, I noted!). But perhaps the delay made the homecoming all the
sweeter, and the scenes recorded by TV and newspapers were heartwarming.
At the same time, everybody will have spared a thought for IX Squadron's lost
pilot and navigator, especially in such tragic circumstances. Our boys would
have known them well, and will share their families' grief. But overall, the
feeling at Marham will have been of a job well done.

"Whatever you may think of the political run-up to the use of force at this
juncture, the air and land campaigns certainly seemed to go off just as well as
they possibly could have done in the circumstances. So perhaps the MoD's
customary 'lessons learned' exercise will be less painful this time than has been
the case on a number of recent occasions. Of course the press carried its usual
quota of 'squaddie has to buy his own desert boots' stories, but it was good to
see that the Tornado element appeared, to the layman as well as to us ex-oper-
ators, to have had its equipment and tactics perfectly tailored to the job in hand.

"As with all recent campaigns, the issue of media coverage became a major
one, and it must have been incredibly difficult for those doing the command-
ing and fighting to have to bear the spotlight's full glare. We at home were

transfixed by the pictures that unfolded on TV; could anybody forget John Simpson's incredible broadcast minutes after he had been wounded and his translator killed in an attack by a friendly aircraft? But I for one found some of the accompanying comment less enthralling. The endless speculation by 'expert' (?) analysts interspersed with pointless invitations to 'describe the campaign for us, general, in a couple of sentences' was a wearying mixture. Probably the professionals took no notice of the talking heads. On the other hand, I'm certain that many commanders must have come to curse the person who first went public with the intention to 'shock and awe', for that phrase undoubtedly took on a burdensome characteristic.

"Amongst the ex-serving commentators, the BBC's Air Marshal Sir Timothy Garden stood out, for me, as providing a model of reasoned comment. But the majority of the political and military analysts wheeled on to our screens and newspaper pages seemed overwhelmingly carping and negative. The pause taken by the American land forces prior to the entry into Baghdad was deemed to be a 'clear indication that their force level was too low'. The time taken by the Brits (only a fortnight for God's sake!) to root out the bulk of the opposition in Basra 'demonstrated that the wrong tactics had been selected'. That the Iraqis didn't cave in after the first week's bombing 'clearly indicated the failure of the air campaign'. The looting after the cities were liberated 'showed that the allies had no plans or capability to cope with post-hostility situations'. Many commentators, including some in government, made much noise about loss of innocent Iraqi lives during the campaign. That was regrettable, of course; it would always be better not to have to resort to conflict. But the complainers never seemed to balance the debit against the lives which have been taken by Saddam's own people ('Amnesty International has collated information on 17,000 disappearances over 20 years, but it fears that the final figure could be much higher.' *The Times*, 14 May). And Saddam would still have been at it now had the coalition not taken action.

"The criticism still goes on. International charities castigate the coalition for not having sufficient welfare arrangements in place, and complain that there's a danger of starvation and disease. But how were conditions for the majority of the Iraqi population before the war? Feminists (including certain lady politicians) complain that Iraqi women aren't being put into positions of influence in the interim regime. Hang on now, do they really think we can overturn centuries of Arab tradition and artificially impose western concepts of the place of women in society? The liberal left demands instant democracy for Iraq. But it's less than likely that Iraqi society would welcome having a western model of democracy grafted on to it. Truly, there are still many questions to be tackled. It would be nice to think that all these various organisations – governmental, non-governmental and media – will pause from time to time to conduct their own lessons learned exercises – but we won't hold our breath.

"But all that aside, congratulations to our squadron on its professional part in the campaign. Ladies and gentlemen of 31, we salute your work and celebrate your safe return."

A lot of water has gone under the bridge since that editorial was written, but I don't think that hindsight renders it any less valid. Moving on, however, in the winter 2004 edition I commented that:

"Our modern-day military people are no longer conscripts, but they nevertheless have a duty to do their government's bidding in whatever operation they find themselves. During my thirty-two years of 'peacetime' service I was lucky enough not to have any difficulty with the government's rationale for what it was asking me to do. It can't be so easy for today's servicemen and women, given the deluge of media comment and opinion on Iraq. But we laymen must never forget that our successors are doing their loyal duty – putting their lives on the line, and sometimes losing them – at the government's ordering."

The last but one item was headlined 'They're Back', but as we now know the Tornado commitment in Iraq went on for donkey's years. Indeed 'they're back' could have been written several times over – and indeed was. But it was complicated by Afghanistan, that 2009 Tornado commitment, taking over from the Harriers and continuing for a full five years. So by the time I wrote the winter 2014 editorial I was becoming wise to the pointlessness of believing things were over. At the apparent end of the Afghan commitment I penned the following, somewhat tongue-in-cheek, piece:

"In autumn 2009 I wrote in *Star News:* 'Operation Telic is over. The Tornado GR4s are home from the Middle East for the last time, their mission supporting allied troops in Iraq complete. They first deployed in 1990 and now the job is done. We wish our squadron well on completion of is task. But of course there's always Afghanistan …

"Now let's just change a couple of words and swap a couple of others around. Try this: 'Operation Herrick is over. The Tornado GR4s are home from Kandahar for the last time, their mission supporting allied troops in Afghanistan complete. They first deployed in 2010 and now the job is done. We wish our squadron well on completion of its task. But of course there's always Iraq …'"

Reverting to a more normal tone, the article continued:

"Yes, there's nothing new under the sun. GR4s are, even now, deployed in Akrotiri to conduct missions over northern Iraq. ISIS are the latest bad guys (ISIL and IS being acronyms also used). A deployment to Turkey looks possible, and ops over Syria could possibly follow. Every minor journalist and back-bench MP now seems to be an expert in what should be done, with their knowledgeable utterances being generally summarised as 'a force of eight Tornados is no more than a gesture, and ISIS can't be defeated unless boots are put on the ground'.

"It's clearly not that simple. Not only is the GR4's capability massive, but a substantial coalition effort is being put together. The area is huge, though, and the guerrilla force is dispersed. And to say that the politics of the thing is confusing is very much an understatement; even quoting the old chestnut that 'my enemy's enemy is my friend' doesn't seem to help much here. For example, the Turks don't like ISIS but neither are they keen on the Kurds or the current Syrian government (both of whom could benefit if the current ISIS campaign were to be defeated). Who would be a politician?

"Suffice to say that our squadron has already been involved, kicking off the initial deployment back in August before handing over to others to allow the Goldstars to continue with preparation for the final Afghan push. It seems likely that they will be sent out again as soon as they've been able to draw breath after returning from Afghan.

"This latest operational commitment was quite quickly followed by the announcement that the disbandment of II(AC) Squadron would be postponed for a year, bolstering the available GR4 force. Whether or not the government deliberately wished to give the impression that this was an overall force increase, it was certainly presented in the media as a boost to RAF numbers. [In fact number II Tornado Squadron was subsequently re-numbered 12 Squadron.]

"At the same time as Iraq is starting up again, Afghanistan is in the final wind-down. As it does so a number of eminent ex-chiefs of the general staff chose the moment (in the recent BBC2 documentary 'Afghanistan – the Lion's Last Roar?') to say that both government and military got the Afghan calculations wrong from the outset. Lords Dannatt and Richards, together with Sir Peter Wall, declared the campaign 'ill-planned and under-resourced'. We must hope that not too many of those watching the programme or reading press coverage of it had suffered injuries in theatre or were relatives of those who died there.

"It is worth observing, though, that the servicemen in theatre have, as far as we may see, conducted themselves immaculately. In particular, we have nothing but admiration for what the Goldstars have done, and are delighted to see them home after completing their task. We have little doubt, also, that they will do everything that is asked of them – and more – in connection with the new commitment."

In between times there was Libya – and, after so much serious stuff on Iraq and Afghanistan, you'll perhaps forgive if I slip in a slightly flippant piece I wrote at the time about the detachment. It was entitled 'Mamma Mia – the Brits are back again', and took as its start point a snippet from the *Daily Telegraph* of 26 May 2011 to the effect that 'Two RAF Typhoon pilots who had been due to take part in missions over Libya have been sent back to Britain after an alleged incident involving alcohol'. There were Tornados there as well as Typhoons, and my article went on:

"So what's new? Nothing under the sun! Italian air base Gioia del Colle once again rings to the merry sound of singing and breaking glass as the RAF moves in again. Deployed units were last in residence there during the protracted Balkans troubles of the 1990s, when Jaguars and Harriers took part in the air campaigns. And now they're back, Tornados and Typhoons attacking targets in Libya. And in an echo of days gone by, even our focus on one war criminal, Gaddafi, has been mirrored by the recent arrest of another – Mladic. Truly, the world goes round and round.

"Anyway, we understand that the team is accommodated downtown in the Hotel Svevo. A comment from my bunch of old Jag mates at one of our regular lunches was that mine Italiano host must have licked his lips at seeing the RAF on his doorstep again. For, in my friends' opinion, we must already have paid for his hotel several times over!

"I put this to our man on the spot, who replied with regret that 'I would love to say we are paying to have the place refurbished again this time round – but booze is banned. It all had something to do with an engineer caught with his pants down, quite literally, and a Typhoon mate falling foul of the Guardineri.' Well, I never saw Gioia myself, but this report has echoes of Decimomannu and the Carabinieri. Must be something in the water at these Italian bases!

"A little more research reveals that *svevo* translates as 'ghost'. Ah yes – might that be the ghosts of all those merry Jaguar pilots? But no, my lunch club friends weren't having that. No, they said: 'It sounds as though the new, high tech boys need some training in deportment. Perhaps some grappa management courses would be appropriate!'"

CHAPTER 20
INTERNATIONALISING

During my first three flying tours my RAF squadrons operated pretty well in isolation. Yes, at Coningsby we were assigned to NATO, and in Bahrain there was some kind of loose CENTO connection. But, apart from occasional squadron exchanges we saw little of our neighbours and allies.

But as time went on things changed greatly, and I embarked on a period of intensely international work. Two tours in Germany, a tour in Norway, a year at Canadian staff college, a year in Belgium at NATO's European military headquarters, and a series of deployments to Saudi Arabia lent an entirely different perspective to the scene.

Gulf War One is widely regarded as being the event which began, for the fighter/bomber forces, the idea of flying in big packages with the support of enabling assets – AWACS, tankers, defence suppression aircraft, and so on. But in fact this form of flying had been developing for some years. Exercise Red Flag, in the USA, had been open to UK forces since the mid to late 1970s, while the tactical leadership programme had been underway for almost as long. The latter brought together aircrew from all the air forces in NATO's central region for an intensive month's training. It started as a programme of purely ground seminars, and I recall attending the second course to be held. It was centred at the Luftwaffe base of Fürstenfeldbruck, near Munich, and although one might not think that a bunch of fighter/bomber pilots would enjoy weeks in the classroom, it was incredibly useful. 'Walking through' complex missions and scenarios was something of a novel concept, but we all got a lot out of it.

Of course once it developed into a live flying event its value vastly increased, and I very much enjoyed my later course at Jever, in northern Germany. The programme subsequently moved, still prospering, to Florennes in Belgium. Each nationality was proud of its own equipment, tactics and expertise, and fighter pilots are seldom shy of proclaiming their ways to be the best, so you would be right in imagining that, from time to time, a deal of fiction would be spouted. The classroom was, however, equipped with a 'bullshit flag' for use during debriefings and ground seminars. When the audience detected that presenters were over-egging their own capabilities, the flag would be waved with gusto.

Air combat manoeuvring course at RNoAF base Rygge in late summer 1981. Most of the pilots and GCI controllers are Norwegian; however the author is present, along with two USAF pilots. The F-5E belongs to the USAF.

Canadian Forces Command and Staff College syndicate, 1988. As well as Canadians from all three arms of the services there were students on the course from around a dozen nations. The author's syndicate included a US Navy WSO.

Graduating with, as the Canadians put it, the 'gradumate' – the author's wife Jacqueline.

Italian Tornado, German and British aircrew. The author's course in 1991 at the TTTE.

Formation flying is a well-regulated procedure. It is essential that everybody maintains his prescribed position, and each pilot knows the rules. In my early days mixed formation flying was virtually unknown, but as time went on we began to loosen up a little. Not, it has to be said, without the odd unfortunate incident. One such occurred during a NATO 'tiger meet' – an informal gathering of fighter squadrons which had a tiger as a part of their badge. I partook in one while in Norway. Not that my 336 Skvadron had a tiger badge, their emblem actually being a swallow, but in the absence of any genuine Norwegian tiger squadron they had persuaded the clan that they should be honorary tigers and should be allowed to attend the gatherings. The meet I attended happened to be a purely social affair and was a lot of fun.

The RAF's representatives in the tiger group were, initially, 74 Squadron, and on their demise 230 Puma Squadron stepped up to the plate. Clearly the helicopter boys didn't fulfil the 'fighter' criterion, but I understand that they brought all sorts of alternative spirit to the gathering. In between times there was, I recall, a brief interlude when Gnats from RAF Valley attended, but they seemed not to fit the bill in the sense of disciplined formation flying. As I remember it, one Gnat pilot disgraced himself by getting a little too close to an F-104, bending his pitot probe by jabbing it up the Starfighter's jetpipe.

Yes, formation flying demanded precision, although before I went on my exchange tour I had no inkling of the equally complex rules which define the behaviour of the diplomatic community. But an invitation for my wife and me to dine with the UK air attaché to Norway opened our eyes.

He and I had met many times and had got on well. Although his job was not operationally orientated, on a couple of occasions he had come down from Oslo to see me at Rygge and we'd flown together in an F-5B. He was a helicopter pilot, a Puma specialist, so whether he was really impressed by the little jet I'm not sure. But he appeared to enjoy the trip.

Anyway, to the dinner party. My wife and I pitched up and found that we knew none of the other guests, who were a mix of Norwegian air force hierarchy, the diplomatic corps, and the military attaché elements of various nations. Still, with the aid of a couple of gin and tonics we soon made friends. In fact things began to swing along quite nicely, aided, unsurprisingly, by another round of G & Ts.

Quite soon after those were served we began to discern some consternation in the area of the host, his wife, and the staff. Soon we discovered the source of the unrest, which was that there were two unexpected guests. It transpired that the attaché's PA had phoned one man, let's call him Herr Sandvik, to ascertain availability, but had then sent the written invitation to another Herr Sandvik. Both Sandvik couples had turned up and were happily throwing back the G & Ts.

Now you might think that this wouldn't be a major problem. Clearly there would be food to spare, and chairs could surely be found, so it shouldn't have been too difficult to set another couple of places. Perhaps we'd all have had to shuffle up a little, but that would simply have made it a little more cosy. But in diplomatic circles – just as in close formation – position is everything. The long table had to be laid with strict precision, starting with the host at one end and the hostess at the other. The senior guest had to be on the hostess's right, with the senior wife on the host's right. Then, along each side, it had to go man-woman-man-woman – and so on. I write this in 2016, of course, as I remember it. Maybe today, in these more liberated times, partner and male/female seating might be more flexible. Or more complicated, as the case may be.

Anyway, this was 1981, and the arrival of the extra couple was causing what almost amounted to a diplomatic incident. Because there were, I later learned, only certain numbers of diners which would make such a seating plan work according to the prescription. Apparently ten was a good number, as were fourteen and eighteen. But any in-between numbers of guests would screw things up completely. If you sketch it out on paper you'll see what I'm getting at.

So it wasn't just that two extra guests couldn't be accommodated. The problem was that the whole table plan had to be redrawn to fit, as best it could, a wrong number into some sort of diplomatic acceptability. This was going to take a while, and thus it was that the staff's revised brief was simply to wheel in a trolley loaded with bottles of Gordons, slabs of tonic and buckets of ice. We all happily replenished our glasses time after time until dinner was eventually called, and you won't be surprised to hear that, in the end, nobody really cared where they were sitting. The dinner went with an international swing, and I wonder whether there might be a lesson, there, for diplomacy.

The mid-1990s, when I worked at NATO's Supreme HQ Europe at Mons in Belgium, spanned a time when the Yugoslavia business was brewing up, and NATO was busy seeking commitments from all its member nations in putting together a multi-national force. I spent many of my working hours trying to understand exactly who was doing what to whom in the region, but as anybody who has ever worked in Balkan affairs would probably agree, to describe the politics of the area as complex is vastly understating the case.

Anyway, during quieter periods I unwisely used the office computer to do a little bit of private work, and the inevitable happened: a virus crawled out of my personal floppy disk and into the office system, infecting NATO's darkest workings. You'll be pleased to hear it wasn't the nuclear strike programme that was corrupted. Rather, it was matters much further down the scale; not exactly the wives' club coffee morning and flower arranging rota, but somewhat in that direction. It still attracted the

Top: Refuelling from the hose adaptor fitted to the boom of a USAF KC-135, Operation Southern Watch, spring 1993. The 135 was unlike anything else – and great fun. The Tornados belong to 17 and 617 Squadrons, the crews could have come from any of the RAF's GR1 squadrons.

Bottom: The boomer's-eye view. The customer on this occasion is an F-18 of the US Navy. Photo taken over Kuwait by the author during his KC-135 flight from Riyadh in October 1995.

attention of the resident snoops, though, and I was hauled up in front of the general for an interview. It wasn't too painful, as he didn't understand computers any more than I did, and we finished up by having a convivial Scotch together.

For part of my time at SHAPE I was also the secretary of the officers' club committee. I wrote the minutes of our meetings, and each time I would take them to the club president for signing. He was Turkish, and would invariably ask for changes. "No sir," I would say; "I've reported a true record of the meeting, and you're asking me to write something inaccurate." "I am general," he would reply, tapping the rank tabs on his shoulder; "you write what I say, not what happened." Well, his English wasn't great so I could always find a form of words which allowed him to believe I'd done his bidding as well as letting the truth filter through, so everybody was happy. I'm tempted to say that it was an interesting insight into the way our south-eastern friends do things, but I ought not to generalise. Suffice it to say, however, that it was an example of the cultures of nationalities being completely different. It is truly miraculous that an organisation such as NATO has managed to accommodate such variations for so long.

And if NATO differences were substantial, they almost pale into insignificance when compared with Middle East business. While I was running the British corner of the Southern Watch show in Saudi Arabia I had to work closely not only with our partners the Americans and the French but also with our hosts, the Saudis. In this latter endeavour I soon learned that there was absolutely no point in looking for our way of thinking in the Saudi psyche. They were different, full stop, and only by acknowledging that difference could one move forward. Even their business ethics are different, and in saying this I'm not implying that their ways are inferior to ours – or better. Simply that they're different, and if one didn't acknowledge that it was impossible to get along. I often wonder whether this fundamental is appreciated by those who would haul BAE Systems over the coals for alleged bribery during their Middle Eastern dealings.

It's worth saying, also, that I found it a mistake to characterise 'the Saudis' as a homogenous group. They are, of course, individuals just as we are, and there were undoubtedly among those I met some whom I would very much have liked to have got to know better.

A completely different bunch of friends were the Australians. For whatever reason, several of them were sent to the UK to go through flying training with us. Perhaps their own system had silted up, or maybe we had spare capacity at the time. At any rate four went through Acklington with my gang. They were, by and large, older than us, and had already enjoyed a spot of flying back home on the Winjeel. So it was no surprise to us that they finished in positions 1, 3, 4 and 5 on the course. (Why not second? Believe it or not we Brits had a good pilot, too!). But that didn't really matter; they were lovely guys and we very much enjoyed their company. Not least because they were in receipt of entertainment allowance from their high commission which they had to use or lose before the end of each month. They had no hesitation in spending it on beer for the rest of us – and we always looked forward to the last Friday of the month.

When we moved onwards to RAF Valley for our advanced training the Aussies were sent to the Hunter squadron over on the seaward side of the airfield. For reasons which are not clear to me the RAF always maintained this extra unit scabbed on to number 4 FTS. Were there not enough Gnats for the job? Was it better to keep the foreigners separate? I don't know. It wasn't only the Aussies who flew the Hunters, by the way; many Arab air forces sent their students to fly there, and I remember an amazing incident when one of those pilots called in by radio, whilst airborne, to announce that a 'rudder' was attached to the side of the cockpit. It took much questioning to ascertain that what he was actually saying was that the 'ladder' was attached. How that had happened – how he had been allowed to start up, taxi and take off with the ladder hanging there – would forever remain a mystery. I'm pleased to relate that he landed safely. At any rate our Aussies seemed to enjoy their jet; the view they took, in banter at least, was that Gnats were for boys but Hunters were for men.

Following the wedding I spoke about earlier (page 116) we all decanted southwards for the Aussies' final hurrah. This started on a Friday evening with a happy hour in the office of the Australian air advisor in Australia House on the Strand. A good deal of duty-free Fosters was drunk that evening as I recall (or, alternatively, as I don't recall), before we staggered off to spend the night in our various billets. Then the next morning we all proceeded to Southampton to see our friends off on the MS *Achille Lauro* for their voyage home. I have to admire their style; given the choice between a quick jet trip and a six-week luxury cruise, I think that I would also have chosen the voyage.

Although, perhaps, if we'd known what we know now of the *Achille Lauro,* we might not have been so keen. What with fires on board, a hijacking by the Palestine Liberation Front, and her eventual sinking, she might not have been the luckiest of ships.

Some of us met the Aussies again during our later careers. I know that those of our Lightning boys who were posted to 74 Squadron in Singapore saw quite a lot of them, as the Aussies were regular visitors there in their Mirage IIIs. Many years later while on a lecture tour with the Department of Air Warfare, I found myself on Penang Island for a week. This related to the five-power agreement which succeeded the UK's permanent far-eastern presence. Malaysia, Singapore, Australia, New Zealand and the UK comprised the alliance; I think the UK played a fairly small part. Anyway, I was out there lecturing on weapons effects when I learned that there was still a fighter squadron at nearby Butterworth, just over the water on the mainland. It turned out to be 79 Squadron RAAF, equipped with the Mirage III. Further inquiry showed the CO to be one of our old friends, Bill Fitzhenry, and it was fairly easy to remake contact with him. From there it was but a step to beg a trip in a Mirage, and so it was that Bill and I launched in the squadron's T-bird, Mirage IIID A3-110, across the Malayan peninsula. Given the sleek outline of the jet I had anticipated a very smooth ride. But my recollection is of a thoroughly rattly trip. Still, it was a marvellous experience.

Of late, as fiftieth anniversaries begin to come thick and fast, I've restored connection with several others of those Aussies. To the point where, while visiting my son who has emigrated down under, I've had the opportunity to visit a couple of them in Canberra. Truly great mates.

The introduction of fifth generation aircraft such as the Lightning II across a substantial number of air forces will see internationalising move on a further stage, with networking between units and data fusion becoming the norm. I confess to having no detailed knowledge of such concepts, but I can easily see that, with so much information being available, the trick will be having the system organise and filter it such that a single person in the cockpit will not be flooded. What he or she will need to be presented with will be what is essential – what's really useful and necessary to know. And, given that so many nations are procuring the F-35, the single most important issue to be kept in mind is that, when necessary, all the various forces will need to be on the same wavelength. Upgrades will inevitably occur during the system's lifespan, that will be the most colossal international challenge imaginable.

CHAPTER 21
HAVE HAT,
WILL TRAVEL

I mentioned earlier my long-standing friendship with Rod Hawkins – he of the Canberra trip to Gibraltar. By chance, he would later be posted to my Tornado squadron where we often flew together, so our friendship was renewed. He was not one who relished ground tours and staff work, so he had opted to become what we used to know as 'specialist aircrew'. I believe that, nowadays, a similar group is now called 'professional aircrew'.

Rod met and married a German lady and settled near the former RAF Laarbruch. There, he now finds himself as curator of the RAF museum which is located there in the former station chapel. It's a fine tourist attraction, standing right beside what is now known as Airport Weeze – or, as low-cost outfits with vivid imaginations prefer to call it, Düsseldorf West.

These wise old 'specialist aircrew' birds usually had the experience to teach a little restraint and maturity to the young gods who were reaching for the skies. And in this category I don't only include the first-tourists; the whippersnappers who were rocketing up the command chain needed, on occasions, a little guidance as well. Here we meet Rod in his most 'elder statesman' mood – and I must straightaway issue the disclaimer that the 'boss' in the story is not me! Here's Rod's tale:

"Sometime in the last century my flight commander asked me if I would like an overseas ranger flight. Usually these would be to an airfield that had handled Tornados before. However, this did not appeal to me, and as I had not visited Cairo I thought that would be a good destination. My justification for choosing Egypt was that the RAF regularly flew over the area en route Saudi Arabia in support of operations over Iraq, and I thought it a good idea to brief the Egyptian firefighters on Tornado rescue procedures. Permission was quickly granted by higher command, as at the time the Royal Air Force was attempting to improve and maintain good relations with the Egyptian government.

"I then set out to do the planning, the necessary paperwork, obtaining diplomatic clearances, ordering an imprest and checking the services available at the military airfield we'd chosen. This was Al Birijat, which was just outside Cairo. I had to ensure that the correct fuel was available, containing anti-fungal treatment. Also that they could store and recharge our liquid oxygen pots. Over the weekend oxygen could leak away, so we took an adaptor which would connect to larger bottles.

"The news that I was planning a weekend in Cairo soon caught the attention of the boss, who declared that he would come in the number two aircraft. All the leg-work and planning was being done by the leader, so that decision was easy for him.

"Prior to departure the aircraft were loaded with oils and the appropriate hand pumps, blanks, tape for sealing the cockpits (normally against rain but in this case against sand) and our small bags – the various holes and empty spaces in the Tornados were stuffed full. The excess we placed in the cockpit, either alongside the ejector seat or in the map case. This included my SD hat ('service dress' – the peaked cap). Being of the old school I always travelled with my headdress; we were, after all, visiting a foreign air force.

"We departed Brüggen en route Brindisi, Italy, for our first, uneventful night stop, there enjoying a fine meal. Friday morning saw an early departure for Cairo as we wished to make the most of our short stay.

"On landing in Egypt we had quite a welcoming committee, who seemed to be pleased to meet us. I believe these were the first Tornados they had seen at Al Birijat, and they were very interested. The airfield was in a run-down, almost disused state, but they managed to find some chocks. After putting the aircraft to bed we departed to the ops block to send our arrival signal. The boss, meanwhile, whisked off (wearing my SD hat) to meet the base commander. As we had flown for over two hours and then serviced the aircraft, we needed to use some facilities so we asked for the toilets. At this point OC engineering wing jumped forward and offered his private en suite as the others were, as he put it, 'not suitable for westerners'. After seeing OC eng's facilities we could only wonder what state the others were in! We were offered a drink, but having seen the crew room area we decided to depart for town. There, a hotel had been booked for us by the air attaché, and we thought it safer drinking there as we had all heard of gyppy tummy.

"A driver was summoned and a small man appeared who apparently spoke a little broken English. He deposited us at a hotel in a side street, and asked when we would like to use his services again. We had assumed he would just transport us to the hotel but, oh no, he was our driver all weekend, day and night. We asked him his working hours and he said, 'All day misters, as I sleep in the car. Just tell reception you need me.' So that explained the atmosphere in the car, then! We checked into the hotel and had to hand over our passports 'for police inspection and retention'.

"The next morning we left early for the pyramids and the other touristy bits. Our driver knew everyone and managed to get us into the pyramids before they officially opened, and also arranged a camel ride with a 'friend' of his. (One began to wonder!) The camel chap was a nasty looking man with whom we did not argue when he asked for money.

"We returned to the hotel, where we'd already found that the rooms could best be described as less than one would expect of a no-star hotel in the UK. Now, the boss stated that the hotel was not up to standard and we were going to move to the Hilton. Whilst I was happy to leave the small, smelly, cramped room, I thought we should inform the air attaché of the plan, but I was over-ruled. We checked out but could not retrieve our passports as they were no longer in the hotel. Never mind, our driver could pick them up for us later.

"Late on Sunday night a very irate air attaché appeared asking where we had been all weekend. Apparently the chief of the Egyptian air force and several senior officers had been at the airfield on the Saturday expecting a briefing. This was the first we'd heard of that but nevertheless, come Monday morning, the boss was summoned to the Egyptian base commander to explain himself – in my SD hat again.

"Meanwhile the rest of us went to prepare the jets, and we soon found that the oxygen pots were empty. We asked for charging, which turned out to be impossible as the base oxygen generator was 'broken'. Their bottles had a different screw thread to our adaptor, so we couldn't use them either. After a quick look at the charts I reckoned that, given our fuel load, we could fly at 8,000 feet (low enough to do without oxygen) to Brindisi, so a flight plan was submitted. The boss returned and said no, he didn't like that plan – we would go to RAF Akrotiri and get the pots charged there. But rather than advertise this we would depart Cairo as per the flight plan and just divert at the international airspace boundary.

"So that's what we did, but on reaching the boundary we were surprised when Cairo air traffic wished us a good landing at Akrotiri. Our driver, who had been with us during the discussions, was obviously much more than merely a chauffeur.

"I had problems raising Akrotiri radar on the second radio. But as we let down we noticed a Hercules in the circuit, so we called the tower and asked for a priority landing as we were now low on fuel. We taxied in and were met with only one line engineer – most unusual. We explained our problem and said we needed fuel and oxygen. He said that could take a while as the station was on stand-down; it was May bank holiday. So what about that Hercules we had just seen take-off? Ah, that was a special movement, for which the airfield had opened briefly. Luckily we were able to refuel quickly and replenish the oxygen – quickly enough to allow us to depart for Brindisi within the same short airfield opening window.

"Unbeknown to us, Akrotiri's station commander had been on the beach when we'd arrived. Naturally, he wanted to know why two Tornados had landed with the airfield notified as closed, and he was soon on to the station commander at Brüggen asking for an explanation. So it was no surprise that, on arrival back home, air traffic informed us that a car would be waiting. The boss, once again with my SD hat on, was whisked away to the station commander's office to explain why we had changed hotel, why we hadn't given the briefing and why we hadn't read the NOTAMs which would have told us that Akrotori was closed.

"If only my SD hat had had a hidden recorder!"

CHAPTER 22
BECOMING CIVILISED?

There can't be many fast-jet pilots who didn't, at one time or another, consider switching to civil aviation. Not those, of course, who were solely committed to ascending the greasy promotion pole to the top of the RAF. Perhaps they were the very sharpest and best – it would be nice to think so. But on the other hand it could be argued that the really clever ones stepped across to civil aviation at the right moment and made an extremely comfortable and remunerative living on the flight deck of a major carrier. Who knows who was right? At any rate, most considered the options.

I myself looked at the airlines at several points during my RAF career. When I joined I was offered two contract alternatives. The first was a commitment until the age of thirty-eight. The second was similar, but also gave me options to walk away after eight or twelve years. The incentive to sign on for the long engagement was a difference of £1 10 shillings (£1.50 in new money) per week during the fifteen-week initial officer training course – an increase from £6 8s (£6.40) a week to £7 18s (£7.90). The higher sum was tempting; it would have bought me an additional few pints of beer! But a (perhaps unaccustomed) rush of common sense made me hang on to my options.

So, at several points during my early career I thought about switching to the civilian life. But for various reasons I stayed put every time. During the 1970s things weren't easy; there was the fuel crisis, the three-day week, and various airlines collapsed. Those around at the time will recall SkyTrain and Court Line as being among the airline casualties. I was married and had commitments – not least babies and mortgages. So it always seemed safer to stay.

Did I do right? It's hard to say. I do have ex-fighter friends who lucked in by joining, for example, Cathay Pacific or Virgin Atlantic at exactly the right point. The Cathay pilots' lounge in its early days was, reputedly, similar to an RAF fighter squadron crew room, and the story was that the selection process was akin to that of the Red Arrows: if they knew you and liked you, you were in. Among those early crews was a Buccaneer friend of mine who had found himself gliding his maritime jet one day at low level following a major error with selection of the fuel tank sequencing. He recovered the situation – but the incident marked the end of a promising RAF career, as well as a new and happier beginning with Cathay.

With an airline like Virgin, which started from scratch and expanded rapidly to a steady state, it all depended on timing; if one was in on the ground floor one rapidly became a senior captain – and stayed there. On the other hand I have other friends who mistimed their transfer to the airlines and have spent fifteen or more years in the right-hand seat of a Cathay or British Airways jet. Remunerative, certainly; but not necessarily satisfying.

Anyway, I stayed. The worst of both worlds, one might say. I had no chance of reaching the top of the air force, and I soon became too old for a full airline career. The fact that I'd never really fancied the airline life helped, but nevertheless some hard decisions eventually needed to be taken. By 1997 I was a forty-nine-year-old group captain who hadn't been a station commander (the RAF, in having more group captains than stations, mirrored the old naval adage that there are more admirals than ships). So there was nothing ahead of me but a couple more staff tours before mandatory retirement at the age of fifty-five. I'd been offered for my next assignment a NATO post in Naples – which, I guessed, would be undemanding, but pleasant in many ways. It occurred to me, though, that fifty-five would be a much less favourable age to be seeking a new job than fifty. Should I consider going now? And if so, what should I do?

There were many factors to consider, most notably of a family nature. Going abroad to the sunshine would be pleasant, but would mean we'd have to let our house again. Letting can provide a good income but, as we'd previously discovered, giving over a loved family home to tenants had its drawbacks. It wasn't, as a rule, returned in the desired condition, which tended to bring particular grief to the dearly belovèd. I still had painful memories of a previous homecoming when she had flatly refused to reoccupy the property until it had been fumigated and redec-orated throughout. I'd agreed with her in principle but the timescale, for logistical reasons, had made things well nigh impossible. Nevertheless we engaged a local man with the instruction that "it doesn't matter how much it costs, emulsion the whole house in a day". Amazingly, he did, but for ever afterwards I knew him as 'Our 'Enry'. Remember the boxer Henry Cooper's wonderful TV adverts for Brut aftershave? His punch line was "Splash it all over!"

And there were children's schooling issues. Our eldest had been at boarding school for a while. According to the principle of continuity of education, the service would pay a good part of the bill in recognition of the detrimental effect on children of having to move schools every couple of years as parents were posted. He hadn't been altogether happy boarding, which was an important factor in our discussions on whether to go or stay. It was ironic that, when we finally decided to leave the military and settle, he was happy – but number two boy was distraught. He had been thor-oughly looking forward to the time when he, as a boarder, would have been put on a plane bound for Naples with an 'unaccompanied minor' label around his neck – to join us for a wonderful summer beside the Italian seaside. It just shows that it's impossible to please everybody.

Returning to the time I was pondering the factors, I spoke to an old friend who was working for a locally based airline. Would they, I wondered, be interested in a relatively old codger like me? He thought they might, and arranged an interview for me. "Yes", they said, "get your licences and we'll take you on. We recruit in September for the spring and summer season and in March for the following winter." It all sounded impressively orderly, and September would suit me perfectly. I'm in, I thought. With the benefit of hindsight I realise that they were actually saying that if I got my licences they would put me on their list if they had one at the time; and then, if I still wanted to join on the day they happened to be recruiting, I'd be in with a chance.

Over a bottle of wine the following Friday evening I chewed over the options with the *memsahib*. Should I jump ship and give it a go? We thought so, and on the Monday I put the wheels in motion.

I'd followed many friends and colleagues through the civilianising process and knew that the first thing was to enrol for a course in preparation for the CAA theory exams. No problem; I'd done an open university degree a few years previously in my spare time and had no doubt that distance learning was the way for me. But immediately the first package of what was to become a torrent of course material dropped through the letterbox it became apparent that I hadn't paid enough attention to what those colleagues could have told me about scheduling the work. I'd bitten off far more than I could chew.

The stuff was incredibly voluminous and detailed and, to my mind, mostly way over the top. When I'd started in the RAF it had been a standing joke that we had to learn, for example, how to build a turn-and-slip indicator before attempting to fly on instruments. As time had gone on, however, RAF instruction had become far more pragmatic and realistic; in later years there was quite enough essential stuff to be absorbed without cluttering our minds with unnecessary trivia. But this mass of civil aviation ground school material was taking me back to the bad old days. There seemed to be volumes of theoretical rubbish along the lines of whether, in an inverted left-hand turn with the North Pole on one's right, the compass would lead or lag. Desperately esoteric and, in practical terms, irrelevant stuff.

I guess they were doing it partly as a means of filtering out time wasters – those who couldn't, or weren't willing to, absorb technical detail. But whatever the reason, I was going to have to fall in with it. My self-imposed retirement timescale was now fixed, but I knew immediately that I'd got no chance of absorbing all this junk in time to take the exams. So I had a look at where I could take a chance. Navigation, I thought; I've spent thirty-two years navigating, so I'll wing it in that exam. And there were other subjects to which I could opt to give minimal attention, so I filtered the material accordingly. Even so, that left a lot to cover. With a busy day job to hold down there was only so much I could do in the evenings.

An added requirement for me, on a ground tour, was to regain airborne currency. I needed fifty hours flying 'recency' for my new licence, and the only practical way of achieving that was to volunteer to fly air training corps cadets at one of the RAF's air experience flights. I'd done this several years previously at Cambridge, in the old Chipmunk, while on a ground tour at Cranwell. At that time it had made for a pleasant couple of days each month out of the office, and I knew the chap who was still running the show. The Chipmunks had, by now, been displaced by Bulldogs, a type I'd never flown, but he nevertheless agreed to take me on. Fine, I'd get my fifty hours. But what with the day job, the evening theory study, and the weekend flying, there wasn't much time left for family.

However, I did take the opportunity of my temporary position on the air experience flight to satisfy a yearning my number two son had often expressed – to 'see what dad does'. To make himself eligible he joined his school cadet corps, which permitted him to accompany me to Cambridge. And one fine Sunday he was able to fulfil his ambition by flying with me in a Bulldog. He loved the experience, as amply demonstrated by the picture I took at the time. I often thought, in retrospect,

that I should have sent a copy to the Air Training Corps publicity people, for I've never seen a happier advert for the cadets.

Before I finished my RAF time, there were a couple more requirements to complete. The first was the civil instrument rating, for which I enrolled on a fortnight's course at a training outfit at Exeter Airport. Strange and unusual flying to a fighter pilot. As related earlier,

Top: The author about to launch in Bulldog XX516 with son Rob on 12 August 1998.

Bottom: Could there ever have been a happier flying picture? Rob enjoys his flight over the Cambridgeshire countryside.

I had an inkling of procedural work from my time with the Norwegians, but now I really had to get to get to grips with it. On my first trip in the Beech Duchess we set off on the take-off roll. At about 50 knots the cabin door flew open and my immediate instinct was to abandon the take-off. But no, my instructor seemed accustomed to such events.

"I have control," said he. "Just drag it back in and secure it as best you can."

I struggled for a moment; "OK, I think that's got it."

"It often does that," he said, "nothing to worry about."

We were now doing 60 knots, just approaching rotation speed. "Are you ready to take it back?"

"Yep."

"OK, you have control." And with that introduction to civil aviation, the flight proceeded.

An unfortunate interruption to the instrument flying course came by way of the civil requirement for me to be current by night as well as day. I needed five recent night take-offs and landings as pilot in command. The only aircraft I was current on was the Bulldog, and we never flew cadets by night. But there was a possible opening. Trainee instructors at the Central Flying School did a brief night phase, and an old friend there agreed that I could muscle in on their next session. These only occurred a couple of times a year, and as sod would have it the next opening would be halfway through my Beech flying. There was no option, so one day, after flying an instrument trip in the morning, I took the train from Exeter to Cranwell to fly at night. On arrival I found the overcast lowered to the deck. I sat in the mess all evening reading the papers, with the weather showing no sign of improvement. The silver-tongued met man promised that things would improve the next night, so I opted to stay on. But the weather didn't get better, and the whole thing was postponed until the following week. Back I trundled to Exeter, flew another few trips, and then returned to Cranwell for a second go. This time I was luckier and got my five 'stop-and-goes' done. In fact I could have done them all in one length of the runway. What an effort for not much. Never mind, back to Exeter again, and I finished the instrument rating. The boxes were getting ticked.

Now for the theory exams. As mentioned, I was going to have to take a gamble on a couple of subjects, and I turned up at Gatwick pretty open minded. I knew that the answers were all multiple-choice and that, given four possible answers per question, I could score around 25% by just ticking random boxes. The pass marks were in the region of 50% and so, even with my limited study, I was in with a chance.

The results came a week later and, as expected, I'd failed a couple. Still, there was time for retakes. But a closer look at the check sheet showed that things were worse than I'd at first perceived. My particular combination of failures meant that I would, in fact, have to retake the lot.

A disaster really, but things got better. Now I was on terminal leave, with only the theories and a little more Bulldog flying to be done. With the experience of the first time behind me and more time to spare I was able to complete the requirements. Before long an air transport pilot's licence (aeroplanes) was in my pocket.

Now I was ready to go back to the airline with, as promised, my licence. There, I soon found that they had spoken with forked tongue. Never mind the allegedly orderly plan to recruit in the autumn for the winter and spring. As I soon found, airlines live very much the same reactive life as does the military. One moment there's a surplus and they lay people off. Then there's a desperate shortage and they recruit like mad. And they recruit those on their list who happen to be on the end of the phone when they ring. If there's no reply they move on to the next name, so woe betide anybody who takes time off to go to the bathroom (the subsequent invention of the mobile phone must, I suppose, have eased that problem!). As it happened they took me on just ten days after I finally left the RAF. But, as I was to learn several times during my twelve-year airline career, luck plays a huge part in these things.

Now I was to be a turboprop captain. I don't think it's permitted, now, for fast-jet pilots to step straight into the left-hand seat of an airliner, as there's a new requirement called 'multi-crew cooperation' training and qualification that needs to be hurdled. Even in my day it wasn't all that common for airlines to take direct-entry captains, for they naturally preferred to promote their own first officers to the left-hand seat rather than have outsiders parachuting in.

In this case they must have been short of home-grown candidates, so I was in – and a most interesting experience it turned out to be. As you might expect, merely flying the machine wasn't any particular problem. But running the operation – mastering the unfamiliar procedures and getting the show on the road on time during a twenty-five minute turn-round – was another matter. During the early months I leant heavily on some very good first officers, who willingly passed on all the tricks of the trade.

They included, I must add, some who had been fast-jet navigators in the RAF. Earlier, when I spoke about RAF pilots considering jobs in civil aviation, I was remiss in omitting mention of my navigator friends and colleagues. But I do know several who made the switch to become airline pilots, and I hugely admire their determination. Not only did they have to go through the same sort of rigmarole that I did to get a civilian licence, but they also had to go right back to 'go' and learn to be pilots. A massive commitment, for which they deserve every reward.

And talking of commitment, what about the colossal financial outlay for an ab-initio civil pilot? To get him (or her) to the stage of being employable by an airline the candidate must be prepared for a near six-figure outlay. And that with no guarantee of a permanent contract, or even a job, at the end of it. Youngsters I flew with had, in many cases, relied on the bank of mum and dad. But I also marvelled at those who had switched career paths in mid-stream. For example I regularly flew with an ex-police sergeant who had chucked in his career with the force and mortgaged his house to fulfil his dream of becoming a pilot. What an understanding wife and family he must have had.

So now I was happily trucking around the airways of eastern UK and the near continent. By and large I felt comfortable, but I'd been picking up an undercurrent of vibes related to 'ex-jet jockeys' coming into the airline. For example, very early on I'd been regaled by stories about an ex-Harrier chap who, a year or so ahead of me, had apparently failed to drop his single-seat habits. He'd riled the training staff and his first officers – indeed he'd annoyed pretty well the whole pilot force of the airline and had left for another company after only a short stay. Whether he jumped before he was pushed I'm not sure, and neither do I know whether he learned from his experience and mended his ways. But certainly, his name lingered in the collective consciousness of my airline for an inordinate time.

I also heard some quite bitter stories of ex-military people, including one which told of 'Squadron Leader Scarcely Worthit' who, apparently, irritated his flight deck colleagues by donning a pair of cape leather gloves prior to each approach and landing. He must, I think, have been ex-Transport Command, as I do recall even the military jet community being amused by some of the idiosyncrasies of the shiny fleet. Indeed, just to digress, I must relate a story of the time when the ground-attack Hunters at RAF West Raynham were transferred to 38 Group of Air Support Command – that, essentially being a renaming of the former Transport Command. These fly-ing-suited Hunter jocks would then insist, when deploying for overseas exercises through Akrotiri or Muharraq, on making themselves comfortable in the 'Air Support Command captains' lounges'. Yes, there really were such things. And the smartly-uni-formed shiny fleet captains occupying them were far from pleased when these Hunter characters swaggered in, polluting the air with their sweaty flying suits.

Anyway, donning one's gloves prior to landing doesn't, in the end, seem the most heinous of crimes. But I guess it was perhaps just one of many mannerisms exhibited by the afore-mentioned pilot which, taken together, made him an object of ridicule, scorn, or even dislike.

By way of further digression, the only piece of 'glovery' I ever saw during my military career that struck me as in any way incongruous (but more amusing than anything else) was during a Nimrod flight. That type came within my sphere of responsibility during my last MoD tour and, as part of my familiarisation process, I was treated to a couple of flights in the beast. The first was a straightforward role demonstration over the North Sea, but the second was an operational mission seeking out shipping in the Arctic. Including, by the way, parachuting a Christmas pack to an RN frigate which was on patrol up there. That was quite a long trip and required air-to-air refuelling. At that time not all Nimrod crews were AAR-qualified, and on this sortie they had to carry an extra man who was. He slept from take-off at RAF

Kinloss to the refuelling area off north Norway. Once the RV with the tanker was well underway the great man was awoken with a cup of tea and invited to take the captain's seat. As they performed the pre-AAR checks he reached into his pocket and pulled out an immaculate pair of white, cape-leather gloves, which he donned with some ceremony. After flexing each finger to his satisfaction he took control and did the prodding. On completion he backed away from the tanker, handed over control, returned the gloves to his pocket and retired to his bunk. I had never before or since witnessed air-to-air refuelling from the viewpoint of a large receiver, and was mightily impressed. The pilot handled that huge piece of machinery with consummate skill and finesse – it must have been the gloves!

Returning to the airline crews' views of the military jet community, what perhaps wasn't appreciated by all in those days was that the way to get the best out of a crew was to keep them alongside you rather than trying to drag them in your direction. Following any airborne incident which required subsequent discussion it was, I must say, self evident to me that one couldn't adopt the blunt, RAF debrief style of simply telling crew members they'd screwed up. First, because they probably knew that without being told. Second, one had to analyse what had happened and find a constructive way ahead. Or, if they had simply blundered for no obvious reason and needed telling, then they had to be told in a manner which wouldn't destroy them. All that sort of thing, in the airline business, is what's called 'crew resource management'. Indeed, some years into my airline career when I was preparing for a position as a line-training captain, I attended a course on 'crew resource management facilitation'. Even 'teaching' CRM was, by then, a no-no; one had to 'facilitate' learning! Dare I say that much of this was what we in the RAF had called 'leadership'? Probably not, for that word didn't appear in the airline dictionary.

Before leaving the subject I must relate the tale of a friend of mine, an ex-Lightning and Jaguar pilot. He had joined the airline a few years before me and had in fact facilitated (!) my introduction. He'd also become interested in the work of the pilots' union and had been elected to the company council. Incidentally, I found it odd that, in the airlines, pilots, cabin crews and engineers all had separate unions, each with their unique agendas. It had always seemed to me in the military that the interests of one were the interests of all. But that's by the by.

One aspect that attracted my friend's attention was the way the seniority list was arranged. Now 'seniority', in the airline pilot world, is extremely important; it determines, inter alia, who has first bid for basing or for promotion to the left-hand seat. I'm not implying, of course, that first officers would get promoted to captain if they didn't merit it; certainly, they all had to reach a prescribed standard. What I am saying is that there was no mechanism for those of special ability to jump the queue. Quite simply, of those who met the standard, those highest up the list would be promoted first.

There were other elements to seniority. It might affect bidding for holiday dates or the ability to choose particular trips on the roster. In at least one of the UK's major airlines, some first officers chose to remain as such rather than accepting the chance to move up to captain. Because, as very junior captains, they'd lose their chance to bid for all the lifestyle choices they'd been enjoying as senior first officers.

Anyway, my friend thought he would have a stab at converting his new airline colleagues to his idea of a 'meritocracy', and it seemed to him that the simplest way would be to split the airline's single seniority list into two – one for captains and one for first officers. The idea would be that first officers would rise towards the top of their area and then, once they'd moved to the left-hand seat, they'd start at the bottom of the captains' list.

The first officers immediately smelled a rat. They could see that once they made it to captain, with perhaps already half a dozen years with the company behind them, they'd find themselves lower on the new seniority list than a recently joined direct-entry captain. Indeed they'd be below the likes of my friend. They were not having that, and the idea was thrown out.

That proposal could have breathed fire on any embers there might have been of anti-military feeling, but at any rate it sets the scene for one of my early airline trips, on which I had in the right-hand seat a line-training captain from another base. We had been getting along pretty well, I thought, and during quiet periods had been talking about the afore-mentioned, awkward, ex-Harrier pilot. This character had clearly left a deep impression on my instructor, and we'd agreed that the airline had been well rid of Mr Harrier. We'd also agreed that I was showing no signs of ploughing a similarly lonely furrow without reference to my crewmembers.

Later in the trip, as we were preparing for approach and landing at Amsterdam, my training captain decided to play dead – to test my ability to cope alone with the whole operation. Now, Schiphol is a very busy airport, and arguably, although the chap was awake and ready to snap into action if required, we shouldn't really have been enacting such a scenario with a cabin full of passengers. I don't think that such exercises are permitted nowadays on commercial flights; they might not even have been then. I myself believe that the simulator is the place for such exploits, and when I later became a line trainer I never played dead on a commercial flight when training any of my newbies. Anyway, in this instance I coped and landed safely, following which he 'recovered' and asked me how I thought I'd done. In view of our earlier conversations I bantered back that perhaps it proved that an ex-single-seat pilot didn't need a crew after all. Off we went for a beer together in the hotel and that, I thought, was that.

How wrong I was, and how unwise I was to assume that the chap had a sense of humour. It all came back to me a few weeks later when I'd completed my training and had been operating in command for a while. One day I received a message that

I had an appointment with the fleet manager at HQ. 'Now that you've been on line for a while,' the note said, 'it would be a good time to discuss how things are going and for you to ask any questions you have about the job.' What a friendly boss, I thought, and how nice of him to be concerned for my welfare.

In his office he came straight to the point (no messing around with CRM!) "I've been hearing tales from another base that you've been operating in single-seat fashion and not bringing your crewmembers into the loop. I won't have some jet jockey upsetting my crews. Any more of it and you'll be out." Taken aback, and puzzled as well, I asked for something more specific. Who was upset? What was the alleged incident? "I'm not able to betray confidences," he said, "but just watch it." I racked my brains, and the 'dead pilot' incident came to mind. Taking a stab in the dark I related the circumstances and asked whether this was what he had in mind. "I can't say, but others from that base have also complained." Ah, so it seemed I might be on the right track. Again I checked my memory for other flights I'd done with crewmembers from the same place – and another Amsterdam approach soon swam out of the murk.

A couple of weeks earlier I'd been in the ILS pattern there with my crew. My experienced and fairly senior first officer, who was flying the sector, helped himself to a swig of coffee. The autopilot was engaged but, nevertheless, I asked him fairly gently (I thought) whether this very busy airspace was really the place to be drinking coffee. He put his cup down, but not without shooting me quite a look, and nothing more was said. Now, I can't recall whether that particular airline had a 'no food or drink below 10,000 feet' policy or not, but I've certainly worked with airlines that had. Indeed, some airlines discourage even casual chat at that stage of the flight – they call the concept the 'sterile cockpit'. Certainly, applying the general principle that one hundred per cent concentration should be devoted to flying while in the busy, terminal phase of a flight seems to me to be a fundamental requirement.

So I tried this story on the fleet manager, who again failed to comment – but I got the distinct impression that I was getting warm again. It seemed that there might have been a spot of gossip going on at that base, but of course I had no means of confirming my suspicion. Anyway, the uncomfortable interview was terminated and I never heard any more about it.

These tales from my early airline experiences to some extent illustrate a misconception held by many civilian crews – and, quite likely by much of the population in general – that fast-jet pilots are very much loners. Whilst there may be the odd individual who operates in that fashion, it couldn't be further from the truth in the case of most of the fighter pilots I've known. Like me they've spent their careers working in formation with other aircraft, many of them operating with navigators, and cooperating with other airborne and ground agencies, so they have a more than excellent understanding of how to get the best out of a team.

CHAPTER 23
WEATHER OR NOT...

It doesn't seem all that long since British weather forecasts were something of a joke. Whether it was a general bulletin on the BBC or a specialised aviation briefing given by the local 'cu-nim Jim' at a military airfield, we could never be sure of getting anything like an accurate picture. The reason was obvious: the UK's weather originates, by and large, over thousands of miles of Atlantic Ocean, and in earlier days there was nothing but a few weather ships sending intermittent information to inform the gurus who would forecast what we were about to receive. Not surprisingly, they were often wrong, and we aircrew regarded what we were told with a good deal of well-justified scepticism.

By contrast, today's forecasts are magnificent. The advent of satellites and computer analysis of weather trends and patterns has transformed things, and most would probably agree that we now enjoy an excellent service. As long, that is, as we still remember that a forecast only offers the likeliest scenario; no reasonable person should expect every prediction to be fulfilled one hundred per cent.

But back then the forecast was routinely regarded with a sideways look. How often I heard that 'the cold front is expected to come through at 1000 hours Zulu'. 'Zulu' time was Greenwich Mean Time, the time base used, worldwide, in aviation. To be pedantic, we now use 'UTC' –universal time coordinated – but it's still Zulu. In my day the promised 'ten-Z clearance' was something of a running joke.

In the business of launching when the destination weather was close to minima there was a fundamental difference between fighter-bomber and commercial flying. The airlines had a schedule to keep to and passengers to deliver. Therefore, if conditions and forecast at destination and alternate were legal, we would go. And quite right too; on ninety-nine percent of occasions we got in. And if we had to divert, the commercial department accepted that they'd deal with the aftermath. In the military, unless there was a war on (or another operational mission, such as the QRA Lightning scramble mentioned earlier) there was rarely any necessity to launch when there was a chance of not getting back in. Why press the limits when we could equally well get on with the mass of ground training which had to be done?

Thus I can almost count on the fingers of one hand the number of times I diverted in my 4,500 hours of military flying. But some of those diversions were memorable.

As with the time when twenty or so Jaguars launched on exercise from Brüggen with little chance of recovering. The whole of north Germany was weathered out, with the exception of the Luftwaffe base at Jever. We all landed there and were stuck for several days. Buses were organised from Brüggen to bring us clothes, wash bags and, most importantly, deutschmarks. It was just before Christmas, and I'm sure it was the threat of another bus arriving full of wives and kids that eventually got us launching homewards.

Curiously, it's Jever that provides another weather story. While I was on 6 Squadron flying Jaguars I was sent there on the NATO tactical leadership programme. It was a December course and, by contrast with the previous tale when Jever was open, in this case we were subjected almost every day to North Sea fog drifting inland and preventing flying. The forecast was always uncertain, so every evening we'd go to the bar with the intention of taking it easy in case the weather would clear for the following day. But invariably, at about 7 p.m., somebody would venture outside and report that "the fog's rolled in again". Our inference was that the early wave would be scrubbed … and the *Jeverpils* would begin to flow at an increasing and unstoppable rate.

Usually we'd be vindicated, and the following morning would see more ground school – albeit through bleary eyes and with sore heads. On the odd occasion, however, we'd be caught out. We'd be woken up to the unwelcome cry that "it's gin clear – launch the early wave". A horrible feeling initially, but we were well practised so we got on and did it.

Wind wasn't something we took great notice of in the RAF. When it was very strong the turbulence at low level, especially in the mountains, could be horrendous – but we just put up with it. In the late 1970s or early 80s, though, there were a couple of incidents which made everybody think. Landing in the sea after ejecting had always been a chancy business, and pilots had been lost when their parachutes had dragged them under in choppy conditions. But parachuting over land had been regarded as a generally safe option. OK, perhaps a broken ankle from the landing – but that was accepted as a small price to pay for survival from a crashing jet.

But what changed everybody's thinking was a Jaguar accident in the Scottish highlands. The pilot ejected safely but was killed when he, in his parachute, was smashed into the side of a mountain in gale-force winds. Although such an incident had a small probability of occurring (both the need to eject and the high wind needing to coincide), a 38 Group air staff order subsequently decreed that we should not fly training sorties at low level in areas where the wind was forecast to be greater than (I think) 40 knots.

Soon afterwards I was running the flying programme when we were scheduled to fly army cooperation sorties with the brown jobs in north Wales. The wind in Snowdonia was forecast to be gale force, and I cancelled our missions. Which decision immediately provoked a phone call bearing a message from no less than our master, the AOC 38 Group, to the effect that we couldn't possibly cancel trips just because of wind when our army brethren had taken the trouble to go out into the hills to provide us with targets. Notwithstanding that those targets, usually rubber inflatable tanks, had probably blown away into the middle distance by then, it was very hard to argue with an air vice-marshal. Orders, if one was an AOC, were clearly open to interpretation.

The types of airliners I flew were not equipped with autoland, so I never had the pleasure(?) of landing in zero-zero conditions. But nevertheless a landing at cat II minima (100-foot cloudbase and 300 metres visibility) was far more exciting in its own right than any bad-weather landing I had ever done in the military. From those minima there was very little time to decide, and the whole approach procedure was extremely carefully designed and rigorously practised. Because barometric pressure altitude (the reference for a normal landing) could not be relied upon to an adequate degree, the minima and decision criteria were based upon the true height above terrain as registered by the radio altimeter. Thus the terrain itself had to be surveyed minutely, which is one reason why only certain runways and approach paths are cleared for cat II landings.

To watch the radalt counting downwards while monitoring the other flight parameters and looking out for the runway lights was very definitely a two-person job and demanded the utmost concentration. And the most interesting place to do such an approach for real was, in my limited experience, Leeds Bradford Airport. There, on runway three-two, one is faced with a very steep upslope towards the threshold. On an approach using the barometric altimeter, the land below would be irrelevant; the altimeter would count down steadily as the glide path headed towards the runway threshold. But on a cat II approach to RW32 one would be monitoring radalt height above terrain which was sloping up so steeply that the radalt height would rush down through 500 feet and 300 feet – to minima – with incredible speed. In low cloud or thick mist it was a most exciting and demanding approach.

Icing was another aspect which was very different between civil airliner and military jet flying. I know that Canberras, for example, were prone to engine icing (we had done some sort of complicated 'anti-icing' arrival at Wildenrath on my one and only Canberra trip), but generally speaking the fast jets just weren't bothered by icing. Perhaps that was partly because we spent very little time in cloud – by and large we popped up through it to get visual on top, then plunged quickly downwards to land. But also, I guess, the wing profiles on our jets weren't particularly prone to icing.

As soon as I started on the turboprops, though, I became very conscious of the problem. Ice build-up on the leading edges of our straight wings was significant, and correct use of anti-icing systems was vital. A malfunctioning anti-icing system could be a major problem, while even a fully operative system sometimes wasn't enough; I recall, for example, the day when my little Fokker 50 simply couldn't maintain cruising height, such was the ice accretion.

I mentioned earlier the legal requirement to have, for a commercial flight, suitable forecast weather at nominated alternate airfields and to carry sufficient fuel to be able to hold off and/or divert as necessary. Many civilian pilots would like to carry more fuel than the mandated minimum on the belt-and-braces principle that one can never have too much. If the flight is already operating at maximum take-off weight that wouldn't be possible, but on other occasions there is capacity available. However, taking extra fuel conflicts with airline management's desire for economy, for of course each extra kilogram costs something to lug around.

I was not one who liked to take unjustified fuel loads, but I do recall one flight when an additional quantity proved handy. On this occasion the extra on board was there as a result of a quite separate airline practice known as 'tankering'. Fuel prices are different at each airport, and if one had extra payload and tank capacity available on a leg originating at an airport where fuel was cheap it was sometimes, even allowing for the cost of carting it about, worth loading up with enough to make the return trip on the same tankful. Such was the case one dark winter's night when I headed off from Aberdeen to Stavanger, which turned out to be useful when we arrived to find Stavanger solidly out in snow. Our nominated alternate, Kristiansand, was usable, so we declared our intention to divert. Unfortunately, because the snow had become widespread, Kristiansand was now the only airfield open in the whole of south Norway. ATC informed us that the world and his brother had already diverted there, all the stands and parking spaces were full, and they wouldn't accept us. As it happened we still had our planned return fuel on board, so we set course back to Aberdeen (naturally, much to the displeasure of our passengers).

The reader might infer from this that, if we'd only carried the legal minimum we'd have run out of fuel, but that's not quite true. If that had been the case we'd have declared a 'Mayday' emergency and Kristiansand would have been bound to accept us; they would, I'm quite certain, have found some kind of makeshift parking space for us. So even this kind of unforeseen situation is still not really grounds for carrying unjustified amounts of fuel.

CHAPTER 24
TRUCKIN' AROUND

"Good afternoon, ladies and gentlemen, and welcome aboard for this flight from RAF Horsham St Faith to RAF Dyce. En route we'll be calling at RAF Kirmington, RAF Middleton St George, RAF Finningley and RAF Turnhouse."

Familiar names to those of a certain age – but I guess that many readers born after, say, 1960, would have difficulty placing some of them. Not the last two, perhaps; Finningley stayed with the military until 1996, and I'll tell a story about it shortly. The RAF maritime headquarters kept the Turnhouse name alive until late in the twentieth century, and of course it's Edinburgh Airport. As well as landing there many times in my civil aviation days I can also claim to have flown a single sortie from RAF Turnhouse in a Bulldog. Having Edinburgh family, I must say I always enjoyed flying in there. The scenery, from the Forth Bridges to the city itself, is absolutely incomparable. And when civil flights are proceeding in a routine manner it's often the scenery that makes the trip.

As for the other fields on our notional flight, I think I'm right in saying that most had lost their original handles by the mid 1960s. And some considerably before that. A pity, as they were evocative names, but the airfields live on. Respectively, they are now Norwich, Aberdeen, Humberside and Durham Tees Valley Airports – all one-time prime destinations on my turboprop network.

What's left of their illustrious pasts? Well Norwich, firstly, is still easily recognisable as an ex-RAF station, although most of the old buildings have found other than aviation uses. The familiar hangars have been absorbed by an industrial estate, from whence substantial concerns such as Anglian Home Improvements ply their trade, and the old station headquarters is still identifiable, finding gainful use in the service of a commercial enterprise. Until relatively recently the NAAFI shop was still an active grocery store (probably still stocking the same horrible old pork pies!) serving the small number of quarters retained as housing for the radar station at RAF Neatishead. That station, now, is simply a remote facility feeding data to other sites, and the NAAFI shop is closed, but the original married quarters, with addresses such as Dowding Road, have been sold off and are still occupied. The messes and barrack blocks provided, for many years, accommodation for the University of East Anglia, but when asbestos was discovered in the structures they were vacated. They lay, boarded up and derelict, for ages, before being demolished to provide space for a thriving new private housing estate.

Whilst I can, just about, claim to have been conscious of RAF aircraft – Javelins – being operated from Horsham St Faith in days gone by, I can't say the same of Kirmington. It was a Lancaster bomber station, but closed as the Second World War ended. It was a satellite only – of RAF Killingholme – which perhaps explains the lack of recognisable infrastructure. Humberside's radio beacon, though, still coded K-I-M while I flew there, and a kind of 'hutted' atmosphere prevailed about the place even then. Nothing one could put one's finger on, but somehow parts of the terminal gave that impression. Especially on a damp and misty winter morning – and, come to think of it, most mornings of the year seemed to be like that in the Grimsby area. Indeed, one wonders how any wartime aircraft, without modern approach aids, ever managed to find their way back in the murk to land. Sorry – we'd better move on before I cause offence to the management of Humberside International and the good people of north Lincolnshire.

Aberdeen Airport bears few traces, as far as I detected, of its military past. By contrast Teesside (that's what it was called when I flew there, although it's subsequently been re-branded as Durham Tees Valley) could almost pass during my airline days as RAF Middleton St George. From its original hangars, which were still in use by Cobham Aviation, who operated electronic countermeasures aircraft on contract to the MoD, to the control tower – and especially to its authentic domestic site – it still lived. A variety of businesses occupied the red brick domestic buildings, and the surrounding grass was beautifully manicured – as though the SWO still cracked the whip over his working parties. And the whole was capped off by a lovely Lightning gate guardian – that being the final RAF type based at RAF Middleton St George.

There's bags of history there; indeed I believe that the St George Hotel, which is based in the former officers' mess, boasts several aviation-related memories. One reputedly derives from a Meteor pilot who, it is said, took a bet in the bar late one evening that he could take off on one engine, do a single-engined circuit and land. Well, he tried it the next morning, and I gather his circuit was shorter and tighter than even he had imagined it would be. After lift-off he veered sharply towards the mess and impacted, bizarrely, exactly through his bedroom window. The new bricks used in the repair show, some say, a Meteor-shaped patch.

RAF Finningley is now Robin Hood (Doncaster Sheffield) Airport, a place where I flew the Chipmunk for a while on odd days when I managed to escape from my office while on a ground tour. When I first knew it the base was the home of the Vulcan OCU, but by the time I was flying there it was the training school for pretty well every non-pilot flying trade. My later trips there with the airlines were few, but I absolutely must relate the story of one memorable visit; or, as it would turn out, non-visit.

It was Christmas Eve and I was rostered to fly four sectors: Gatwick-Jersey-Robin Hood-Jersey-Gatwick. I planned to follow that with a drive home to Norfolk, but the weather was disgusting and predicted to get worse. My first officer was inexperienced and, looking at the forecast, I reckoned that his categorisation would give us little chance of getting into Robin Hood. I called ops to ask them to call in a first officer who was cat II qualified. This would permit us to make approaches down to one hundred feet cloudbase and 300 metres visibility, which would give us a fighting chance of landing. There was no-one available at Gatwick, but Jersey's weather was reasonable and they promised to whistle up the Jersey standby to fly the sector to Robin Hood. Fine; off we set.

At Jersey the new man hopped aboard. He was a recently qualified skipper so, as I was right-hand seat qualified, it seemed best if he sat in the left seat and I in the right. Then we'd have a cat II crew, yes? No. Although he had been cat II qualified as a first officer in the right seat, he hadn't yet got the tick in the left-hand seat. So could we do it the other way around? No – having just converted to left seat he was no longer qualified right seat. So he was no use whatsoever; I thanked him for turning up, but said that he might as well go home and enjoy his Christmas Eve. I called crewing to ask whether they had any other ideas. Answer, no. So we set off northwards with my original first officer, and with optimism running out.

And so it turned out. The weather was close, but not close enough. We hung around in the Robin Hood overhead for an hour or so, hoping for a gap in the clag, but it wasn't to be. So, with our eighty-odd passengers anxious to get to their destinations in Lincolnshire and south Yorkshire, we headed off to Manchester. Given the poor weather to the south and east, Manchester was chock-a-block with diverted aircraft and it took an hour to get our punters disembarked. They still had a couple of hours' bus journey on the M62 ahead of them, so by the time they left us they weren't exactly full of seasonal cheer. But of course each passenger's air trip is their only one of the day, and they seldom think of the crew who might be running several sectors. I take my hat off to the cabin attendants who manage to put on a bright, welcoming smile to each new passenger. On days like that they bear the brunt of the aggro which comes in return; the lucky pilots shelter behind the flight-deck door.

Anyway, we were now over two hours behind – and things weren't about to get back on schedule. There had, of course, been eighty punters at Doncaster eagerly awaiting our landing so that they could embark for their trip to Jersey – and their own festivities. We now heard that they were somewhere on the M62 heading west, so our instructions were to wait. We checked our watches and the weather reports, which didn't bode well. Gatwick was going down in mist, which would thicken to fog with time. Other fields in the south were similar; worse, being Christmas Eve, many of them were closing early. We nibbled unhappily on our crew meals.

Eventually the buses arrived, fought their way onto the overcrowded airport, and delivered our new – and somewhat agitated – passengers. I mouthed honeyed words of apology and reassurance to them across the PA, and off we shot. Jersey weather was OK, so at least those passengers were somewhat appeased; their Christmas started only three hours late. The Jersey turn-round team did us proud and we were off again within twenty minutes.

So now we were on the home straight, with only Gatwick's mist to worry about, as well as conditions at the dwindling number of alternate airfields still available. But at last the weather gods smiled, and we slipped in first time. Great; only a three-hour car trip left. All I will say about my arrival at home is that it was well after Santa Claus had been and gone.

Have I banged on a bit about this day? Probably, but I just wanted to paint a picture of the different type of challenge experienced by civil crews compared with those in the military.

Many people recall clearly where they were when the Twin Towers were attacked, and I am no exception. I had flown a sector from Schiphol to Leeds, and while the passengers were boarding for the return flight we could clearly see from their faces that something was going on. There was every shade of expression, varying from very animated to tense. We enquired the reason, and it turned out that they'd been watching live news pictures in the departure lounge which had shown the horror unfolding. We lost no time in tuning the trusty ADF to the BBC – and soon caught up with what they already knew. With another sector imminently due, it offered huge food for thought.

One fallout from the event was a complete change of policy regarding passengers on the flight deck. Whilst one could easily see the reasons behind the new 'locked cockpit door' policy, it was nevertheless a pity that we could no longer show passengers the ropes. Those who had hitherto visited us had invariably been grateful, interested and enthusiastic. I recall one occasion when we'd had a steady stream of guests on a Norwich to Aberdeen night flight. The aurora borealis was in full glory; as we headed north the view ahead was absolutely spectacular and deserved sharing with the maximum number.

With my first airline, sometimes a passenger would be with us for the whole sector. This would happen when the flight was full, for if there was more business standing by the company would then sell the jump seat as well. In such cases the crew always retained the right to refuse the extra punter if, for some reason, they didn't want a body up front – perhaps, for example, if we were training a new pilot or if the weather on the flight was going to be particularly tricky. On one occasion I had my dentist on the jump seat, which was an interesting reversal for the two of us of the relationship between practitioner and victim. Most times, though, I didn't know the passenger, but we nevertheless weren't reliant on the check-in desk for selecting our guest. We could always leave the cabin crew to choose someone 'suitable', and we'd sometimes prompt their choice by taking a crafty squint at the passengers as they came up the steps before making our recommendation. I'll leave the reader to speculate on the type of criteria we might have applied!

The subject of airline security regularly provides newspaper fodder, as, for example, in a story when an airline threw a female 'celeb' off a flight for spending the flight kissing her lady friend a little too enthusiastically. It wasn't so much the kissing that was the problem, but the ensuing language and commotion when the couple were asked to cool it. "The conversation escalated to a level that was better resolved on the ground rather than in flight," commented a spokesman.

A minor event and it's hard to argue with the airline's stance. But security does sometimes seem to assume all-consuming proportions in the world of civil aviation. It certainly appeared that way to me during the few months of my employment when I worked from one of the south-east's major airports. Security ruled like it was going out of fashion. Not just in quantity, but more in the all-pervading unpleasantness of the whole security organisation. It took the pleasure out of nearly every flight, and guaranteed that crewmembers often arrived at their aircraft in a disgruntled state.

Before those months I had operated from a small, regional airport. The crews there knew the security staff well and they knew us. I'm not suggesting that familiarity made them more lax in checking us or that we paid only lip-service to security requirements. Merely that they did their work in a pleasantly efficient manner, avoiding the over-bearing rudeness and arrogance one so often finds at mainstream airports. In consequence, we flight crew cooperated willingly, and our two related worlds revolved and intermeshed harmoniously.

One morning I was going through the check at oh-dark-thirty hours, chatting idly with the crew while my favourite little grey-haired old security lady cast an idle eye over my flight bag. "Do you mind if I have a look inside, dear?" she asked, somewhat apologetically. "It's the snoops, you know," she added, throwing a disdainful glance at the CCTV camera on the wall. "We're supposed to open a percentage of bags, and *they* check the video from time to time." I continued my chat while she got on with her work.

But after a short period I became aware of some 'tut-tutting' as my security friend rummaged in the depths of my bag. Oh no; what oversight could have upset this sweet little old lady? Could it be the suspicious-looking remains of yesterday's crew lunch? Had she found a pencil sharpener which could be construed as an offensive weapon? Was I carrying a millilitre more than the permitted amount of aftershave?

(My wife always questioned the necessity, by the way, for me to take aftershave with me on short-haul flights – but that's another story.)

Soon, all became clear as she extracted my uniform jumper from a dark corner of the bag where it had been unceremoniously stuffed after the previous flight. "Dear oh dear!" She continued to 'tut' as she spread it on the counter, smoothing out the creases as best she could. "Now we can't have you looking all untidy, can we?" she added, folding it neatly and re-stowing it. "What would the passengers think?" "And," she continued, a twinkle in her eye: "I'm sure your wife would be horrified after all the time she spent ironing it."

She was right, of course. My wife continues to be regularly horrified by the way I treat my clothes. Suitably chastened, I departed for the flight. But nevertheless cheered by the lighter moment security had provided for me on that dark and dirty morning.

Of course we all know that the checks are there for a reason, and I've little doubt that the job's not much fun. But wouldn't it be nice if all airports kept their staff and public onside by ensuring the process is carried out in an affable manner? Do big airports really have to make the whole business so unpleasant? At times it almost takes the pleasure out of travelling.

CHAPTER 25
IT'S ALL GONE QUIET UP THE ROAD

As I write this I hear the sound of jets practising air-to-air combat overhead. They're above the overcast so I can't identify them accurately. Could be Typhoons, or perhaps my old mates on the Tornado? More likely, though, they are F-15s from Lakenheath. And yes, as they power back and drift off towards the south-west, I can hear the distinctive deep hum of Eagles at low power. I bet they've had fun; I envy them in a way.

This part of East Anglia used to be thick with air bases, with my own particular village lending its name to RAF Coltishall. I paid my first visit to that base during Lightning days – when it was the home of the iconic fighter's OCU. Back then, I was on a cadet camp, and I clearly recall watching with awe as the Lightning students were shown their first rotation take-offs into vertical climbs. One day during the week we sprogs were bussed across to RAF West Raynham where we saw the Hunters of 1 and 54 Squadrons in action – and were also taken into the hangar to get a glimpse of the Kestrels of the Tripartite squadron – British, American and German. An extraordinary aircraft at the time, whose design evolved into the even more extraordinary Harrier. In fact West Raynham (now closed) briefly saw some early Harrier operations. That outstanding Easter camp was, unsurprisingly, one of the triggers that persuaded me to join the RAF.

Would it distract too much from the story if I told of another element in my recruitment process? Bear with me; it won't take long. At my school it was compulsory to join the cadet corps. In the first year there was no choice but to join the army section. I wasn't impressed by this; not only was there endless marching up and down and cleaning of webbing, but field days were spent crawling around the forest on our stomachs, leaves and twigs stuck in our helmets. Most importantly, though, the hairy brown shirt with its tight collar was a source of intense irritation to my neck. And this last factor provided the vital element in my decision, at the end of that year, to make the now-available switch to the RAF section. I had noted that the RAF boys wore nice smooth poplin collars, so the choice was an easy one.

I often marvel that seemingly trivial matters can have major ramifications downstream, and it's undoubtedly true that this decision pointed me first towards RAF

The next generation. The author's eldest son, second from right, and friends enjoy an event at RAF Coltishall in about 1988.

field days, spent pleasantly and excitingly on air experience flights in Chipmunks. And then, of course, to a developing love of flying and, ultimately, to an RAF career. How could such a small thing as an itchy collar have whole-life consequences?

Back to Coltishall. Despite not having flown Jaguars myself since 1985, I've continued to live in this particular corner of Norfolk, off and on, for thirty-five years. The sound of jet noise always seems, to me, particularly evocative in spring. For, despite the first cuckoo and the cheerful sounds of new-born lambs and chicks that mark the season, 'my' spring sound was always the gradual realisation each year that RAF Coltishall's Jaguar aerobatic pilot was working up for his approval to head for the display circuit. Every year there would be a moment when, whatever I might be doing, I would suddenly become conscious of the unmistakable sound of jet aerobatics in the high overhead. I'd run outside, and after much squinting and craning of neck would eventually pick up and follow the distant spot through his sequence up in the heavens.

Over succeeding days he'd work down to five hundred feet or so until, having been given the AOC's stamp of approval, he'd be blasting through my neighbours' chimney pots practising his full display. With my background, I never minded the noise. The sound of spring! And, in general, the local people didn't object either. They loved their air force. And they loved their local air stations.

Coltishall. Like so many others, closed now or turned over to other roles. I think of South Cerney, Acklington and Church Fenton from my training days. Of the Hunter pilots who, like me, will remember Chivenor, Brawdy and Muharraq. My memories of Brüggen are shared with so many Jaguar and Tornado crews. I think of Gütersloh where I flew my Lightning, of Wittering where I drank the Harrier hover pot, and of Wildenrath from where I launched in my Canberra.

But most of all I think of Coltishall, the spiritual home of the Jaguar. The Battle of Britain base which, I believe, survived longest as a fighter station was finally declared surplus to requirements in 2006, and its last aircraft left. This is not the place to go into the rationale for the present and future size of the military. Except to comment that, notwithstanding the incredible capability possessed by each Typhoon and Lightning II, the plan seems to call for incredibly small numbers.

I only did one tour at Coltishall, so why did we settle here? Like many things in life, we were probably led by events rather than making a conscious decision. I was posted here at the point in my life when we needed to buy a house. And our firstborn went to his primary school here – with his mum making many friends among her contemporaries at the school gates. Although we subsequently had overseas post-ings – to Germany, Canada and Belgium – we always maintained this local base and were delighted to come back, to catch up with old friends and acquaintances, and to revisit familiar haunts. Certainly, the most pleasant memories of my staff tours in the MoD were always of the train journey home to family and friends in Norfolk each Friday evening. All of which indicates that the roots, however inadvertently put down, grew strongly.

As well as flying Jags from Coltishall, I also from time to time flew the next gen-eration's cadets from the station in the little Chipmunk. There was never much time to admire the scenery from the cockpit of a jet, but it was different in the old piston trainer. There would be my wife and children, looking up from the garden as I departed with my young passengers on our trips over the Norfolk Broads. Even later my vantage point was an airliner flight deck, and as I looked down during the approach to Norwich Airport it seemed unnatural to see the deserted aprons at Coltishall. Such a vibrant location, quite suddenly stopped in its tracks.

But not forgotten, for sure, and the celebration of Coltishall's passing was quite something. To give you an idea of the spirit of the closing-down party, a note from the invitation to the final ball read: 'drinks will be free from 7 p.m. until 4 a.m.; after that there will be a cash bar'. It was a fabulous evening. Indeed, a wonderful and memorable couple of days. Old friends re-met. Those no longer with us remembered. A new squadron standard presented. Another handed over to a new unit. Immaculate parades and fly-pasts. The chief of the defence staff and the chief of the air staff present – both ex-Coltishall Jaguar pilots. A most moving service in Norwich

Cathedral, led by the bishop. Lumps in throats, but no tears. Truly, nobody does these things better than the RAF.

Such events have happened all over the country and abroad over the past few years as the forces have contracted and units have closed. Local communities and enthusiasts' groups have, without exception, grappled with the problem of what should be done with the remains. My opinion is that, of course, we should be permitted our little spot of nostalgia. But I don't think we should get carried away, nor should we become maudlin over it. That's why, despite the many cries around Norfolk that Coltishall was special and should be turned into some kind of a shrine, I didn't agree. There are already many locations where the Battle of Britain is commemorated and, with Duxford not so very far away, it didn't seem to me that we need another museum right here. And, despite the fact that Douglas Bader spent a while at Colt, I believe that there were many more significant locations during the battle.

Another point was that, although it seemed that Coltishall had been there forever, its entire lifespan was only around seventy years – just the blink of an eye in the big scheme of things. So the fact that the air defence radar museum at the nearby site of RAF Neatishead has a section dedicated to Coltishall is, to my mind, just about right. Among its memorabilia is displayed an item I recall very clearly; it's the framed map from the officers' mess notice board which was marked up with all the local hostelries. Although, as if to reinforce my remarks about the temporary nature of things, many of those fine pubs have also subsequently closed. Naturally, it crosses my mind that the closing of the pubs might have been precipitated by closure of the base.

After several false starts with plans for new uses for the real estate, an alternative site for Norwich Airport being one of them, we now have several going concerns on the former airfield. There's Her Majesty's Prison Bure, which utilises many of the old airmen's blocks (many former airmen might argue that their blocks might not have needed much modification to make them suitable for prisoners!) The perimeter track is planned to form the basis for something special by way of cycling venues. And the bulk of the grassed area is now covered with solar panels. Really and truly, I feel that the former base is being put to productive use, and the ghosts of all those Spitfire, Jaguar and Lightning pilots who enjoyed their service there should be able to rest easy. But still I get the inescapable feeling that it's all gone quiet up the road.

I mentioned former RAF locations where I've served, and there were others, too, where I flew regularly: Ouston; Rufforth; Sharjah; Masirah. But one which rivalled Coltishall in meaning a lot to me was Brüggen. When it closed, in 2001, this is what I wrote in the squadron association newsletter:

> "An era is nearly over. It's hard to believe it's coming to an end. The Goldstars are leaving Brüggen, and the RAF's leaving Germany. The last one out will,

no doubt, turn off the lights. The job's been well done for over half a century, and there will certainly be much written about it in due course. I've known the area, off and on, for the past thirty-two years, so here are a couple of my own snap-shots.

"I first visited Brüggen as a very young acting pilot officer, sent to Germany on a short holding posting following advanced flying training. I travelled in an Argosy from Northolt; we had waited most of the day for the weather to clear, and eventually arrived in early evening. Snow lay a couple of feet thick on the ground as I humped my bag to a room in one of the blocks opposite the mess, and the place looked like fairyland. I had never been abroad before, or for that matter ever ventured out of the cloistered world of Flying Training Command and into the operational air force. The whole thing was an eye-opener. Within a day I'd taken the dreaded BFG driving test and been issued with a left-hand drive Land Rover – with orders to move over the coming weeks to Gütersloh, Rheindahlen, and Wildenrath. I loved it: the culture; the food; the beer; and the whole atmosphere within 2 ATAF and RAF Germany. I flew in a Canberra, a Hunter, a Lightning, a Beaver, and in a Wessex helicopter. I made friends and spent Easter skiing in the Alps – getting a burned face to prove it, as one easily can on the high slopes in the spring. And I got a taste for serving abroad, which never left me.

"My next stint at Brüggen took in the late 1970s, at the height of the Cold War. I flew Jaguars on 20 Squadron, with the famous 'Whisky' Walker as station commander. He was a hard and ruthless man, whom some called something other than 'Whisky'! We worked incredibly hard – but got amazing results in exercises and were, I think, very professional. It was sobering to think that there was an opposition 'over there', armed and ready just as we were. Sitting on QRA, facing them, was a major part of our existence. I spent one Christmas Day in the 'shed' – but no, we didn't ring up our oppos on the other side and sing carols with them. That story is possibly an apocryphal one, and I certainly never met anybody who admitted to doing it. I've no idea whether we 'won' the Cold War, although it can't be denied that we played a major part in keeping the peace. But the whole Brüggen experience – including the hectic socialising – took over our lives. We lived, ate and breathed the squadron and station. It was a wonderfully enjoyable and fulfilling time.

"When I returned to post-Cold War and post-Gulf conflict Brüggen in the early 1990s to join the Goldstars, the place had undergone a metamorphosis. Not because of the switch to the Tornado – that was just another strike/attack jet, after all – but because of the change in role and world politics. Friday nights in the bar just weren't the same; whilst all four Jaguar squadrons had been almost permanently in residence and happy hours had always been riotous, more often than not at least two of the Tornado squadrons were on the road. And, being away so much, people tended to look more for family time when they were back at home rather than for happy hour. Low flying in Germany was finished – partly, and inevitably, due to the cumulative nuisance caused over the years to German villages by our aircraft. Not to mention by the Starfighters and F-16s of the Dutch and Belgians. Well, those church steeples made such excellent navigational turning points! But it was still very satisfying and enjoyable work, not least because this time I had a squadron to run. And the marvellous holiday opportunities remained, with those autobahns leading virtually from doorstep to Alps and Côte d'Azure. But the station had a very different character.

"There have been further changes since I left. Almost ironically, given the ostensibly more peaceful world situation, it's during this last period that Brüggen launched its first and only live operational missions – to the Balkans. Apart from the Falklands Vulcan raids, the only RAF offensive missions launched from either the UK or Germany since WWII. [note: the Libya raids from the UK followed later.]

"I for one will never forget Brüggen and RAF Germany; it was a wonderful place to serve."

But now it's gone quiet up the road there, too.

CHAPTER 26
SOMETIMES IT GOT EXCITING...

Civil flying was, by and large, a matter of routine, but occasionally there was something special about a trip which made it stick in the mind. Perhaps it was the place; or maybe, as in an earlier chapter, the weather. I'll tell you a couple of stories. The first relates to two cities I used to visit in my little turboprop. Well, one actually – London. But such is the contrast between two of its airports that it might as well have been two.

Let's start by smoothing our way up west to the sophisticated home of BA – Heathrow, of course. When adopting my new airline persona at advanced years I believed that I was signing up for a pottering life up and down the North Sea, and I never expected to feel Heathrow's tarmac under my wheels. But my airline was, after a while, merged with another (some would say swallowed up by) and I suddenly found myself visiting a whole new set of destinations. One of the new sectors was Rotterdam-Heathrow, and on several occasions I found myself venturing in on what was, I think, LHR's last turboprop schedule. My aircraft felt minute amongst all those Jumbos and Triple Sevens, but we made up for that with our flexibility and manoeuvrability. So we didn't, as you might expect, hold up proceedings. Indeed, it's not so long since the radio rang with the exchange we all love to recall: "Turboprop on final approach, please slow down – you're catching Concorde". Was that a true story? I'm not sure, since all aircraft on approach to major airports are speed-controlled by air traffic to ensure spacing is maintained on finals to land. Perhaps, though, the turboprop captain on that day was a sporty individual.

I suppose there will be readers who remember Heathrow as a sleepy little field, but now of course it's a million miles from that. From a piloting point of view, I must say that, as well as offering an attractive set of views of London and Windsor Castle on the approach, it also functions like a well-oiled machine. Passengers, though, might not see things quite that way, for sheer traffic volume inevitably causes delays. After a forty-five-minute flight from Rotterdam it was quite common to have to hold for almost as long over north London before starting the approach. Orbiting in the 'stack' was the place to get the most vivid impression of the bulk of those Boeing 747s and 777s as they passed overhead, just 1,000 feet separated.

Even after landing further delays could occur, and I have known a fifty-minute wait before a stand became available for disembarkation. Very frustrating for passengers with an onward connection to make – or not make, as the case might be. Especially when they had to face a time-consuming transfer to another of the five terminals. What price the hold baggage, too, making the tight connection? Long odds against, I'm afraid, when delays built up. Ah well, all part of the joys of air travel.

I wonder how the third runway will affect things? In itself it won't make much difference, I guess; for all that there will be extra capacity, I've little doubt that it will soon be taken up by extra arrivals and departures. One sure thing is that I'll never have to cope with it as a pilot; I'll simply be one of the millions of unfortunate passengers who struggle with five terminals and an overcrowded transport system. One day technology will permit finer control of departure times and en route speed, so the pre-landing hold might become a thing of the past. For now, though, I confess to seeing the attraction of Eurostar for those short, cross-Channel trips.

Anyway, let's move quickly down river to the east – to the second 'city', London City Airport. Located in altogether homelier surroundings, you might recall it being known as 'Docklands' in its early days. It's built on the old quay which stood between the Royal Albert and King George V Docks, which seems a fantastic concept. Many readers will have watched *Eastenders* on TV. If you have, you'll have seen it right in the centre of the aerial view which forms the opening sequence, just to the east of the Dome – or the O2 as it's currently known.

No-one who remembers the real and symbolic importance of London's docks – the pounding they took during the Blitz and the effort put into defending them – could have imagined they'd close soon afterwards. Being an 'Eastender' myself (well, just about) I remember the tail end of the grand maritime era. Treats for me every school holiday in the 1950s were outings to see the ships. There were two ways of doing it. One was to take a river trip from Tower Pier down past the Millwall, India and Surrey docks and into the Royal group. The sightseeing boat would spend an hour or so prowling around under the towering hulls of those ocean-going

Splendid views over Westminster while on approach to runway 10 at London City Airport. The author's old office block, the Ministry of Defence, shows up well between Horse Guards Parade and the river.

monsters – the Blue Star liners on the South America run and the Union Castles, whose work was largely down to Africa – before heading back up river to the Tower. I can still recall the smells and sounds, the slap of dirty water and the scent of foreign produce, backed by the hubbub of machinery and raucous cries of stevedores.

The other option was to take the number 101 London Transport bus down East Ham High Street. From our vantage point upstairs at the front, cranes and ships in the docks would begin to dominate the skyline as we

Fokker 50 on final approach to LCY. A painting by Ian Wilson-Dick, GAvA, which was exhibited in 2004 at the summer exhibition of the Guild of Aviation Artists.

drew closer to the Thames – until eventually the great lilac hulls of the Union Castles and the towering Blue Star funnels would fill the field of view. If we were really lucky, a swing bridge would open and the bus would be held up while a liner was inched out by tugs before starting down river on its ocean voyage. Then on we'd go towards the terminus at North Woolwich, take a five-minute trip across the Thames on the ferry (having a peep below at the great engine cranking around), and finish with a walk down Woolwich High Street for an ice cream or an orange squash at a 'Lyons' teashop. Wonderful!

But soon the ships had all gone, and dereliction ruled for a decade or so. Miraculously, a phoenix arose from the ashes in the form of regeneration as a business area, and City Airport became its main international connection. It was my part of the world, and I loved to fly over my childhood house, my old school, and the park where I played my schoolboy football. It was a fascinating airport to fly into, not least for the stunning close-up of the Canary Wharf skyscrapers on final approach. I was always amazed that we were permitted to do visual approaches, and on occasions we'd position right-hand downwind to runway one-zero. We'd track along the south bank of the Thames and then turn in, arcing around the towers such that we could almost read the secrets being written on computer screens by all those naughty bankers. That particular procedure stopped, of course, after 9/11, but it was good while it lasted. (I mean the visual approaches stopped then; according to what we read in the newspapers, the naughty banking continued at least until 2007/2008's financial crash!)

As a noise abatement measure the glidepath at LCY is, at 5½°, almost twice as steep as normal, and leads to a short, narrow runway. No place here for Jumbos, and the little turboprop was in its element. But when there was pouring rain, a 400-foot cloudbase, visibility of only one kilometre and a twenty-five knot crosswind, it could be quite a white-knuckle ride. The worst wind was a south-south-westerly, which brought turbulence off the nearby sugar factory, and I often thought that it was just as well the passengers couldn't see too much.

An eerily exciting time was when we were approaching from the west and there was a layer of mist or low cloud. Sometimes, on those occasions, we would have a good view of the skyscrapers poking through the undercast just a little off to the right, and then we'd bore into cloud, losing sight of them completely. One could trust the instruments, of course, but it was still an odd feeling.

Even operations on the ground were different, being extremely cramped and busy. Because the runway's so short and the surrounding buildings so high, performance could limit payload, and we were always juggling fuel load against passenger numbers in an effort to get the best out of the situation. Kilograms mattered, and we sometimes had to take desperate measures to make it work. On occasions we even had to off-load the bar trolleys!

So there you have my 'tale of two cities'. Not quite Charles Dickens, nor a parallel-track, night four-ship across Labrador with 1,000-pound bombs – but it still kept me amused.

There were many in the RAF who regarded air traffic control as the 'flying prevention branch', and there was often talk to the effect that it should be renamed ATA – air traffic advice. There were many fine ATC personnel, but in general aircrew seemed to think they knew much better than ATC what needed to be done.

I admit to tending towards this attitude, but very soon after taking the airline route I developed an enormous respect for civilian air traffic control. To listen to one of the London or Manchester sector controllers handling the deluge of traffic was something to wonder at, and I have nothing but the greatest esteem for those people. Such was the volume of chat that it was sometimes well-nigh impossible to check in on a new frequency. I know that English is the prescribed language of the skies and that all crews entering UK airspace must have a certified proficiency, but I reflected on many occasions how glad I was that it was my native language. It must be hugely demanding to cope with the likes of London ATC in one's second language.

The days when those controllers really earned their crust were those when conditions were out of the ordinary – for example when there was a lot of thundery activity. Every pilot worth his salt would have one eye on the weather radar at a time like that and, with his passengers' comfort in mind, would not be shy in requesting a new vector to route around an ugly-looking build-up. So rather than the semi-ordered flow a controller would normally cope with, on days like that the work would be doubled.

Talking of thunderstorms I do remember one particular trip when everything happened. By this time I was flying the Bombardier Dash 8 Q400 which, by turboprop standards, was a powerful beast with many modern characteristics. But it had its idiosyncrasies, both in the airframe and avionic departments, caused to some extent by long evolution during which developments had been tagged on one by one. Most Q400 pilots would agree that, at some point,

The author on the flight deck of a Bombardier Dash 8-Q400.

it would have been better to have started again with a clean sheet. Certainly, in my time, crews were always being hauled over the coals at head office for misdemeanours which were, to a great extent, induced by the aircraft's peculiarities. Systemic problems, in other words; just as in the military, pilot error wasn't always as clear a cause of incidents as would appear at first sight.

Thus the Dash took more crew attention than it should have needed to keep it out of trouble. But it was nevertheless an interesting machine to fly. On this particular day, I was heading down to the Alps with a cabin full of skiers looking forward to their hols. Our destination was Chambéry, in France, located near the Swiss border and situated at the far end of a long, steep-sided valley. The only way in was also the only way out, thus the traffic flow was approximately half that of a conventional airport. Flights were scheduled accordingly, but it was still not unusual to be asked to hold before one's approach to permit departing traffic to clear.

So it was on the day in question, and on first contacting the airport we were told to enter a holding pattern well off to the north-west of the field. It was a relatively clear day and we could, for the most part, enjoy a grand view of the Alps. Approaching the eastern end of the holding pattern we flew into a little bit of thin alto-stratus; nothing to fret about, and we still had sight of the mountains through the haze. Then ... crack! We received a massive lightning strike.

There had been absolutely no warning, either on the weather radar or visually, and it certainly wasn't the sort of cloud in which one would expect thunderstorm activity. Everybody jumped like hell, not least me. After 4,500 hours of military flying and a further few thousand with the civilians, this was my first strike. Anyway, we shook ourselves, regained our composure, and asked for clearance to an alternative holding area; we certainly didn't like that one.

Off we went towards our new hold, checking the systems en route. Lightning strikes rarely cause serious damage to an aircraft – they just scare the pants off crew and passengers. And so it was on this occasion; one of the ADFs appeared to be out, but otherwise we were OK. Systems-wise, at any rate, but not necessarily weather-wise. For as we headed south-eastwards towards the new holding area we entered thick, turbulent cloud, and by the time we were established in the alternative pattern things were quite uncomfortable. But we knew from listening to radio traffic that it wouldn't be long before we would commence our approach. Just one more departing aircraft to go and then it would be our turn.

As we turned inbound in the holding pattern the day suddenly got even more exciting. "Climb, Climb!" The collision avoidance system was yelling at us. There was no time to question it; no option but to immediately pour on power and pull up. No sooner had the warning popped up than the kit gave us the all clear; following a call to ATC we gingerly eased ourselves back down to the assigned level. Neither cabin crew nor passengers would have known about this incident, which was a relief; what with the lightning strike and the turbulence, they'd already had quite enough drama for one day. But on the flight deck we were thoroughly shaken up by this time, and very relieved to hear that we were now cleared to land. In the circumstances, you'll not be surprised to hear that it was something of a no-frills approach, and I have seldom been so pleased to feel the tyres kiss the runway. Things improved, though, when we received the best news of the day. A lightning strike meant a mandatory technical inspection, and an engineer couldn't arrive until the next morning. So rather than the usual thirty-minute turn-round and homeward sector we were off to a hotel for the night. And I for one had never been more in need of a few beers!

A word about the collision warning system, which is a most magnificent piece of kit. By and large one would expect a potential conflict to be signalled first by a cautionary, amber warning, which would prepare the crew. If the conflict subsequently entered the 'red' area, then everybody would be primed to take action. In our case the intruder had come at us steeply from below, giving little or no 'amber' phase – I certainly don't recall seeing or hearing any significant warning. To all intents and purposes the kit had jumped straight to red. What had happened had been a result of our second holding area being located directly above the climb-out lane from the field. That shouldn't have been a problem; there was a height limit on departing traffic until clear of the hold. But, as I mentioned earlier, the valley sides were steep, high and hard. Aircrew, when in cloud and sensing the proximity of 'cumulo-granitus', have a natural instinct for self-preservation. Although the standard instrument departure procedure took account of terrain, there must have been in the minds of the crew of the departing aircraft an urge to steepen their climb – and they had 'busted' their cleared altitude. The given excuse in their subsequent report was 'weather avoidance' – but I'm afraid that just didn't wash. One must not avoid weather without first receiving clearance that one isn't going to collide with other traffic. I doubt whether the incident had much to do with anybody but the crew concerned, but nevertheless it seemed poetic justice that the airline concerned went out of business soon afterwards.

Oddly, after so many years without ever being troubled by lightning, I had another fright caused by a second strike just two weeks later. This time it was just off the Norfolk coast. And, equally curiously, although lightning is almost always associated with thick, cumulonimbus cloud, this second one also occurred in almost clear air.

CHAPTER 27

GIRLS IN THE COCKPIT

When writing *Tornado Boys* I was conscious that there are girls involved these days, and I was determined to include a female view. In the end a lovely woman pilot whom I know fairly well gave me an excellent chapter. In discussions with the publisher we agreed that, although the series of books is known by its 'Boys' tag, the presence of girls on the force would be highlighted in the sub-title on the cover.

In a related incident, I had to submit a couple of the chapters of another book to the MoD to gain approval to include words by serving personnel. They came up with very few comments, but one of them was a recommendation that I should replace all mentions of 'girls' with 'women'. Presumably they saw something frivolous in the term 'girls'; or perhaps they felt I was somehow diminishing the value of the women employed in the services. Maybe, even, they saw the word 'girls' as having, however remotely, something of a 'page 3' connotation. I had no wish to trip up in the political correctness area, so I wrote back to say that I noted their concerns. I did, though, test their sense of humour by pointing out that the book contained dozens of references to 'boys'; would they, I wondered, like me to change all those words to 'men'? The airwaves, at that point, went quiet.

Of course we all accept that girls in the workplace are a routine part of today's scene. From a personal viewpoint, though, I somehow doubt whether female numbers in the military and on airline flight decks will ever rise much higher than they are at present. In fact I believe that there was an initial rush of girls wanting to go flying once it became apparent that the services and civilian airlines were accepting them, but that numbers have dropped off since. Similarly, and perhaps more seriously, I believe that the Royal Navy, having converted mess decks on a number of ships to make them suitable for the fairer sex, subsequently found that numbers fell away and they had difficulty in crewing those ships.

My service life ended somewhat before the female invasion started, and I never had the pleasure of flying with an RAF girl. With the airlines, though, I flew with many female first officers, and I must say I found them indistinguishable from the blokes. No ... I didn't mean that! I meant of course that their flying was indistinguishable; equally competent.

I had a good deal to do with a female friend of one of my sons, who was dead keen to join the military; while she was busy sending in her application I was very pleased to provide a reference for her. Several references, in fact, for it turned out that she had to demonstrate more than the usual amount of those admirable qualities, determination and perseverance. First she applied to the RAF to be an air traffic control officer, but was rejected. In her defence, I should say that rejection doesn't always imply that a candidate is inadequate; the laws of supply and demand mean that, in some phases of the cycle, almost all applicants are rejected, while at other times they'll take anybody who barely meets the standard. Recruiters tell me that one of the biggest factors is the state of the general labour market; when unemployment in the country is low, it's hard to find the required numbers of good applicants, and vice versa.

Anyway, following that disappointment she applied to the Royal Navy and was accepted as a trainee seaman officer. In fact I met her during her work-up period when her frigate docked in Bahrain – I was at the time running the RAF's Operation Jural, the effort to police the southern Iraq no-fly zone. It was a great pleasure for both of us to do the ship tour together, and I could see her pride as she showed me around. Sad to relate, she was suspended from training not long afterwards.

Following that she tried the army where, I'm pleased to report, she made it. I was a guest at her graduation parade at Camberley, and now, many years later, she is a senior officer. A triumph for tenacity, and she no doubt learned much from each stumble that could subsequently be applied to the next stage.

CHAPTER 28
TWO, ONE, ZERO...

Towards the end of this decade my nearest RAF base, RAF Marham, will receive its first single-seat type. And my guess is that, in the messes, the eternal argument over whether two seats are better than one is already raging. As editor of my association's newsletter I always steered well clear of navigator (or should I say WSO?) jokes. In some ways that was a pity, as there's a rich vein of humour there, but the subject always has the potential for causing offence and I had no wish to start a war with my one-winged friends.

The operational arguments are relatively simple. It's indisputably an advantage to have extra human brains on board. On the other hand, weight and space matters in a tactical aircraft. No, to any navs reading I'm not suggesting that you're all over-weight – but it's undeniable that by halving the requirement for life-support systems and so on the thrust-to-weight ratio is improved. And as in many related arguments, much comes down to cost. In this sense there are direct economies from having a smaller airframe, but probably the greater savings come from all the peripherals like housing, training, salaries and pensions. And of course, not least, the fewer people we have to risk in combat zones the better.

Straightforward, eh? Well, that hasn't stopped the RAF changing its mind many times over the years, often on the premise that advancing technology would substitute for human input. In the air-to-ground role we moved from the two-seat Phantom to the single-seat Jaguar – but then back to the two-seat Tornado. Now it's to be single-seat again, with the Lightning II. In the air defence world we've gone from two-seat Javelin through single-seat Lightning and two-seat Phantom and Tornado F3 to single-seat Typhoon. Clearly, there are no absolute answers.

I personally have no axe to grind one way or another, having enjoyed front-line tours on three single-seat types and two two-seaters. And in any case, far from poking fun at the demise of the navigator, I acknowledge that it looks as though the joke will soon be on the single-seaters. For who would bet against the next generation of tactical aircraft having no pilots either? Taking all the arguments I've just touched on to their logical extremes, an unmanned air system has enormous advantages: the requirement for life support systems is zeroed; if it's shot down its crew isn't killed; and so on.

Of course something similar happened in the 1950s in the air defence arena, with the notorious announcement that we would move towards an all-SAM interceptor force. That policy was rapidly reversed, but now, in the attack role, remotely piloted air systems are already demonstrating that it's possible to do without on-board pilots in some circumstances. We can still argue that having a human brain on board is an advantage we can't ignore. And political discussion still rages about accompanying issues such as the morality and legality of RPAS, but we nevertheless must acknowledge that the way ahead appears to lie towards the unmanned direction. Indeed recent Marham squadrons, numbers 13 and 39, have already converted to RPAS.

The viability of operating without pilots on board is, then, hardly in question. So if machines undertaking complex military missions can do so, why can't those performing the relatively simple task of, say, flying from Heathrow to New York's JFK Airport? Because, of course, the paying public won't have it. Even reducing crew numbers is a step too far, as the outspoken Michael O'Leary of Ryanair found when he – provocatively perhaps – floated the idea of one-pilot flight-deck crews.

Conventional wisdom has it that passengers would never stand for an empty cockpit, and one can understand the psychological barrier. On the other hand, most people would, in principle, also be unhappy with the concept of an unmanned train, but nevertheless such things already exist to all intents and purposes. Both the Docklands Light Railway and the Victoria Line in London have 'drivers' on board for little more than cosmetic reasons. Spacecraft (arguably performing even more complex missions than tactical aircraft) seem able to perform equally as well with no humans on board. So it seems inevitable that, one day, the RAF will see an almost wholly unmanned tactical force. Perhaps the only thing which could stop a total changeover would be the need to maintain our sacred cow ... the Red Arrows.

CHAPTER 29
OVERSTRESSING?

The term 'overstress' generally referred, in my military flying days, to pulling G beyond the permitted airframe limit. This could reduce airframe life; occasionally it would cause damage; at the very least it would demand an inspection. Although overstressing was sometimes hard to avoid it was rightly frowned upon; it hinted at inattention or carelessness and caused unnecessary work. On some squadrons one was punished by having to buy a slab of beers for the ground crew who had to do the inspection.

But that's not the type of overstress I wanted to address here. One of the commonest questions a pilot or ex-pilot is asked is whether he/she finds/found the job stressful. The general expectation is that the answer will be affirmative, and that is particularly the case if the enquiry comes from the media, for there's nothing the ladies and gentlemen of the press like more than a gee-whiz pilot story. Now, stress can vary in grade from post-traumatic stress disorder to, it seems nowadays, a general feeling of dissatisfaction that one's mobile phone isn't quite as smart as one's friend's model. That last remark may seem flippant, but it has to be made because the range of situations which attract the description 'stressful' does impede a sensible answer to the pilot question.

Real stress takes so many forms. Being seriously unhappy at work, for example; or being out of work. A deep and genuine fear of failure can be debilitating, as is the worry that one cannot feed one's family or pay the mortgage. Prolonged bullying in school or workplace (not just the routine ragging experienced by every new boy) is terrible, as is the unexpected death of a loved one or the break-up of a relationship. And of course combat and fear of violence are categories of their own.

It's sometimes difficult to find a reasonable reaction when somebody tells you they're in a stressful situation. Should one be sympathetic? Perhaps not always in the pilot situation, given that it's a career he or she has chosen. But what if a medical diagnosis of stress has been made?

A chap I know, who has a top job in a respected profession, is currently off work through the complaint. His doctor has prescribed rest and relaxation, so he's playing lots of golf. He's also got plenty of time to supervise a programme of alterations and upgrades to his home. Now, an active leisure life will no doubt keep the man's mind off his work, and it could help him resume his career. But many would feel uneasy with the situation. Perhaps it's in my upbringing, but I think of the business partners who are left to carry the additional burden, as well as the clients who have to accept delays to the service. I can certainly empathise with feeling pressure of work, for I experienced plenty of that in running a squadron and in the MoD. But I and my colleagues thrived under those pressures; we took pride in being able to cope despite the ridiculous workload. Achieving success in adverse circumstances was called job satisfaction and we did, after all, have the option of asking for postings to less demanding positions – just as this chap could, if he'd wished, have opted to go part time. Of course, we might have reduced our career or promotion prospects, just as he might have had to take a salary cut. So perhaps it's sometimes not only the workload which applies the pressure, but rather one's ambition and the family's expectations of lifestyle. I know I appear to be lacking sympathy; the remedy's always clear, isn't it, when others have the problem? But couldn't we, maybe, find greater contentment without some of this artificially applied 'stress'?

A young acquaintance of mine set off last month for his first term at university to study the subject of his dreams. Blow me, he was back the next day. "He's decided it's not for him," said his friend. "He's never been away from home before and found the environment and all the unknown faces very intimidating. Besides, the coursework looked fearsome. He's right to drop out. If it's causing him stress, there's no point in forcing himself through it."

Pardon? Isn't a degree course meant to be demanding? Shouldn't one have to put oneself out a little to get through it? And didn't we all find starting at each new school – and our first days in the RAF, too – immensely frightening experiences? Most of us rode those 'new boy' periods, generally treating them as a challenge. At the very least, even if uni didn't appear 'right' for the lad at first sight, didn't it deserve more than a day's trial before being jettisoned?

Business and university are desk-bound situations, but this chapter is really aimed at a working life in another sort of office. The layman certainly views life in a fighter-bomber cockpit as being 'right on the edge' and, consequently, stressful. It's difficult to put an alternative perspective on the business without appearing to be artificially modest, but as readers who have themselves flown would agree, most flying is exciting rather than stressful. I'm not talking about combat, for I'm certain that, had I ever found myself over enemy territory with people firing high explosive at my little pink body, I would have felt something else entirely. Truly, combat stress is a conundrum which we struggle even now to rationalise. After all, less than a century ago they executed men for 'cowardice' who were, in all probability, exhibiting no more than extreme battle stress. It's something we often reflect upon at the remembrance time of the year – particularly when our current forces are enduring difficult duties in, for example, Afghanistan or Iraq. But aside from combat and other operational situations, we (ex) military airmen generally found enormous satisfaction in the successful completion of a complex mission in demanding conditions.

Other real stresses in the military are caused by government policies. Readers will recall 2010's defence review, which was largely driven by financial pressures. Cuts were made, although commitments weren't reduced accordingly. The pressures on the remaining units increased, as outlined in 2011 by one of my successors as squadron commander, Jim Mulholland:

> "At this current rate, if nothing changes, every Tornado front-line squadron will spend eight months away on operations in the next twelve, in addition to the exercise and work-up programme; the effect that will have on families and morale should not be underestimated. When you add the uncertainty of redundancy, which was recently announced, into the context above, the stress which my men and women are coping with is unhealthily increasing. There is little certainty about their future, other than that it is uncertain, and many are talking about their concerns openly to colleagues. This gives me a difficult management challenge, because I am asking them to do more and work harder without being able to assuage their future concerns. The initial trawl for voluntary redundancy did not get the numbers that were required, so we are now entering a period for this first round where compulsory redundancy boards are sitting; we are asking a lot of our people at the moment."

In fact, as mentioned earlier, one additional Tornado squadron was subsequently run on to cope with the unforeseen commitment to counter ISIS, and this has served to reduce the time away on operations for personnel on the Marham squadrons to four months per year. But with other commitments and operational work-up continuing, the people still face huge amounts of time on the road.

We shouldn't, either, underestimate the effect on service people's nearest and dearest. When a family member is away too much, those behind are left under pressure, and of course, unhappy families at home reflect anxiety back to the one who's away with the squadron. I particularly remember this from the time of my squadron command. Many of the young wives back at our German base found themselves not only without their menfolk but also far away from their own families. My wife and the senior NCOs' wives at the top end of the squadron put in endless hours as unpaid counsellors, and it's no exaggeration to say that they were essential to the functioning of the organisation. Maybe it's different now; the RAF is home-based, and people tend not to marry at such a young age. But on the other hand those away nowadays are often in combat zones. So I can't but think that family stresses still exist.

Civil flying brings its own pressures, and I sometimes daydream about the apparent glamour of airline life in days of yore. Perhaps I'd have been a flying-boat captain, and I picture myself taxiing my stately machine into a sleepy lagoon somewhere in the tropics for a night stop. My bunk would be mahogany-panelled, and a steward would prepare dinner for me and the dozen or so rich widows and heiresses who would be the passengers. We'd watch the sunset ... and there my daydream ends abruptly! Because there must have been patchy weather forecasting, dodgy navigation aids, dubious mechanical reliability and inadequate autopilots. So perhaps, after all...

The public, occasionally encouraged by lurid press stories, believe that an airline pilot, even now, battles daily with endless hazards. There are of course occasions when crews are called upon to dig deep into their skill banks, but I'm certain that passengers would feel more comfortable knowing that it's not only 'by the skin of their teeth' that they reach the destination. So perhaps I should offer a word of reassurance; airline pilots rarely have to scrape in on a wing and a prayer.

The times when the heart beats faster were, for me, vastly outweighed by the hours spent gazing out of the window and drinking in those amazing and constantly-varying skyscapes. And there were still stand-down periods spent in pleasant locations. However, I should say that those stand-downs aren't always, these days, as generous as might be imagined, and often encompass time-zone changes or uncomfortable split shifts. So now we're getting to the heart of today's pressures. Tight rostering overflows into flight-deck stress, and civil flying undoubtedly has its fatiguing and frustrating moments. Rostering up to the limit, stemming from airline commercial departments' efforts to increase profitability is, rather than airborne drama, what generally induces today's airline stress.

Long-haul pilots do say that they get fed up with the eternal living in hotels out of suitcases. It's tempting to retort that they could always switch to short-haul flying if they preferred, although they might not like that either. One short-haul airline I flew with was in the habit of rostering six-sector days; each of the scheduled turn-round times was tight, and I can certainly confirm that those days were exceedingly wearying. So is there any glamour at all left in the job?

The question puts me in mind of a marvellous article which appeared in BALPA's magazine *The Log* to mark the demise of the flight engineer trade. It was long ago and I can't quote it precisely, but the premise was along the lines of a retired flight engineer being asked whether he missed his job. "Whenever I think I do," he said, "instead of going to bed at 10 p.m. when I'm tired I pretend I'm on an eastbound Atlantic crossing. I go to the cupboard under the stairs and sit on an uncomfortable chair. I read the gas and electricity meters every hour and record the figures. At 4 a.m. I switch on a 100-watt bulb and stare into it for the next three hours. Then I get up and drive twice around the M25 to simulate my commute home. At 9 a.m. I have two or three beers that I don't want, then go to bed and can't sleep. That's how much I miss work."

Leaders of airline pilot unions continually emphasise cumulative stress aspects of the job, regularly playing the flight safety card. It's natural, I think, for airline commercial departments to demand as much as they legally can and for unions to battle for improved lifestyle. What's not so clear is whether the unions or the authorities are on the side of right, safety-wise, in arguing just what should be a sensible maximum.

We've hardly scratched the surface here, but the reader will have gathered from the tone of this piece that I find the s-word often to be inappropriately used these days. But before abandoning it completely may I suggest that, as a rule, we also need a little 'stress' to get the adrenalin racing and to spice up the workplace and family life? Perhaps 'challenge' would often be a better word, and shouldn't we relish it every day? Certainly, from a purely flying viewpoint, that's the way it struck me during my career, which is why I enjoyed the tough missions and bad weather almost more than the routine trips in fine conditions. And why, when obstacles were successfully overcome from beginning to end of a sortie, I always relished the debrief. So did my colleagues, and that's why supplementary debriefs still went on in the bar many hours later.

CHAPTER 30
TRAINS AND BOATS AND PLANES

Flying provided me with well over forty years of enjoyment, but even so I left many stones unturned. I was never driven, for example, to be a display pilot. And when I started airline flying I had no ambition to get into the management area. But often in life it's hard to resist a challenging opportunity when it presents itself – if for no other reason than 'because it's there'.

Doesn't every RAF pilot have an ambition to be one of the Red Arrows? That's often the impression held by people I meet, but in fact it's far from the truth. Like most of my RAF friends, I never volunteered for the team for various reasons. Having experienced many months away from family on operational deployments, I was not about to sign up to the guarantee of spending large chunks of every summer away from home. And, despite the apparent glamour of the posting, I reckoned that performing an identical display time after time might lose its appeal. I'm not really one for cocktail parties and receptions, either, so the endless round would have carried little appeal.

Those not in the business tend to believe that team pilots are some kind of super-men. Of course they are very good, forming as they do what is probably the world's premier military aerobatic team. But in fact every RAF pilot is pretty useful at close formation, practising it daily to get, for example, through cloud expeditiously. Indeed before the Red Arrows were formed as a dedicated unit, each year's RAF display team was simply nominated from among the operational fighter squadrons. Hence our memories of 111 Squadron's 'Black Arrows', 92 Squadron's 'Blue Diamonds', 56 Squadron's 'Firebirds' and so on. Even at basic flying training school, many students were taken through a few formation aerobatic manoeuvres; such activities weren't on the syllabus, but adventurous instructors would nevertheless sometimes slip a few in.

There was, though, an overriding reason for not volunteering for the Arrows. I knew well that the team was something of a club; the members selected their mates, and I have no difficulty with that. If one is going to spend an entire season welded to another eight pilots, it's essential to select those with whom one will be truly comfortable. I was absolutely content to leave it to them.

Neither was I driven to get into the solo display circuit. My first Jet Provost instructor subsequently lost his life in a low-level display, but that wasn't particularly the reason. A big factor was that I was almost never based at a station which had a display commitment. But then the opportunity unexpectedly arose while I was instructing on Hunters at RAF Brawdy. At that stage I was feeling increasingly confident in my ability, so when the call came for volunteers for this new post I stepped forward.

For that 1976 season three of us applied. Curiously, all were from 234 Squadron; there were no takers from either 63 or 79 Squadrons. We were each granted an allocation of flying hours to work up our proposed displays, following which a selection would be made. I flew, I think, three practices before the process came to a grinding halt because of some crisis or other. I forget whether it was money or fuel that ran out, or perhaps we were simply too far behind the line in getting students graduated. Whichever, there was no further capacity to accommodate a fly-off, so the selection was abruptly made without anybody seeing our embryo displays. One went forward, while the other two returned immediately to normal duties; I was not the lucky one.

Ironically, the chosen pilot was sick for much of the ensuing season and unable to display. There was no reserve, so Brawdy was unable to provide much of a Hunter display that year.

When I headed for civil aviation I felt that, having done 'management' in several RAF jobs, I was now just going to enjoy being a line pilot. But in similarly unplanned vein, when the opportunity arose I couldn't resist applying – again, I suppose, because 'it was there'. Or perhaps it was simply that I had seen others doing less than sparkling jobs and I reckoned I could do better!

So against my better judgement I applied for the job of turboprop fleet manager when it became vacant in my first airline. I had no real chance as I was up against a real big hitter, the long-serving chief trainer, who had been with the airline for twenty years. So I was neither surprised nor disappointed not to get that job.

But later, I found myself in contention for the post of director of flight operations with my second airline. I was encouraged to apply by the retiring incumbent, and I could have made the domestic aspects of that post work better than the arrangements then in place (I was commuting to a remote base to work). I made the short-list of two, but fell at the last fence. Not speaking the airline's native language was a bit of a show stopper, as of course it was always going to be. But sometimes one just cannot resist the challenge.

I wonder whether you remember that great 1960s number 'Trains and Boats and Planes' by Billy J Kramer and the Dakotas? If you do, that certainly dates you! But the title encapsulates my current-day activities. Do I fly? Not at present – I just write about flying. Since retiring from the airlines I have been tempted to keep up my private pilot's licence. But I know I wouldn't use it enough. What would I do with it? Just fly around the local area gazing at the scenery? I've done that. Would I rent a plane and cross the Channel for lunch in Le Touquet? No; I don't trust single pistons that much. And besides, I like a glass or two with lunch, so the whole scenario wouldn't appeal.

But the lure of flying is strong, and still I'm tempted. A couple of years ago a small share in a Tiger Moth came up for sale at one of the local flying groups and I came very close to buying in. Membership would have brought with it a reciprocal entitlement to fly the adjacent group's Chipmunk, and both types appealed. I'd flown a Tiger in Norway with a friend (a Norwegian who had done an exchange with the RAF flying Jaguars) who was known for his summer performances at Rygge's 'happy hour' on a Friday afternoon. We would be quietly quaffing our beers outside the squadron HQ when along would come Odd (don't laugh – it's a very common Norwegian name) in his Tiger. He'd appear at about 1,500 feet and begin his aeros display. Tiger Moths are very short of power, and so the ensuing series of loops and rolls would result in a steady loss of height. Before long Odd would be pretty much at ground level, with each manoeuvre attracting cheers from the drinkers. He'd land, step out, take the applause, and enjoy his bottle.

The Chipmunk also had its appeal to me. I'd flown it way back in the beginning, as well as on several occasions later in my career, so I'd have loved to have had another go at it. But just before I was due to sign a cheque the group's Chippy had what seemed to be a minor engine problem. This, following investigation, turned out to be a £20,000 job, with the inevitable invitation to syndicate members to pitch in to the tune of four figures each.

This brought home to me the true nature of private flying; it can be a bottomless bucket into which one pours money. Did I really want it that much? The answer was no, and I counted that Chipmunk episode as a fortuitous lesson.

So what of the 'boats and trains'? Well, I have a forty-plus-year-old motor cruiser on the Norfolk Broads which gives me a huge amount of pleasure. She's plastic hulled, so spares me the enormous work of maintaining wet wood. But nevertheless she has a wooden top, so looks and feels (to my eyes at least) magnificent. I never feel that I have to set out on an odyssey; it's often sufficient just to cruise downstream for fifteen minutes or so, throw down the anchor, put on the kettle for tea, open the daily paper, and enjoy the peace and quiet. Not to mention that some of the chapters of this book have been written afloat.

And the 'trains' aspect satisfies one of my other wishes. Like many others of my generation I was, as a little boy, a train spotter. My fascination for all things technical, and especially those metal monsters, has endured, and now I drive narrow-gauge steam engines at a local museum and visitor attraction. Marvellous fun! Could I ever have asked for more than to be involved with not only 'trains' but also 'boats and planes'?

Was there a favourite jet? Well, the Hunter was lovely to fly and holds a special place in my memories for being my first operational type. The Phantom's sheer power always made it a thrilling ride. And the F-5 formed the centrepiece of a truly wonderful three years for me and my family. But we have no space for too much detail here and those three will simply have to be eliminated at the group stage. Moving straight on to the knock-out competition, therefore, it's Tornado versus Jaguar in the final.

As a Tornado squadron commander, perhaps my greatest love should have been the big fin. It was good of course – great even. It was a far more capable aircraft than the Jag, whose puny engines led to its performance being ridiculed in its early life. And, in common with all those who've ferried a Jaguar across the Atlantic, I'll never forget the experience of flying for seven or eight hours without an autopilot. Also, notwithstanding the Jaguar's fabulous (for its day) navigation and weapon-aiming performance, I've already pointed out that the ergonomics of the original system were a nightmare.

But there's so much more to a tour than the aircraft itself. The package embraces the people you're with, the job you're doing, and where you are. Of course the Tornado 'boss' job was tremendously fulfilling, but both of my Jaguar tours were outstandingly enjoyable. And I collected one, new, from the factory; just as with a new car, you can't beat the smell and feel of that. I know, too, I'm not alone in identifying the fantastic 'Jag spirit'. Perhaps, in the early days, it could be put largely down to the fact that the nucleus of the force comprised ex-Hunter pilots, who knew each other well. Indeed, I was joined on my first Jaguar squadron by no fewer than three others with whom I'd shared instructing duties on 234 Squadron during our previous tours. Then some really sharp and spirited first-tourists also entered the mix.

My very last jet flight in the RAF was in a Jaguar T2. At the time I was working in the MoD, and one of the offices in my department had been busy pushing through an upgrade for the aircraft. I needed to see for myself, and thus it was that one

Left and middle: The new cockpits; the author drives a variety of locomotives at Bressingham Steam Museum, Suffolk. Right: That's the way to relax! The author with Jacqueline on the Norfolk Broads.

afternoon found me at Boscombe Down strapped into a T2 with a test pilot in the other seat. The aircraft was the test bed for the helmet-mounted sight, terrain reference navigation and bigger engines – the package that would eventually form the core of the Jaguar GR3. It was a marvellous flight and I was thrilled to experience the new capability; the avionics were, in some ways, superior at the time to the Tornado GR1's, and the aircraft was truly transformed.

In latter years, a contributory factor to pilots' affection for the Jaguar would undoubtedly have been that the remaining Jag force was so small and was concentrated at the ever-popular Coltishall. So for all those reasons, although I enjoyed my tours on Tornados, Phantoms, Hunters and F-5s, when pressed to decide on a favourite it has to be the Jag which provides the best overall memories.

People in the world of civil aviation often asked me whether I missed the thrill of flying fighter-bombers, and for two reasons my answer was always 'no'. Firstly, I felt I'd done all that and had been lucky enough to be able to make the change at the right time and with no regrets. And secondly, for all the exhilaration of flashing around in the weeds at four-fifty knots, I had become increasingly conscious that each hour's flying was surrounded by several hours of planning, briefing, dressing and de-briefing. In any case, their airships had decided that I was unlikely to fly regularly again in the RAF. So as I passed a certain age, the attractions of the more sedate civilian routine – with flight planning all done remotely and where it was only necessary to turn up an hour before departure – became that much greater. Although I have to say that the so-called 'stability' of airline life which I'd expected when I left the service never really materialised. What with commercial pressures and the turbulence caused by background world events, one could never – even less than in the military – really be sure where one's path would lead next in the civil world.

18 June 2010, the author's final commercial flight. The first officer is Jim Jenkins, formerly of 111 Squadron RAF.

As an illustration of that I could mention the time when the commercial depart-ment of one of my airlines decided to retire three of the turboprops. That meant that a number of pilots would have to be redeployed, and those changes would come from the bottom of the seniority list upwards. Even though I was a line-training captain I was a relatively recent arrival; therefore I would have to convert to a jet aircraft. Which sounds nice, but not only would I have to take a demotion to first officer but I'd also have to operate from a base that wouldn't suit me at all. So, as you would imagine, it was not a happy bunny who reported one Monday morning for technical ground school to study the new aircraft's systems. Only two days into this purgatory, however, the chief pilot walked in and announced that commercial had re-done their sums and reinstated the turboprops. With immediate effect, which had created an immediate and acute shortage of crews. So I was dispatched with no further ado for a quick dual check on my favoured aircraft, followed by a rapid re-ros-tering to operate out of my preferred base. I was happy again, pleased to confirm that it wasn't only the military who can demonstrate the flexibility of air power.

For my last year or so in the airline industry times were quite hard; the recession had bitten and there was the threat of aircraft being laid up and crew redundancies. But I'm pleased to say that the management of my particular outfit were very proactive and secured a contract to wet-lease four aircraft for a year to a Greek airline – which was busy re-inventing itself in a form which, it hoped, would be profitable. Over and above preserving jobs, that gave those of us who chose to volunteer the chance to operate for periods in the Aegean, and I was always keen to try something different.

Thus it was that I found myself regularly sitting by a poolside in a coastal hotel just south of Athens. It was a tough assignment, but somebody had to do it! And I did make myself useful; I often took my laptop with me to the lounger and did quite a bit of work on *Jaguar Boys* right there in the sunshine.

Off duty I was able to do the tourist bit in Athens, and evenings were the time for sitting by the seashore watching the sun go down. Sometimes I swear that, through the gentle slap of the waves, I could hear an old Nana Mouskouri number wafting from a battered Dansette. That was, truly, a time to contemplate the meaning of life. Without, naturally, reaching too meaningful a conclusion.

Away from this silliness, the wonderful scenery of the Aegean provides the overwhelming memory, and my final trip couldn't have been more idyllic. A gentle potter down to Crete from Athens – and back. I was with a very nice first officer who had been, in his previous life, Treble-One Squadron's intelligence officer. Even though he had been in the admin branch then, I could almost count him as having been a Tornado F3 operator, and we passed the trip happily swapping reminiscences. With him, together with two lovely Greek ladies in the cabin and with clear blue skies and gentle breezes, I mused en route that this was how it was always meant to end. My wife joined me for my last few days in Greece, which were partly spent working and partly holidaying on a beautiful nearby island. It was a great way to finish.

The memories – flying suit patches on the den wall.

Who would have thought, when the Tornado entered service, that we'd be at a dinner thirty years later to celebrate its continued operation? And now, as plans currently stand, we can look forward to its thirty-seventh anniversary.

GLOSSARY
ACRONYMS AND DEFINITIONS

2ATAF	Second Allied Tactical Air Force (NATO command)	*bends, the*	Decompression sickness. Complaint, not uncommonly experienced when flying in poorly pressurised aircraft at very high altitude, caused by gasses coming out of solution in bodily fluids. Usually felt as pain in joints
AAR	Air-to-air refuelling		
AC	Army cooperation		
ADF	Air direction finding		
AEW	Airborne early warning		
AFC	Air Force Cross (medal)	*BFG*	British Forces Germany
AFME	Air Forces Middle East (command organisation)	*BITE*	Built-in test equipment
alpha	Angle of attack	*CENTO*	Central Treaty Organisation
AMO	Air Ministry order	*CFS*	Central Flying School
AOA	Angle of attack	*C of G*	Centre of gravity
AOC	Air officer commanding (of an RAF Group)	*CRM*	Crew resource management
APC	Armament practice camp	*CSAS*	Control stability augmentation system (Tornado)
ATC	Air Training Corps		
ATC	Air traffic control	*CTTO*	Central Trials and Tactics Organisation
ATPL	Air transport pilot's licence		
AWACS	Airborne warning and control system	*DDR*	Deutsche Demokratische Republik (East Germany)
BA	British Airways	*DFGA*	Day fighter ground attack
BALPA	British Airline Pilots' Association	*DME*	Distance measuring equipment

EFA	European Fighter Aircraft (later Typhoon)	*IS*	Islamic State (also ISIS or ISIL, Islamic State of Iraq and Syria, or Iraq and Levant)
ERU	Explosive release unit		
F3	Tornado F3 (air-defence variant)	*JFK*	John F. Kennedy Airport
FIN1064	Upgraded navigation and attack system (Jaguar)	*LCY*	London City Airport
		LHR	London Heathrow Airport
Fox 2	Rear-hemisphere AAM launch	*MoD*	(UK) Ministry of Defence
Fox 3	Gun-firing solution (air-to-air combat)	*MPC*	Missile practice camp
		mud movers	(slang) Air-to-surface attack crews
GCI	Ground controlled interception	*NAAFI*	Navy, Army and Air Force Institute
GMT	Greenwich Mean Time	*NATO*	North Atlantic Treaty Organisation
Gulf War 1	(slang) the Gulf Conflict		
Gulf War 2	(slang) the Iraq War	*NAVWASS*	Navigation and weapon-aiming sub-system (Jaguar)
HAS	Hardened aircraft shelter		
HUD	Head-up display	*NDB*	Non-directional beacon
Icarus	Mythical human character who 'flew' by attaching feathers to his arms with wax. Unfortunately he flew too close to the sun, whose heat melted the wax – whereupon he fell to earth	*NOTAMs*	Notices to airmen
		OC	Officer commanding (of a unit)
		OCU	Operational conversion unit
		OTF	Overseas training flight
ILS	Instrument landing system	*PAI*	Pilot attack instructor
INAS	Inertial navigation and attack system	*PBF*	Pilot (or protected) briefing facility (hardened building)
IR	Infra red		
IRE	Instrument rating examiner	*pickle*	To press the bomb/rocket release button
iron bombs	(slang) Unguided bombs	*PIs*	Practice interceptions

QFI	Qualified flying instructor	*TASMO*	Tactical air support of maritime operations
QM	Quartermaster	*TLP*	Tactical Leadership Programme
QRA (or Q)	Quick reaction alert	*TTTE*	Tornado Tri-national Training Establishment
QWI	Qualified weapons instructor	*TWCU*	Tornado Weapons Conversion Unit
R & R	Rest and recuperation	*TWU*	Tactical Weapons Unit
RAAF	Royal Australian Air Force	*UAE*	United Arab Emirates
radalt	Radio altimeter	*UN*	United Nations
RN	Royal Navy	*USAF*	United States Air Force
RNAS	Royal Naval Air Service	*USN*	United States Navy
RPAS	Remotely piloted air system	*WSO*	Weapons system officer (RAF tactical aircraft – second crewmember, formerly navigator)
RSO	(Weapons) range safety officer		
RV	Rendezvous		
RWR	Radar warning receiver		
SAM	Surface-to-air missile		
SAS	Scandanavian Air Services		
SAS	Special Air Service		
SHAPE	Supreme Headquarters Allied Powers Europe		
Sidewinder	AIM-9 air-to-air missile		
SNCO	Senior non-commissioned officer		
STC	RAF Strike Command		
SWO	Station warrant officer		
TACAN	Tactical air navigation equipment		

INDEX